With a new introduc

Narratives of Exile and Return

Mary Chamberlain

Memory and Narrative Series

Transaction Publishers
New Brunswick (U.S.A.) and London (U.K.)

Second printing 2007

New material copyright @ 2005 by Transaction Publishers, New Brunswick, New Jersey. First published by St. Martin's Press in 1997. Copyright @ 1997 by Mary Chamberlain.

This book is printed on acid-free paper that meets the American National Standard for Permanence of Paper for Printed Library Materials.
Library of Congress Catalog Number: 2004058027
ISBN: 978-0-7658-0824-0
Printed in the United States of America

Library of Congress Cataloging-in-Publication Data

Chamberlain, Mary, 1947
   Narratives of exile and return / Mary Chamberlain.
      p. cm.—(Memory and narrative)
   Originally published: New York: St. Martin's Press, 1997. With new introd.
   Includes bibliographical references and index.
   ISBN 0-7658-0824-2 (pbk. : alk. paper)
   1. Caribbean Area—Emigration and immigration. 2. Return migration—Caribbean Area. 3. Barbados—Emigration and immigration—Case studies. 4. Retum—migration—Barbados—Case studies. I. Title. II. Series.

JV7321.C43   2004
304.8'729041—dc22   2004058027

Contents

Transaction Introduction

An appropriate subtitle for *Narratives of Exile and Return* would have been 'transgenerational life stories and the migration journey,' for the focus of the book is as much on the narratives of migration as the ways in which they were played out through families across the generations, and across the oceans. Although the use of life story methodology was to reveal the dynamics of a Caribbean migratory culture (and to challenge many of the former models of migration behavior), what it also revealed was the centrality of families not only in enabling migration, but in the lives of Caribbean migrant people, at home and abroad. It is this latter point, on the importance of families in the Caribbean and its Diaspora, which is appropriate to highlight in the introduction to this new edition.

There is no other region of the world whose character has been so molded not only by migration *into* the area, but equally *out* of it on a long-term and continuing basis, where departing migrants continue to maintain, and replenish family links with the region, and, where possible, return in retirement.[1] Now, the revolution in communications—from cheap flights to the Internet—has facilitated regular telephonic or email contact and easier and more frequent patterns of visiting, to the extent as Nancy Foner[2] has indicated for the United State, that it has diluted the need to *return* permanently by enabling a pattern of migratory *commuting*. A comparable pattern is emerging with British-based West Indians who either return to the Caribbean for protracted periods, or play host to Caribbean family members for up to six months (the legal maximum).[3] As a result, the links between the Caribbean and its citizens abroad have been reinforced, and extended across the generations.

Like their African American counterparts, Caribbean families dispersed through migration (and often generations of migrants) hold regular reunions that bring together kinfolk in their hundreds.[4]

The clue to the importance of the family is found in the seminal influence of migration on the culture of the Caribbean, enabled, facilitated, and permitted by families. In this, the family story is central to the narratives of migration, as well as to the networks and support systems that migrants need and utilize. It is also found, relatedly, in the emphasis placed within Afro-Caribbean families on lineage and descent lines, from either side of the family, the importance of ties of consanguinity and affinity,[5] and the links between family identity and national belongings, at home and abroad.[6] Caribbean families were forged out of the modernizing impulses of slavery which left them, for the most part, bereft of kin,[7] and fused kinship and family practices from African and European influences to create new, unique, Creolized families. From the start, therefore, Caribbean families were creative, transcultural institutions, a heritage that served them well in their subsequent migratory journeys as those transcultural families emerged into modern day transnational families with vibrant links with family members across oceans, generations, and locales. For families formed on the margins, and often forced to live there, the centrality of that history is integral to their sense of self; it contains also a strong message of survival and identity, for the nurturing tradition of Caribbean families ensures a safety net for all its members and a continuing source of cultural and national belonging.

Since the first edition in 1997 of *Narratives of Exile and Return,* a scholarly momentum has emerged on the meanings and implications of transnationalism, particularly transnationalism 'from below,' on the everyday movements of peoples and products, which continues on a regular basis below the visible plimsoll line of major state or corporate involvement.[8] In many ways the Caribbean was an exemplar of transnationalism long before the concept was invented,[9] its families evolving to accommodate daily the emotional as well as material meanings of transnationalism and to resist and overcome its disruptive tendencies. Linda Basch, Nina Glick Schiller, and Cristina Szanton Blanc drew attention to this in 1994 with the publication of *Nations Unbound. Transnational Projects, Postcolonial Predicaments and Deterritorialized Nation States.* [10] In this, they pointed to the complexity of transnational lives and the impossibility of separating the actors either side of a migration divide, for the strength of family ties, the interconnections of experience and the regularity of movement rendered the old paradigm of emigrants and those left behind, of home and host country, meaningless. These insights were further continued by Nina Glick Schiller and Georges Fouron in *Georges Woke Up Laughing. Long Distance Nationalism and the Search for Home.*[11] Although the locus of the research was Haiti and the United States, the links between family and national belongings and pride added a further, and very relevant dimension to the debate on transnationalism and one which had resonances in my work on Barbadian migrants, by pointing to the importance of the imaginary and the emotional life across borders through which 'transmigrants' live and order their lives.

It was through families that remittances—so crucial to the survival and mobility of the Caribbean—flowed. But it was also through transnational families that political ideas and organizational skills flowed.[12] It was also transnational families who challenged, and continued to challenge, the borders of the nation state, by globalizing identities and internationalizing living spaces. And it was through families that culture continued to flow.

Neither the significance of transnationalism, nor the impact of Caribbean migrants to the metropolis was recognized when West Indians arrived in the United Kingdom. The British response was local and parochial. Immigrants, and immigration, needed to be managed to ensure the smoothness of race relations in the country. What migration represented in terms of transnational and transcultural crossings was passed by. It was widely assumed, in the 1950s and 1960s, that the migration of West Indians to Britain was to escape the poverty of the Caribbean. That West Indians arrived from societies where migration, and return migration, had been a feature for at least a hundred years was either not known, or ignored. That West Indians may have *preferred* to go to the United States was beyond British comprehension. It was further assumed that West Indians had no culture,[13] or, rather, that their culture was essentially a British derivative. As a result, it was thought that West Indians would be able to integrate and assimilate into British society far easier than their counterparts from the Indian sub-continent, whose culture, society and family traditions were long recognized and hallowed by the iconic position that the Indian sub-continent occupied in the British Empire. For all that the West Indies were part of the Empire, Britain had no heroic history of them for West Indians represented slavery, and a reminder of Britain's inglorious past.

But West Indians, like Jasper, arrived with

> One little suitcase, one little valise…full of food…there was yams, and sweet potatoes and breadfruit, there was eggs, pumpkins. I'm walking through the airport with a suitcase filled with food. And there's sugar cane syrup…molasses. Molasses is good for the blood pressure in Britain, you know, that sort of thing…. So all that, and…bush, bush tea, the bush for making bush tea.[14]

In the words of the German philosopher Walter Benjamin, there was a 'compressed fullness'[15] in Jasper's suitcase, stuffed not only with food, but the symbols of a family and a culture transported, transplanted, and transformed across the ocean. West Indians arrived with dreams forged in the dichotomized history of the colonial Caribbean: on the one hand, a history and a culture salvaged, and inherited, through families, but vilified, denigrated, and misunderstood by colonial authorities and, on the other, a history of Barbados and the 'Mother Country' and all she represented in terms of justice and propriety, and all she claimed in terms of opportunity and loyalty. These were two competing visions, two ways of looking at the world—what DuBois described, in relation to African Americans, as double consciousness. 'One ever feels this twoness,' he wrote, 'an American, a Negro; two souls, two thoughts, two unreconciled strivings; two warring ideals in one dark body, whose dogged strength alone keeps it from being torn asunder.'[16] It was a familiar theme for the black West Indian, a tension between lived reality and British ideology, and one long articulated by its intellectuals such as C.L.R. James, as Bill Schwarz has argued.[17] It offered particular insights that, alongside the experience of journey (a rarity for most Britons in the 1950s and 1960s) made West Indians particularly sensitive to the nuances of their arrival and its implications for the future.

When West Indians arrived in the Mother Country, they may have been newly enfranchised but they were well aware, and the memories were still living, that enfranchisement had been forced out of Britain by the riots that had racked the region in 1937 and 1938 and had left, in Barbados alone, fourteen dead, and that the struggle for Independence represented the unfinished business of slave emancipation. They may have set off as Barbadians or Jamaicans, Kitticians or Grenadians but they arrived as West Indians, with regional identities, and a burgeoning self-awareness. The distance from home and the homogenizing gaze of the white British ensured this. Furthermore, far from West Indians having no culture, they had a great deal of it and, significantly, were, as Bill Schwarz has pointed out, about to involve 'us' in 'their' journey.[18] Their presence challenged the bulwarks of Empire and the meanings of Britishness as much as it altered the demography of the inner cities, the climate of tolerance, and intolerance and the legislative and employment framework. Britain was never the same again.

Yet, as Caryl Phillips has recently pointed out, the presence of West Indians was rarely reflected in the writings of contemporary British novelists, even though all would have been aware of the West Indian and, later, Asian presence. Phillips argues that in British novels of the 1950s and 1960s, with the exception of Colin MacInnes (who was Australian)[19] there is a significant absence of black West Indians. By contrast, West Indians writers and intellectuals not only wrote about their experiences in England, and reflected on its philosophical and historical significance,[20] but, crucially, as Phillips points out, they wrote about 'contemporary Britain with eyes that take in not only black people but white people too,'[21] in novels,[22] songs,[23] essays,[24] and plays.[25] West Indians, in other words, saw, long before the white British, how profound their impact was to be on the development of contemporary Britain.

Even now, it is the children of those West Indian migrants who continue the tradition of reflecting on the meaning of this migration, this Diaspora, and its connections and influences. It is no coincidence that Paul Gilroy entitled his seminal book on the inter-culturation of black intellectual ideas *The Black Atlantic. Modernity and Double Consciousness,*[26] for West Indians recognized that migration was always a link with abroad, not a severance from home, that the Atlantic was not the divide between nations, but the conduit for people and ideas. It is a theme repeated in other essays and novels.[27] The most recent addition to this genre was *The Big Life,* a musical, which opened at the Theatre Royal, in Stratford, East London, in April 2004. Loosely based on *Love's Labor Lost, The Big Life* was at once a vibrant and witty celebration of those early West Indian migrants to Britain, and a hard hitting punch at the levels of discrimination and prejudice they faced in their everyday lives, along with their shattered dreams and the grinding drudgery of their lives. 'Work, work, work, work,' sings the chorus to one of their songs, 'sleep, sleep, sleep, sleep.'

> I feel so fed up
> Live a lie
> I feel so lonely
> I could cry
> And all the time
> Days pass me by
> All the time
> Life pass me by
> Just pass me by.[28]

Between scenes, one of the characters, Mrs. Aphrodite, a 'member of the audience,' reflected and commented on the distance traveled between the scene just witnessed, and the present, on her own journey to Britain and that of the global linkages that underpinned it. She embodied the dialogue between past and present, the West Indies and Britain, the Caribbean and the world, which the West Indians started with their arrival in Britain in the 1950s, but which had precedents in the Caribbean dialogue with the United States in the early years of the twentieth century.

It was something of this initial encounter, and this spirit, that *Narratives of Exile and Return* sought to capture: the immediate impact of arrival and the trauma as the Mother Country failed to materialize along the lines taught and imagined back home; the encounter with the city and its racialized gaze, the stories sent home, along with the remittances, to disguise the pain, and to encourage others to come, to develop a consoling narrative that could both exonerate and valorize the journey. And all the while, a realization, and then a celebration, of the difference, of the families who had nurtured and encouraged them to come, and which stood as models and metaphors for appropriate and moral behavior, of the village communities that had guided them and taught them the principles of communitarianism and solidarity, of the faith practices that inspired and humbled them, all of which metamorphosed into viable communities which absorbed the migrants and cushioned the experience, but actively participated with the outside world in a constant and restless dialectic, a 'twoness' within as Britain was accommodated and assimilated into the West Indian experience, and a 'twoness' without as Britain, in turn, was forced to confront a world, this time, not of its choosing.

West Indians have reminded us of the long history of Caribbean transnationalism—inextricably linked with Britain's colonial past—and introduced this into the fabric of British lives, in much the same way as they have done for New York, Toronto, and other major North American cities.[29] It is their comings and goings, their busy, living links with families that cross histories and nations, their privileged, critical eye at the margins, which reaffirmed the historical link between the Caribbean and Britain, and ensured that it could never be easily severed again. At the heart of this ever present reminder, were and are Caribbean migrant families, emblems of the possibilities of the cultural mixing and miscegenation that arrived with slavery, and which continues in the creative avenues of transnationalism.

It is particularly relevant that *Narratives of Exile and Return* is to be republished within the *Memory and Narrative* series. Based on life histories across generations of the same family, it explores how narratives link the generations, and how their particular dynamics are inherited through them. In this case, the narrative is that of migration, refracted through memories, where exile and return jostle as real possibilities, but where exile *from,* or return *to,* remains an anxiety and ambiguity, particularly for the British-born children of migrants. I also attempted, through the use of life stories and oral histories, to tease out other, hidden complexities in the story of migration—of the dislocations, as well as the continuities, of generations, of gender, memorized through significantly different frameworks, of young people straddling the paradox of Barbadian, and Diasporic, identities. In the second half of the book, I wished to present the life stories of some Barbadian families, and the full richness of the migrant experience, rooted in Barbados and articulated through those memories and cultural templates. When *Narratives of Exile and Return* was first published,[30] *Memory and Narrative* was not quite born. I am delighted, that the re-publication of its U.S. edition can now be included as part of the series, and that Transaction Publishers, and in particular Professor Irving Louis Horowitz, had the vision and the confidence to re-launch this series (and my book within it) and make it available for a wide audience. I thank him and his colleagues at Transaction.

Mary Chamberlain
London, July 2004

Notes

1. See Harry Goulbourne, *Caribbean Transnational Experience* (London: Pluto Press, 2002), esp. chapter 8, 'Returning "Home" from the "Mother Country" in the 1990s.'

2. Nancy Foner 'West Indians in New York City and London. A Comparative Analysis' in *Caribbean Life in New York City;* Nancy Foner, 'Towards a Comparative Perspective on Caribbean Migration' in *Caribbean Migration. Globalised Identities* ed. Mary Chamberlain (London: Routledge, 1998); Linda Basch, Nina Glick Schiller, Cristina Szanton Blanc, *Nations Unbound. Transnational Projects, Postcolonial Predicaments and Deterritorialized Nation-States* (Langhorne: Gordon and Breach, 1994); see also Carol Boyce-Davis, *Black Women, Writing and Identity. Migrations of the Subject* (London and New York: Routledge, 1994).
3. Dwaine Plaza, 'Frequent Flyer Grannies,' paper presented to the Caribbean Studies Association (1996).
4. Constance Sutton, 'Celebrating Ourselves: The Family Reunion Rituals of African Caribbean Transnational Families,' *Global Networks* 4(3) (July 2004): 243-258.
5. There is a considerable literature on Afro-Caribbean families. For an overview, see Christine Barrow, *Family in the Caribbean. Themes and Perspectives* (Kingston: Ian Randle, 1996); Jean Besson, *Martha Brae's Two Histories. European Expansion and Caribbean Culture-Building in Jamaica,* (Chapel Hill and London: University of North Carolina Press, 2002), 27.
6. Mary Chamberlain, *Love in the Caribbean. African-Caribbean Families at Home and Abroad* (2005, forthcoming).
7. Sidney Mintz, 'The Caribbean as a Socio-Cultural Area,' *Journal of World History,* 9, 4 (1966): 914-5
8. Useful summaries of this literature can be found in the various working papers of the ESRC *Transnational Communities Research Programme* and the journal *Global Networks* which evolved from it. See also Arjun Appadurai, *Modernity at Large: Cultural Dimensions of Globalisation* (University of Minnesota Press, 1996); Ulf Hannerz, *Transnational Connections: Culture, People, Places* (London: Routledge, 1996); Alejandro Portes, Luis E. Guarnizo, Patricia Landolt. 'The Study of Transnationalism: Pitfalls and Promises of an Emergent Research Field,' *Ethnic and Racial Studies* 22, 2 (1999): 217-237; Deborah Bryceson and Vuorela Ulla, eds., *The Transnational Family. New European Frontiers and Global Networks* (Oxford: Berg, 2002).
9. Don Robotham, 'Transnationalism in the Caribbean: Formal and Informal,' AES distinguished lecture *American Ethnologist* 25, 2 (1996):307-321.
10. Linda Basch et al, *Nations Unbound.*
11. Nina Glick Schiller and Georges Eugene Fouron, *Georges Woke Up Laughing. Long Distance Nationalism and the Search for Home* (Durham/London: Duke University Press, 2001).
12. Constance Sutton, 'Some Thoughts on Gendering and Internationalising Our Thinking about Transnational Migrations' in *Towards a Transnational Perspective on Migration. Race, Class, Ethnicity and Nationalism Reconsidered,* eds. Nina Glick Schiller, Linda Basch, and Cristina Blanc-Szanton (New York: New York Academy of Sciences, 1992); Constance Sutton and Elsa Chaney, eds., *Caribbean Life in New York City: Sociocultural Dimensions* (New York: Center for Migration Studies of New York, 1994 [1987]); Mary Chamberlain, ed. *Caribbean Migration. Globalised Identities.*
13. See, for instance, the West India Royal Commission 1945; Thomas Simey *Welfare and Planning in the West Indies* (Oxford: Clarendon Press, 1946).
14. Cited in Mary Chamberlain, 'The Family as Model and Metaphor in Caribbean Migration to Britain,' *Journal of Ethnic and Migration Studies* 25, 2 (April 1999): 251.

15. Walter Benjamin, *One Way Street* (London: Verso, 1997 [1974]), 75.
16. W. E. DuBois, *The Souls of Black Folk* (New York: Signet, 1995), 45.
17. Bill Schwarz 'Crossing the Seas' in *West Indian Intellectuals in Britain*, ed. Bill Schwarz (Manchester: Manchester University Press, 2003), 2-30.
18. Bill Schwarz 'Crossing the Seas,' 2.
19. Colin MacInnes, *City of Spades* (London: Alison and Busby, 1993 [1957]).
20. The most prominent intellectual to have done so is the Jamaican, Stuart Hall, in a long and distinguished career that has spanned over fifty years of critical reflection, which has included the formation of cultural studies as a viable discipline, and which has contributed immeasurably to an understanding of race, colonialism, and cultural contact. See also the novels of Sam Selvon, V.S. Naipaul or George Lamming; for non-fiction, see George Lamming *The Pleasures of Exile* (Ann Arbor: University of Michigan Press, 1992 [1960]).
21. Caryl Phillips 'Kingdom of the Blind' *The Guardian Review* (17 July 2004): 4-6
22. Sam Selvon, *The Lonely Londoners* (London: Longman, 1956); George Lamming, *The Emigrants* (Ann Arbor: University of Michigan Press, 1994 [1954]); *Water with Berries* (New York: Longman, 1971).
23. See, for instance, the calypsos of Lord Kitchener which reflect and reflect on the experiences of West Indian migrants to London. These calypsos, and others of the period, have been brought together in *London is the Place for me. Trinidadian Calypso in London, 1950-1956* (Honest Jon's Records, 2002).
24. Lamming, *The Pleasures of Exile*; Donald Hinds, *Journey to an Illusion* (London: Heinemann, 1966).
25. *The Motherland,* based on the life experiences of West Indian women to Britain in the 1950s was first performed at the Oval House Theatre, South London, 9 July 1982. Eylse Dodgson, *The Motherland. West Indian Women to Britain in the 1950s* (London: Heinemann Educational Books Litd, 1984).
26. Paul Gilroy, *The Black Atlantic. Modernity and Double Consciousness* (London: Verso, 1993).
27. See Caryl Phillips, *The Atlantic Sound* (London: Faber and Faber, 2000); Mike Phillips, *London Crossings. A Biography of Black Britain* (London: Continuum, 2001); Zadie Smith, *White Teeth* (London: Hamish Hamilton, 2000).
28. Paul Sirett, *The Big Life* (Stratford: Theatre Royal Stratford East, 2004), 77. *The Big Life* was first performed on 17 April 2004.
29. Philip Kasinitz, *Caribbean New York. Black Immigrants and the Politics of Race* (Ithaca: Cornell University Press, 1992).
30. Mary Chamberlain, *Narratives of Exile and Return,* Warwick University Caribbean Studies (London: Macmillan, 1997); *Narratives of Exile and Return* (New York: St. Martin's Press, 1997).

Abbreviations

BDA   Barbados, Department of Archives

MTIL   Ministry of Trade, Industry and Labour
           (Barbados Government)

OPCS   Office of Population, Census and Surveys (UK)

Acknowledgements

I owe huge debts of gratitude to the many people who contributed to the making of this book. First, I must thank the many Barbadians, here and in Barbados, who welcomed me into their homes, who willingly and trustingly allowed me to interview them, often for hours (and sometimes days) on end, and who were so generous with their time and their hospitality. Although in the text I have changed names and identities, and although not everyone I interviewed has been quoted directly, I owe a very special and heartfelt thanks to the following, without whose experiences, memories and insights this book could not have been written. George Adamson, Eurene Alleyne, Garfield Alleyne, Mrs Agard, Muriel Alder, Vita Ashby, Clarice Best, Carole Boulemnakner, Carlotta Boyce, Beulah Boyce, Edwardine Boyce, Franklyn Boyce, Beryl Bovell, Grantley Bovell, Arthur Brewster, Thelma Brewster, Verona Broomes, Edgerton Broomes, Coleridge Burke, Levi Burnett, Genetha Callender, Claudette Carrington, Vere Carrington, Coreen Chandler, Simon Chandler, Pauline Clarke, Tracey Clarke, Ursula Clarke, Averil Corbin, Fitzgerald Corbin, Christopher Cumberbatch, Eldridge Cumberbatch, Violet Cumberbatch, Marva Duguid, Radcliffe Duguid, Mr and Mrs Franklyn, Carmen Francis, Greta Garnes, Elaine Goddard, Ellen Lynch Goddard, Joseph Goddard, Earl Harewood, Vere Harewood, Alison Hewitt, Charles Hewitt, Lionel Hewitt, Andrew Jordan, Hansell Jordan, Vas Jordan, Daisy Kellman, Alison Layne, Maria Layne, Semele Mandeville, Conrad Marshall, Douglas Martindale, Kathleen Mayers, Jennifer Mayers, George Medford, Olga Medford, Iris Neblett, Roy Newsom, Leon Norville, Sylvia Norville, Elise Odle, Stanley Odle, William Parris, Carl Rice, Stephen Rice, Iris Rice, Charles Rock, Delbert Sandiford, Linda Sandiford, Elaine Scantlebury, Elmer Scantlebury, Valmay Scott, Everil Springer, Mark Springer, Charles Stuart, Vivien Stuart, Marjorie Todd, Newton Todd, David Williams. I would like to make particular thanks to Coreen Chandler, Christopher Cumberbatch, and Lionel Hewitt who went out of their way to introduce me to members of their families and communities, to Hansell Jordan and Jean White who helped to introduce me to Barbadians in Birmingham and Leeds, and to Victor Jackman in Barbados for the same.

xvii

A special thanks is also due to Leroy Bowen who not only supplied me for several years with fresh eggs, chickens, lamb and the Christmas Turkey but who also introduced me to some of the elderly residents of St. Philip in Barbados whom I interviewed for earlier research on the Barbadian Plantation Tenantry System. It was their memories from this project, which included tales of the migration of their parents and their children, which inspired me to do this research.

I must also thank the Nuffield Foundation, without whose grant this research would not have been possible, the National Life Story Collection of the National Sound Archive of the British Library for administering the grant, and with whom the tapes and transcripts are deposited, and the School of Humanities of Oxford Brookes University for research funding which contributed to transcription costs. Transcribing tapes is a laborious, time consuming and often difficult task, particularly when neither the accent, nor the experience, is familiar and here I must thank Marion Haberhauer who transcribed most of the tapes with considerable efficiency, enthusiasm and good humour. Mrs Christine Matthews, and other members of the staff of the Department of Archives in Barbados, took on board my research and, with great fortitude and courtesy, helped to direct me to the relevant archives and to secure other documents from the appropriate ministries, and to her and her staff I am especially grateful.

Over the years I have presented various chapters as conference papers to the Annual Conferences of the Association of Caribbean Historians, the International Oral History Conference, and the Society for Caribbean Studies or at research seminars at the University of Essex, the University of Delaware, University of the West Indies, St. Augustine and Cave Hill, London History Workshop Seminar, the University of North London and the Humanities Research Centre at Oxford Brookes University. The opportunity this provided, and the individual comments, insights and suggestions which they offered me, were much appreciated. Similarly, Gert Oostindie and Paul Thompson made very useful editorial comments and criticism on earlier articles published in the *New West Indies Guide* and *The International Yearbook of Oral History and Life Stories, Vol III*.

I would also like to thank the British Academy and the School of Humanities of Oxford Brookes University for travel funding to attend the conferences, and to my colleagues for covering my teaching (and examination marking!) in my absences. I am aware that conference trips from England to the Caribbean rarely inspire sympathy, particularly in the late winter, but I hope that this book, in addition to the rum, will persuade them that it was all for a worthy cause.

There were many other friends who over the years have contributed, wittingly or unwittingly, to the formation of this work. Bill Schwarz and Raphael Samuel generously dropped other commitments to read the entire first draft and to comment magnificently and magnanimously. Their insights and criticisms were particularly valuable and always welcome. Similarly, Alastair Hennessy, Gad Heuman and Robin Cohen made invaluable comments on the manuscript and James Walvin and Catherine Hall on individual chapters, and I am grateful to them all for the time and effort they expended on my behalf. I may not have taken all their many helpful and astute suggestions entirely on board, so responsibility for the final product must rest entirely with me.

In addition, a special thank you is due to Sally Alexander, Alessandra Cummins, Anna Davin, Harry Goulbourne, Catherine Hall, Keith Laurence, Bill Schwarz, Raphael Samuel, Paul Thompson and Woodville Marshall whose friendship, over many happy years, and sometimes decades, has always been an inspiration and support, both professionally and personally. Alessandra Cummins must have a special mention for extending unending generosity, patience and politeness while I stayed with her (and her family) for considerable periods in Barbados during 1992 and 1993.

Finally, I must thank my family, my husband Peter and my three wonderful daughters, Rosie, Kate and Alice, for tolerating my sojourns to the Caribbean, my moments of stress, my demands for silence, my minimalist cooking and my sometimes negligent laundering, while I was writing this book. But most of all my thanks are due to the people of Barbados, with whom I lived from 1987–1991, and to whom this book is dedicated.

PART ONE

Introduction

Our family love to travel ... My grandfather was in Cuba and
send for my two uncles ... He leave the girls ... with his wife.
Then after my mother could get grown up, then she went to
Trinidad ... and leave me very small, as a baby ... (My mother)
was working in Trinidad .... Then she ... went on to Panama
and meet her husband there. He took her from Panama to
Jamaica .... I come up to England, 1958 ... and came home to
Barbados in 1987.[1]

Between 1948 and 1973 approximately 550,000 people of Caribbean
birth migrated to Britain, the majority arriving before the 1962
Immigration Act effectively cut off further immigration. The first immigrants came from Jamaica, and they remain by far the largest group of
Caribbean nationals in Britain. The 1971 census (which first differenti-
ated Caribbean nationals by island of birth) revealed that Jamaicans
comprised 171,775 of the total Caribbean population in Britain, Barbadians 27,055, Trinidadians and Tobagodians 17,135 and the Guyanese
21,070.[2] By 1981 the Jamaican community stood at 164,119 or 55.6 per
cent of the Caribbean population, Barbadians 25,247 or 8.55 per cent,
citizens of Trinidad and Tobago 16,334 or 5.53 per cent and Guyanese
21,686 or 7.35 per cent,[3] with the remainder from the Leeward and
Windward Islands. Although the Caribbean community in Britain repre-
sents less than one per cent of the population of Britain, migrants as a
percentage of the population of the *home* countries are large. Between
1951 and 1971, 7 per cent of the population of Jamaica, 12 per cent of
the population of Barbados and 1.5 per cent of the population of Trinidad and Tobago migrated to Britain.[4] These figures suggest that very
different cultural and economic pressures operated in each of those
islands to encourage migration. Equally, although figures on return
migration are difficult to ascertain, nevertheless there has been a significant reduction in the size of the Caribbean communities in the last
decade, some of it as the result of death, but mostly due to re- and return
migration. There are also significant differences. Between the census

2

points 1971 and 1991, the Barbadian and Jamaican communities have declined by 17 per cent (from 27,055 to 22,294, and 171,775 to 142,483 respectively).[5] The Trinidadian community has remained not only stable, but appears to show an increase from 17,135 in 1971 to 17,620 in 1991.[6]

Such significant differences in the patterns of migration, settlement and return require explanation. At the same time, the migrants who arrived in Britain during the 1950s and 1960s are now comfortably into middle-age. Many of their children were born and brought up in Britain. Many are now grandparents. There has been a qualitative change in the structure of the Caribbean community in Britain. At one level it is a stable community with established lineages and networks; at another, it clearly retains elements of transnational mobility. Both features require fresh investigation and raise the question of the extent to which the Caribbean communities in Britain retain or adapt features of their distinctive cultures and traditions. Recent research such as that by Philip Kasinitz[7] or Constance Sutton[8] or Ransford Palmer[9] in the United States, where migration from the Caribbean has been a feature for nearly a century, suggests that these migrants retain a Caribbean identity across generations and remain centred within kinship networks which link the Caribbean and North America. Indeed, it is the resilience of these family networks, the frequent traffic between the Caribbean and North America, and the constant replenishment of Caribbean influence which distinguishes Caribbean migrants in North America. The ease of contemporary communications has strengthened, rather than diminished, these features. It is my contention not only that the Caribbean community in Britain now displays elements which parallel those of North America but that these elements are neither random nor coincidental. Rather, they contain elements common to a Caribbean *migratory* culture which not only functions as an explanatory factor in migration itself, but continues to function as a cohesive and distinctive force within the host society. It may be modified by local conditions, but not eradicated by them.

Much of the early literature on the Caribbean community in Britain privileged the Jamaican community above other communities. Jamaicans had been the first and most numerous to arrive. They became exemplars for the Caribbean. At the same time, the prevailing climate of race awareness and racism in Britain in the 1950s, fuelled by a history of Empire (a poor apprenticeship for racial harmony) and the fall-out from decolonisation, presented all West Indians as ethnically homogenous, devoid of an autonomous historical identity and potentially unsettling. Integration was the goal and the key to successful 'race relations.' The West Indies was British and West Indians were 'Black

Britons.' Joyce Egginton's *They Seek a Living* (1957),[10] Ruth Glass, *London's Newcomers* (1961),[11] Sheila Patterson, *Dark Strangers* (1964),[12] R.B.Davison, *Black British* (1966),[13] Ceri Peach, *West Indian Migration to Britain* (1968),[14] Dilip Hiro, *Black British White British* (1973),[15] Frank Field and Patricia Haikin, *Black Britons*, (1971),[16] Nancy Foner, *Jamaica Farewell*[17] are all testimony (the titles alone often suggesting the theses, if not the assumptions) to these early concerns with settlement and harmony. Written often from the perspective of sociology or social geography, the intellectual framework itself determined the enquiry, and shaped the conclusions.

The migration from the Caribbean was subsequently supplemented by that from the Indian subcontinent and by the 1970s it was no longer possible to equate all migration with that from the Caribbean. Integration as a goal was replaced by 'multi-culturalism.' The apparent differences in educational and occupational achievement between the Asian and Afro-Caribbean communities led to a more considered analysis of ethnic communities in Britain and attempts by, for instance, John Rex[18] or Malcolm Cross,[19] to tease out the historical, social and cultural factors which may account for Afro-Caribbean 'under-achievement', pointing their conclusions towards a differential distribution of public resources while geographers such as Ceri Peach[20] indicated the ways in which the spatial distribution of migrants contributed towards, or detracted from, achievement. Other recent studies have (rightly) distanced themselves from the old race relations paradigm. Embedded in a post-colonial perspective, they focus on the issue of diaspora and on rethinking the notion of identity. Harry Goulbourne's *Ethnicity and Nationalism in Post-Imperial Britain*[21] investigates this from the perspective of a political scientist, looking at the ways in which ethnicity has played into British politics and into a construction of British as well as immigrant identities, echoing in some ways the arguments presented by the historian Catherine Hall on the importance of Empire (and the Caribbean) in the construction of British (and in particular, English) identity in the nineteenth century,[22] and other trends towards discovering a 'pluralist conception of the national past.'[23] For scholars such as Stuart Hall[24] or Paul Gilroy[25] this contemporary focus is an attempt to move beyond the location of ethnicity, and to leap the borders of the nation-state, into a construction of identity which stresses culture, mobility and hybridity. A more empirically based study by John Western[26] also takes identity as its central issue. The majority of *Passage to England*, however, charts the geographic and social mobility within Britain of a small group of Barbadian informants and makes little attempt to address the historical, cultural or ethnic context of Barbadian migration to Britain or the lingering context of Imperialism in which the migrants found themselves in Britain. Its strictly geographic definition of identity lacks the conceptual punch of Hall or Gilroy or, from a different perspective, Homi Bhabha.[27]

Although the debate may have moved from migration to diaspora – in itself a profound and significant shift – nevertheless, it does not answer the question, why do people migrate? Posing the question itself presupposes that migration is an abnormal condition. A cursory look at the modern history of (certainly) Europe and America suggests, however, that migration was the precondition for capitalism, industrialisation and the emergence of the modern nation-state. (A theme touched on in Chapter 1.) Nevertheless, while the historical models of migration – the search for economic improvement or political and religious freedom – persist, migration is still viewed as an aberrant act, the last resort of the desperate. Nomad capital is acceptable, but nomad labour is not.

Why do people migrate? The prevalent economic and structural models of migration behaviour in the 1950s assumed that all migrants were motivated by economic necessity, the result of economic deprivation (unemployment, over population) at home, and the promise of abundant employment elsewhere. That most migrants in the post-Second World War environment appeared to come from underdeveloped nations and gravitated towards developed nations added potency to the premise.[28] Based on observable and objective scientific principles, qualitative and subjective variables such as culture, history or preference found no place within these formulae. This notion found particular echoes within studies of Caribbean migration to Britain. Certainly it lies at the basis of the work by Davison,[29] Glass and Ceri Peach. The postwar migration from the Caribbean to Britain was 'powered by free market forces.'[30] West Indian migrants came at a time of labour scarcity in Britain and surplus in the Caribbean and the patterns of settlement which ensued appeared to support the thesis.[31] Studies based in the Caribbean, such as that of W.F. Maunder,[32] or Gene Tidrick[33] added weight to the argument by highlighting the employment profile of the migrants at the time of departure. In Maunder's survey, for instance, most were un- or underemployed, and the majority were unskilled or semi-skilled.

Most economic models assumed a global dimension and pointed to the cyclical demands and dimensions of international.capital. In this view migration from the Caribbean was either the rational response to labour shortages elsewhere, a natural process in the maintenance of economic equilibrium and thus a form of aid from the First World to the Third or conversely, it was part of a neo-colonialist conspiracy, a form of aid from the Third World to the First.[34] As a refinement on these theses, some scholars, such as Dawn Marshall,[35] have pointed to the policies of the receiving countries as a determinant in migrant destination, and/or to migration as a way of relieving the social pressures created by over-population, and to the role of the state in the construction and direction of labour requirements.[36]

Seductive though these arguments are in terms of explaining migration and highlighting its implications on the host as much as the home society, these models of migration (cyclical labour demands of international capital, policies of receiving countries, the 'pressures' of over-population and unemployment) finally only explain the timing and the scale of specific migratory movements. They fail to account for ways in which migration engages historically with other social and cultural goals, including the 'open' goal of migration *per se*. Critiques of economic and structuralist explanations of Caribbean migration have refocussed on causation by pointing to the links between the environment, culture and migration. Bonham Richardson's *Caribbean Migrants, Environment and Human Survival on St. Kitts and Nevis* indicates how migration is integral to the survival and social renewal of some Caribbean islands, pointing to St. Kitts and Nevis as case studies[37] and elsewhere investigating the impact of migration from Barbados to Panama.[38] A similar theme is explored by Elizabeth Thomas-Hope. Migration, particularly from the Caribbean, is assumed to be 'the movement of labour' where, as she comments 'interpretation (of migrant behaviour) at the level of societal meaning and personal consciousness has scarcely been touched upon.'[39]

As a result, geographers such as Thomas-Hope, or anthropologists such as Karen Fog Olwig[40] point to explanation in migration as a response not just to local 'push' factors of over-population, un- or under employment, or even political repression, and the 'pull' of employment elsewhere, but as an individual choice informed by cultural values and social pressures which encourage and enable such migration.[41] Within this framework, what Thomas-Hope terms the 'homeward orientation' of migration becomes paramount. It helps explain the circularity of Caribbean migration, usefully chronicled by Palmer,[42] and indicates new directions in studies of migrant Caribbean families by highlighting the internationalisation of those families through the extension of the domestic unit abroad.[43]

Although the work of geographers such as Richardson or Thomas-Hope and anthropologists such as Fog Olwig introduce a vital cultural and historical dimension into the debate, for the most part, there have been few studies which place migration within a continuing historical perspective. G.W. Roberts essay on migration from Barbados[44] is one of the few notable exceptions, although the emphasis is heavily chronological and echoes, rather than analyses, the sources used. Mainly governmental, these reflected the concerns of the Barbadian government with the labour supply and over-population. On the other hand, Peter Fryer's *Staying Power: The History of Black People in Britain*[45] or James Walvin's *Black and White: The Negro in English Society 1555–1945*[46] are both excellent investigations into the history of black people in Britain, but are not, as such, histories of Caribbean migration. There has, however, been considerable research on the impact of migration to the Caribbean, particularly that of East Indian migration, usefully summarised by Alvin Thompson in his long bibliographic review essay.[47] Three recent publications, Verene Shepherd, *From Transients to Settlers*,[48] Keith Laurence, *A Question of Labour*,[49] and Walton Look Lai, *Indentured Labour, Caribbean Sugar*[50] all attempt to broaden the debate on migration to the Caribbean beyond the economic impact of East Indian migration to plantation economies by investigating the social and cultural impulses of migration from India (and China), the dynamics between the Colonial Office and the colonial authorities, and the adaptation of Asian migrants within the Caribbean. They are exemplary models of historical migration research which have not been emulated by studies of migration from the Caribbean.

The recent emphasis in Britain on (to simplify crudely) identity, however, while making a valuable and exciting contribution to debate, does not address completely Thomas-Hope's notion of 'societal consciousness' and, with its focus on response rather than motivation, does little to explain the cause or process of migration, or the impact of both on migrants and their families, or indeed the extent to which a migration ideology continues to shape the perspectives, behaviour and identities of Caribbean migrants. Nor does it fully investigate the contemporary historical development of Caribbean communities in Britain. Indeed, there is little synthesis between these 'revisionist' studies of Caribbean migration, between the focus on the 'societal consciousness' of the Caribbean, and issues of ethnicity and identity which occupy much of the contemporary debate in Britain. Yet manoeuvring between and around these models and explanations are the migrants themselves, their children, and sometimes their grandchildren, occupying serial positions of identity and consciousness, moulded in the Caribbean and modulated across the generations and across the seas. The story of Caribbean migration is an international one, and a continuing one.

This research is based on a quota sample of eighty five life-story interviews across two and three generations of migrant families which originated in Barbados. Contact with informants in Britain and Barbados was made initially through membership of, or an association with the members of, various branches of the Barbados Association, of whom the majority had family members of previous generations migrate. The sample ensured a balance of class, gender, occupation and educational attainment. In all, 85 interviews were conducted, 39 with migrants to the United Kingdom, 23 with their parents in Barbados, 20 with children born in Britain or brought here as young children, and three with children left in Barbados. This is not an attempt to provide a grand theory of migration, nor a universal model. Rather, it focusses on the responses and perceptions of migrants and their families to the particular process of migration from Barbados to Britain. It is an attempt to convey and analyse the social character of that experience, which was – and remains – uniquely theirs. It is as much to do with understanding the history and culture of migration as the process by which such a culture is transmitted and transformed.

It does so in two particular ways. The story which opens this chapter was one I was to hear many times again. Its significance lay, I believed, in the challenge it offered to the assumption that migration arose from an historical, rather than an economic, vacuum. This was a *family* which for three *known* generations had migrated. This was a family which 'love to travel.' The significance of the family has long preoccupied the social and behavioural sciences. For sociologists and social anthropologists the connection of family, culture and memory to socialisation and cultural transmission is clearly recognised.[51] Similarly, within psychoanalysis and psychology the role of the family and, in particular, generational relationships, role models and the family stories (and secrets) which transmit and mediate them, have been recognised as pivotal in the shaping of personality and behaviour.[52]

Historians have been slow to recognise the significance and usefulness of the family in understanding, indeed driving, historical transmission, behaviour or movement. Family structure, household organisation and demography have been legitimate areas of historical concern but as indicators of social change, rather than its engine. Even those historians who use oral sources, whether engaged in social history or gender history, have used the family and the detail collected either as the gauge by which social mobility is measured, or the stage on which identities of class, race and gender are located, and social roles reflected. Overall the family assumes at best an indicative role in the formation of social behaviour, at worst an indirect or passive role. Its role as an active agent, its central position as cultural mediator, if not agitator, and the vitality of family dynamics in directing social and individual behaviour, seemed not to have engaged the research imagination of historians. The emphasis, and the debate, has been around the substance of memory, rather than the historical *context* in which memory is formulated and reformulated.

It is this context which now needs to be examined. This research, using oral life-stories and engaging with different generations of a family is an attempt to see the family as both the tool *and* the material which creates and shapes historical mentalities and identities. It recognises that the family is not merely the bridge, but the conduit, between the individual and the collectivity. Since many historians are concerned primarily with social movement, the family in terms both of its outer structure and inner directives may offer a key to understanding historical change and perception.

Thus, drawing on insights from both the social and behavioural sciences, this suggests several important dimensions. First, the existence of a family dynamic, in this case, a migration dynamic which both determined behaviour and gave it meaning; second, the interplay between this migration dynamic and other family dynamics (such as colour), and family goals, (such as social mobility); third, the importance of the family in approving and enabling migration; and fourth, an ethos reflecting and reproducing a broader culture of migration which perhaps ran parallel with, but did not necessarily conform to, the vagaries of international labour demands. Indeed, once family stories and memories are taken into perspective then the motives for migration become more complex, ambiguous and culturally specific.

Although the original motivations of migrants may be 'history' for their children, nevertheless the dreams and aspirations which were forged by them may retain their momentum translated and transformed by subsequent generations. The global dimension of migration, played out in international labour markets, and mediated by the manoeuvrings of the host polities, engages with a home-based social and cultural history which has furnished and continues to furnish Caribbean migrants and their children with their own agenda. In this agenda, the family can be seen to play a role as both the end goal, and the means to achieve it. It is worth reconstructing those motivations, for the historical insights they may bear on present and future migrant behaviour. In the case of Barbados, it can show how the links between family and migration continue to play a role in the motivation of migrants and thereby contribute towards a contemporary understanding of the hopes, aspirations and lifestyles of the Barbadian community in Britain, including the emergence of Caribbean family structures in Britain, and demographic change. Moreover, by focussing on one Caribbean community, rather than a conflation of the community as a whole, it is possible to isolate features which may link, and distinguish, behaviour. For, whatever the reason for migration, migrants come from somewhere. They arrive with a cultural suitcase, made locally. They arrive caught in the tension between the global and the local, between the international and the

national, between *their* idea of the global and *their* idea of the local.
They are not acultural itinerants, international vagrants with no fixed
abode, but rational human beings driven by complex and mobile strategies, fretworks of dreams and aspirations, calculations and plans, ob-
scure directives and unarticulated responses, changing and changed by
their journey. The key to all this lies within memory in its twin role as
agent of socialisation and historical evidence. The migration narratives
demonstrate the historically socialising function of what Maurice
Halbwachs describes as the 'collective memory.'[53]

Memories contain historical memory, the cumulative imagination
of others. We remember earlier generations, and their memories are
incorporated into our own. Their past elides into our present. Pierre
Bourdieu suggests that we call carry, to a certain extent, the collective
history of our group or class, and, as Raphael Samuel reminds us,
history is 'a social form of knowledge; the work, in any given instance,
of a thousand different hands.'[54] To the categories of group or class
should be added gender, as one of the central organising structures of
society. Not only therefore do gender, class and ethnicity shape that
social knowledge, they also determine response to it. They are the
imaginative categories through which experience is organised, recalled,
recounted and passed on. They constitute the framework of narrative
and operate in and through the experiences of migration, as one experience in a set, to shape memory and explain events.

The narratives recounted provide not merely rich empirical data,
but are important cultural constructions in themselves. What we remember and recall is not random, but conforms and relates to this social
knowledge of the world. Memory and narrative are shaped by social
categories, by language and priorities, by experience and tense, by
choice and context. They are shaped also by imagination, by dreams and
nightmares, hopes and fantasies which, however private they may feel,
are moulded by culture. We recall past events through present time, and
the present always anticipates the future. The past also contained at
some stage a future, what might have been and what may yet be.
Memory not only recounts; it also explains as it measures and judges. In
the process, it necessarily selects and re-presents, what Alessandro
Portelli calls the 'uchronic imagination.'[55] Memory is essentially (as the
Romantics from Wordsworth to Freud have attested) a function of the
imagination. This does not invalidate it as a source (for there are few
historical sources devoid of imagination) but rather alerts us to its
potential. Memory not only recounts events, but offers also the attitudes
and emotions which surrounded events, then and now. It alerts us to
individual consciousness, subjectivity as well as to a collective consciousness, a culture.

At the same time, as particular themes can be found repeated across generations, they are sometimes repeated within generations. They may be reinterpreted and reinvented, yet still conform in structure, if not always in detail. The words may change, but the melody remains. There is a narrative repertoire of explanation and account, genres which, in oral narrative as in literature, reflect social practice as well as classify it and which convey vital social and historical information.

In the United States, the migration narrative of African Americans with its movements from South to North, from rural to urban, from liberation to alienation, has been a theme within literature, art and music.[56] The migration narratives of the Caribbean may not have captured the attention of scholars and critics and they may not have shaped the Caribbean aesthetic in such a central way. They are, nevertheless, there, these narratives of movement and freedom, exile and return, success and failure, told through families and by example and reflected, from time to time, in the literature of Selvon or Lamming, or in rare autobiographies such as Donald Hinds, *Journey to an Illusion*,[57] Louise Shore, *Pure Running*,[58] or constructed biographies such as Elyse Dodgson, *Motherland*.[59]

It is these twin themes – family dynamics and narrative genre – which are the concern of this book. It is an attempt to draw out and explore some of the migration narratives and reinstate them alongside those other dominant narratives of migration and modernity. Chapter 1 sets the historical context, of the migratory history of the Caribbean and of Barbados within it. Chapter 2 details the contemporary context of the postwar migration from Barbados to Britain. In this, I have found Raymond Williams' notion of a 'structure of feeling' an useful device for highlighting both the migratory 'mood' of Barbados in the 1950s and 1960s and the climate of reception of Britain in the same period. Chapter 3 uses a case-study approach to explore the role, importance and variety of family dynamics, while Chapter 4 returns to the theme opened in Chapter 2 and looks at the responses of the migrants to their reception in Britain. Chapter 5 opens up the theme of genre and in particular looks at gender as an explanatory tool and an organising principle of narration and response. Chapter 6 concludes with more case-studies which look at the importance of family in shaping the responses of the generation born (or raised) in Britain to those Barbadians who came here earlier.

Part Two presents the edited transcripts of two and three generations of five Barbadian families, drawn from the sample as a whole. Some of the individuals have already been introduced in the text of Part One. These narratives are necessarily the result of my interviewing practice and editing priorities. They are also the result of what was told to me, though a series of open-ended questions designed, as far as possible, to allow my informants to control the agenda and content of their life's narration. But that was not, nor ever can be, neutral. In addition to the collectivity of memory, the chemistry and the politics of the interview contains within it the interplay, and autonomy, of gender, race, class, education, culture, and subjectivity. It also contains the wishes and motives of the individual to present themselves in a particular way to an outsider, and to the unencountered world beyond. The narratives contain commissions. They also contain omissions. These were memories told to me. But they are not distortions. They are what they are: edited interviews, based on memory, which contain empirical data on the social history of Barbados and of Barbadian migrants to Britain. They are expressive autobiographical tracts. I hope my editing – to reduce the spoken word to a literary form, in a reasonable length – has remained as far as possible true to my source.

References

1   B5/1/A/9,2. Barbados Migration Project (M. Chamberlain). Tapes and transcripts deposited at the National Life Story Collection of the National Sound Archive of the British Library. References refer to interview number, tape number, side, and page references.
2   1971 Census for England and Wales. Office of Population Census and Survey (OPCS).
3   Percentage figures quoted in Ceri Peach, *The Caribbean in Europe: Contrasting Patterns of Migration and Settlement in Britain, France and the Netherlands*, Research Paper in Ethnic Relations, No. 15, Centre for Research in Ethnic Relations, University of Warwick, 1991.
4   Figures calculated from Caribbean census and OPCS census data.
5   UK census returns 1971, 1981, 1991. OPCS.
6   Figures computed from UK census returns 1981–1991, OPCS.
7   Philip Kasinitz, *Caribbean New York: Black Immigrants and the Politics of Race*, Ithaca, Cornell University Press, 1992.
8   Constance Sutton and Elsa Chaney (eds), *Caribbean Life in New York City: sociocultural dimensions*, New York, Center for Migration Studies of New York, 1994.
9   Ransford Palmer, 'Caribbean Development and the Migration Imperative' in Ransford Palmer (ed.) *In Search of a Better Life: Perspectives on Migration from the Caribbean*, New York, Praeger, 1990.
10   Joyce Eggington, *They Seek A Living*, London, Hutchinson, 1957.
11   Ruth Glass, *London's Newcomers*, Cambridge, Mass., Harvard University Press, 1961.
12   Sheila Patterson, *Dark Strangers*, London, Penguin, 1964.
13   R.B. Davison, *Black British*, London, Institute of Race Relations/Oxford University Press, 1966. See also R.B. Davison, *West Indian Migrants*, London, Oxford University Press, 1962.
14   Ceri Peach, *West Indian Migration to Britain: A Social Geography*, London, Oxford University Press, 1968.

15 Dilip Hiro, *Black British White British: A History of Race Relations in Britain*, London, Pelican, 1973.
16 Frank Field and Patricia Haikin (eds), *Black Britons*, London, Oxford University Press, 1971.
17 Nancy Foner, *Jamaica Farewell: Jamaican Migrants in London*, London, Routledge and Kegan Paul, 1979.
18 John Rex and Sally Tomlinson, *Colonial Immigrants in a British City*, London, Routledge and Kegan Paul, 1979; John Rex, 'The Heritage of Slavery and Social Disadvantage' in Colin Brock (ed.), *The Caribbean in Europe*, London, Frank Cass, 1986.
19 Malcolm Cross, 'Migration and Exclusion: Caribbean Echoes and British Realities' in Colin Brock op. cit.; Malcolm Cross and Han Entzinger (eds), *Lost Illusions: Caribbean Minorities in Britain and the Netherlands*, London, Routledge, 1988.
20 Ceri Peach, 'Patterns of Afro-Caribbean Migration and Settlement in Britain 1945–1981' in Colin Brock, op. cit.
21 Harry Goulbourne, *Ethnicity and Nationalism in Post-Imperial Britain*, Cambridge, Cambridge University Press, 1991.
22 See, for instance, Catherine Hall, 'White Visions, Black Lives: the Free Villages of Jamaica', *History Workshop Journal*, 36, Autumn 1993.
23 Raphael Samuel, Editorial, *History Workshop Journal*, Issue 40, Autumn 1995.
24 Stuart Hall, 'Cultural Identity and Diaspora' in J. Rutherford (ed.), *Identity: Community, Culture and Difference*, London, Lawrence and Wishart, 1990; or 'The Local and the Global: Globalization and Ethnicity' in A.D. King (ed.) *Culture, Globalization and the World System: Contemporary Conditions for the Representations of Identity*, Basingstoke, Macmillan, 1991.
25 Paul Gilroy, *The Black Atlantic: Modernity and Double Consciousness*, London, Verso, 1993.
26 John Western, *Passage to England: Barbadian Londoners Speak of Home*, London, UCL Press, 1992.
27 Homi Bhabha, 'Between Identities' in *International Yearbook of Oral History and Life Stories*, Vol III, Migration and Identity. Oxford, Oxford University Press, 1993.
28 M.P. Todaro, *International Migration in Developing Countries*, Geneva, International Labour Organisation, 1976; I. Wallerstein, *The Capitalist World Economy*, Cambridge, Cambridge University Press, 1979.
29 R.B. Davison, *West Indian Migrants*, London, Oxford University Press, 1962; Ceri Peach, *West Indian Migration to Britain: A Social Geography*, London, Oxford University Press, 1968.
30 Ceri Peach, *The Caribbean in Europe: Contrasting Patterns of Migration and Settlement in Britain, France and the Netherlands*, Centre for Research in Ethnic Relations, Research Paper in Ethnic Relations, No. 15, October 1991.
31 See also Ruth Glass, *London's Newcomers*, Cambridge, Mass., Harvard University Press, 1961.
32 W.F. Maunder, 'New Jamaican Emigration', *Social and Economic Studies*, (4), 1955.
33 Gene Tidrick, 'Some Aspects of Jamaican Emigration to the United Kingdom 1953–1962', *Social and Economic Studies*, (15) 1966.
34 Hymie Rubenstein, 'Remittances and Rural Underdevelopment', *Human Organisation* 1983, 42(4); Hillbourne Watson, 'Theoretical and Methodologi-

cal Problems in Commonwealth Caribbean Migration Research: Conditions and Causality', *Social and Economic Studies*, Kingston, 1982, 31(1); E.M. Petras, *Jamaican Labor Migration: White Capital and Black Labor 1850–1930*, Boulder, Westview Press, 1988; E.M. Petras, 'The role of national boundaries in a cross-national labour market', *International Journal of Urban and Regional Research*, 4(2), 1980, pp. 157–194; Elsa M. Chaney, 'Peoples on the Move: An International perspective on Caribbean Migration' in Richard Millett and M. Marvin Will, *The Restless Caribbean: Changing Patterns of International Relations*, New York, Praeger Publishers, 1979.

35   Dawn Marshall, 'The International Politics of Caribbean Migration' in Richard Millett and W. Marvin Will, *The Restless Caribbean: Changing Patterns of International Relations*, New York, Praeger, 1979.

36   Robin Cohen, *The New Helots: Migrants in the International Division of Labour*, Aldershot, Avebury Press, 1987.

37   Bonham Richardson, *Caribbean Migrants, Environment and Human Survival on St. Kitts and Nevis*, Knoxville, University of Tennessee Press, 1983.

38   Bonham Richardson, *Panama Money in Barbados 1900–1920*, Knoxville, University of Tennessee Press, 1985.

39   Elizabeth Thomas-Hope, *Explanation in Caribbean Migration*, London, Macmillan Caribbean, 1992.

40   Karen Fog Olwig, 'The Migration Experience: Nevisian Women at Home and Abroad' in Janet H. Momsen (ed.) *Women and Change in the Caribbean*, Kingston, Ian Randle/London, James Currey/Bloomington and Indianapolis, Indiana University Press, 1993.

41   Elizabeth Thomas-Hope, *Explanation in Caribbean Migration*, Warwick University Caribbean Studies Series, London, Macmillan, 1993; Elizabeth Thomas-Hope 'Caribbean Diaspora, the Inheritance of Slavery: Migration from the Commonwealth Caribbean' in Colin Brock (ed.), op. cit, 1986; Karen Fog Olwig, 'The migration experience: Nevisian women at home and abroad', in Janet Momsen (ed.), *Women and Change in the Caribbean*, Kingston, Ian Randle, 1993.

42   Ransford Palmer, 1990, op. cit.

43   Karen Fog Olwig, 1993, op. cit.

44   G.W. Roberts, 'Emigration from the Island of Barbados', *Social and Economic Studies*, 4(3), 1955.

45   Peter Fryer, *Staying Power: The History of Black People in Britain*, London, Pluto Press, 1984.

46   James Walvin, *Black and White: the Negro in English Society 1955–1945*, London, Allen Lane, 1973.

47   Alvin Thompson, 'Historical Writing on Migration into the Commonwealth Caribbean: A Bibliographic review of the Period c.1838–c.1938', *Immigrants and Minorities*, Vol. 5, No. 2, July 1986.

48   Verene Shepherd, *From Transients to Settlers: The Experience of Indians in Jamaica 1845–1950* University of Warwick/Leeds, Peepal Tree Books, 1993.

49   Keith Laurence, *A Question of Labour. Indentured Immigration into Trinidad and British Guiana 1875–1917*, Kingston, Ian Randle Publishers/London, James Currey Publishers, 1994.

50   Walton Look Lai, *Indentured Labor, Caribbean Sugar: Chinese and Indian Migrants to the British West Indies 1838–1918*, Baltimore and London, Johns Hopkins University Press, 1993.

51   Elizabeth Tonkin, *Narrating our Past*, Cambridge, Cambridge University

Press, 1992. John Davis, 'Social Relations in the Production of History' in E. Tonkin, M. McDonald and M. Chapman (eds), *History and Ethnicity*, A.S.A. Monograph, London, Routledge, 1989. E. Ardener, 'The Construction of History: Vestiges of Creation', in E. Tonkin *et al.*, 1989, op. cit.

52 John Byng-Hall (interviewed by Paul Thompson) 'The power of family myths' in Raphael Samuel and Paul Thompson, *The Myths We Live By*, London, Routledge, 1990.

53 Maurice Halbwachs, *The Collective Memory*, New York, Harper and Row, 1980. See also Elizabeth Tonkin, *Narrating our Past*, Cambridge, Cambridge University Press, 1992; John Davis, 'Social relations in the production of history', and E. Ardener, 'The construction of history: vestiges of creation' in E. Tonkin, M. McDonald and M. Chapman (eds), *History and Ethnicity*, A.S.A. Monograph, London, Routledge, 1989.

54 Raphael Samuel, *Theatres of Memory*, London, Verso, 1994.

55 Alessandro Portelli, 'Uchronic Dreams', in Raphael Samuel and Paul Thompson (eds), *The Myths We Live By*, London, Routledge, 1990.

56 Farah Jasmine Griffin, *'Who Set You Flowin'?'*, Oxford/New York, Oxford University Press, 1995.

57 Donald Hinds, *Journey to an Illusion: The West Indian in Britain*, London, Heinemann, 1966.

58 Louise Shore, *Pure Running: A Life Story*, Hackney Reading Centre at Centerprise, Centerprise, 1982.

59 Elyse Dodgson, *Motherland: West Indian Women in Britain in the 1950s*, London, Heinemann Educational, 1984.

1 | Migration and Modernity

It was an old man in St. Philip, Barbados, who first told me the story:

> My father ... (who) was a labourer ... been to Panama ... and British Guiana ... (and) America. He die over in America ... I had a uncle over there too, my mother brother was in America ... I went to America in 1944 and ... in 1945. I have thirteen kids by my wife ... some out in England.[1]

This narrative of Barbados, like others from the Caribbean, has been overshadowed and displaced by the grander narratives of migration – the heroic narrative of America, the homogenising narrative of Empire – which shaped the modern nation-state and captured the modern imagination, elaborate *unifying* metaphors which inverted and subsumed the destabilising *diasporic* heart of migration, and which centred, settled and domesticated the nomadic essence of capital and labour which gave rise to it.

Migration and modernity, the nation-state and Empire, all came of age together. The great migrations which began in the sixteenth century from Europe and then Africa and Asia to the Americas and the Caribbean were central to the development of the European states involved, and formed the basis of those nations which subsequently evolved in the New World. The culture in which the nation-state was nurtured, and in which its defining characteristics matured, was a global and a migratory one. It was also a culture where at first the destination for those migrants was not a stable state, but random and mobile, where Barbados or Virginia, New England or Jamaica offered different but equal opportunities and where sojourners and slaves alike settled, moved and returned. It was a culture of *several* migrations, and re-migrations, of European sojourners, of political and religious dissidents, of miscreants and paupers, of buccaneers and adventurers, of indentured servants and enslaved Africans, a culture in which voluntary and involuntary migration was intertwined, where slave or indentured migrant labourers produced the raw materials and trading commodities through which capitalism developed and upon which European industrialisation depended. Capital itself was nomadic, part of the migratory framework, creating new markets, feeding old, embracing the lucrative, releasing the redundant, hopping within islands, to and from America, back to England, back to Africa, cargoes of slaves or copper, indigo or tobacco, sugar and cotton, while the ballast was recycled in the colonies and even today serve as an odd reminder of ancient trades: the floor in the old Dutch fortress of St. George in what was British Guiana is built of slate (did it come from Spain or Wales?); the pathways of the Barbados Wildlife Park are paved in old London stock brick.

Such activity was not confined to Britain. The French, the Dutch, the Spanish, the Portuguese, were all equally mobile, moving within their own territories in the Caribbean and the Americas, and into other peoples. Hobbes summed it up in the seventeenth century, when he likened his hypothetical state of nature to the real turmoil of the international world as he saw it. For the New World had exploded as a contested, nomadic arena of fierce territorial and trading disputes where there was 'no Propriety, no Dominion, no *Mine* and *Thine* distinct; but only that to be every mans, that he can get; and for so long, as he can keep it.'[2] Although no global Leviathan emerged to create or impose security, the nation-state and its Empire, as it began to evolve in the eighteenth and nineteenth centuries, began to assume the role of regional contender. As civil societies based more or less on the accepted rule of law, they had a mission to consolidate, often through expansion, their territorial dominion. Acquisition, plus labour, in the philosophical mind of the eighteenth century, meant possession. The narrative of migration and modernity which emerged was that of Leviathan, the narrative of the victor, not the vanquished.

America was the first to show that a Commonwealth could be created out of a State of Nature and the State of Nature that was America was as much the vast tracts of uncharted land and the tribes of 'savages' who inhabited it, as the Europeans who had migrated there to cultivate and appropriate it;

> ... the vast country ... was inhabited by many indigenous tribes ... the Indians occupied it without possessing it. It is by agricultural labour that man appropriates the soil, and the early inhabitants of North America lived by the produce of the chase. Their implacable prejudices, their uncontrolled passions, their vices, and still more perhaps their savage virtues, consigned them to inevitable destruction .... In that land the great experiment was to be made, by civilized man, of the attempt to construct society upon a new basis; and it was

there, for the first time, that theories hitherto unknown, or deemed impracticable, were to exhibit a spectacle for which the world had not been prepared by the history of the present.[3]

Neither savage nor civilised, the labour of the African slave could claim neither occupancy nor possession, to the land, to the 'great experiment', to the narrative of migration which had given birth to it. America's great experiment belonged to the European.

Nor could the African slave find a place within the subsequent homogenising narrative of Empire whose imperatives were concealed behind a grand civilising mission to which all well-behaved colonists were permitted to subscribe. It was, as Lord Elton described it (in 1945), part of Britain's 'high destiny', to 'deliberately spread the idea of liberty through the world and ... unlike previous Empires ... to protect and educate backward races, and not merely to exploit them.'[4] It was the ending of the slave-trade and the abolition of slavery which enabled Britain to claim the moral high ground for her grand civilising mission, even while the use of Empire as a pool of surplus labour, and Britain's ability to move labour from one continent to meet its requirements in another, had become a central feature of her (home and) colonial economy. Nor, within Barbados and the British West Indies, were the slaves and their nineteenth century descendants provided with a narrative of belonging and begetting within the society which had evolved. They were excluded from the mores and institutions of the planter elite. They were excluded also from the tensions in which that elite were caught. For the white elite were neither colonised nor coloniser, neither independent nor subservient, and their struggle to establish an autonomous identity through which political autonomy and cultural hegemony could be established and maintained, created a narrative of white creole which silenced that of the black, labouring majority. *Their* struggle for autonomy took, finally, a very different route.

From the beginning, Africans and Asians in the New World were placed in an epistemological vacuum.[5] Their migratory journeys could fit neither of those narratives. Neither visionary nor missionary, migration to, from and within the Caribbean was viewed in a more venial light. Those who came to the Caribbean entered a 'social system' which, as Sidney Mintz observed, was 'powerfully constrained to produce nothing but cane cutters, and more cane cutters, and more cane cutters.'[6] Their migration was simply the relocation of savages and heathens within the places where Britain, as the Mother Country, chose to produce her tropical commodities.

Even those who subsequently left the islands, voluntarily, after Emancipation, did so 'casually' and for individual 'betterment,' as the

1895 Barbados Emigration Commission put it, or, alternatively, were forced to migrate to avoid the inevitable and fatal consequences of over-population, as the Governor of Barbados, Governor Rawson, perceived it in 1871. They are views which in varying forms continue to dominate contemporary discussion of Caribbean migration: over population is the push, high wages are the pull. Caribbean migration is viewed now, as always, as 'the movement of labour.' The universal mythologies of citizenship and mobility, of heroism, exploration and conquest which accompanied the modernising impulses of European migrations were deemed irrelevant to the West Indies. The exchange of people between metropole and Empire was one way – of Europeans to the Empire, of Africans and Asians, within it. Caribbean migration is not a narrative of statehood, or citizenship or loyalty. It was viewed as an altogether more iconoclastic movement, unprincipled, untrustworthy and potentially disruptive.

I want to reinstate the old man's story, to remember that there were several routes into modernity, with different impulses, agendas and origins. Those tell-tale gatherings of clouds which heralded land long before land could be spotted, those natural navigational signposts which guided the indigeneous peoples of the Caribbean as much as the Euro-pean explorers, must also have excited the imaginations of the slaves, the unwilling migrants to the New World. There was always somewhere else within sight, another place, another horizon, a different future, elsewhere, across the sea. But there was also a past, locked into place as much as time, a memory of where you had come from, in opposition to the dominant framework of conquest, capital and colour.

On the Eastern edge of the Caribbean and the first port of call from Europe, Barbados was charted and named by the Portuguese in 1536. It was not until 1627 that the British claimed the island for themselves. Both the Portuguese and the British recorded that the island was un-inhabited, but archeological evidence now suggests that there had been settlements of Amerindian peoples who had been migrating there from South America for at least a thousand years. By 1655, there were 23,000 British and 20,000 Africans in Barbados, a population density, inciden-tally, which far exceeded that of any European city in the period. It was a settler society, shaped by the migration of the English, their Irish and Scots indentured servants, and the enforced migration of Africans. Many of the Scots and Irish were alienated political dissidents and all, though for different reasons, were exiled from their home society. Barbados was created out of a rootlessness. By 1712 nearly a third of the British population had already moved on, to other Caribbean islands or to North America, leaving the remainder to consolidate their holdings and their interests. At the same time, the African population as a result of the slave trade had more than doubled in size, to 41,970. Migration, exile, alienation, rootlessness were all central to the formation of this plantation society (whose industrial production and social organisation, incidentally, prefigured that which was to characterise nineteenth century Britain), while trade itself was the major impetus of migration.

But while production and politics were consolidated in the eighteenth and nineteenth century, and assumed an aura of stasis, the African population continued to arrive, and leave. With a high mortality among slaves, the core concern for the planters in the Caribbean was to maintain the level of slave labour. At the same time, with slaves as a commodity in themselves, expanding the slave-trade suited the labour needs of the planters and the profits of the traders. The central position of Barbados in the Atlantic slave-trade ensured a regular turnover of labour, while its policy from the eighteenth century of ameliorating conditions for the creole slaves to encourage reproduction, guaranteed that its slave population would continue to expand. Indeed, long before the abolition of the slave-trade in 1807, Barbados had more than enough slaves to meet its own labour requirements and a healthy surplus of Creole slaves, with a high economic premium, to export for profit. If trade had been the engine of migration, migration itself was also a highly lucrative trade.

In 1844 – six years after the ending of Apprenticeship in 1838 – the population stood at 122,200. Barbados was the most densely populated island in the Caribbean. A surplus of slave labour was one thing, but a surplus of free, poor, black labourers posed very different issues. The planters feared that emancipation would result in labour being reduced by migration away from the plantations and even off the island altogether, or seduced by ideas of insurbordination, fears fuelled by recent memories of revolt, and images of massacre. The planters were a very small elite. British Guiana, Trinidad, Jamaica were witnessing what in the eyes of Barbadian planters was evidence of both a reduction and seduction of their own labour forces and had been forced to take active steps to promote immigrant labour from overseas, first from China and then from India. This situation, of labour desertion and importation, was one which the Barbadian planters did not wish to see emulated at home. Early signs, however, provided an indication that unless action was taken swiftly, Barbadians would, indeed, follow their counterparts abroad and leave the plantations.

By 1838 numbers of Barbadians had already left Barbados for plantations in British Guiana which promised not only higher wages, but the potential for land. The House of Assembly moved fast passing laws in 1838, amended in 1840, which on the one hand aimed to regulate and restrict out-migration and the activities of recruiting agents and on the other, the notorious 'Contract Law', restricted internal mobility within the plantations on the island. Indeed, this law – not repealed until 1937[7]– subverted the notion of 'free' labour implied at Emancipation by coercing the former slaves/apprentices into becoming 'tenanted' labourers. These labourers worked under a contract, which tied them exclusively to the plantation with whom the contract was held. Under the terms of the contract they were required to live on this plantation, and were not permitted to seek additional or alternative work elsewhere, even in the 'hard times', when employment on the plantation was irregular or unobtainable. Breach of contract resulted not only in eviction, but prosecution and economic sanctions.

Most of the land at the time of Emancipation was under white planter ownership. At the same time, the planters' control over the land was mirrored in their absolute (and constitutional) control over the political and economic life of Barbados. Unlike those in Jamaica, Guyana or Trinidad, the ex-slaves had, simply, nowhere else to live or find alternative employment other than on and through the plantations. However punitive the Contract Law, the former slaves had little alternative but to accept it. Wages were kept artificially low, and were lowered further by the deduction of land rent. There was no security of tenure and labourers were not permitted to plant permanent crops, or build permanent homes, on the ground rented from the plantation. The Barbadian Plantation Tenantry System which evolved through this law was unique to Barbados. It transformed chattel slaves, effectively, into chattel labourers.

Although the House of Assembly recognised the levels of poverty among the black labouring class, it refused to recognise that underemployment or unemployment or, simply, low wages were contributory and related factors. On the contrary, it insisted that the huge reserves of labour were vital to the plantation economy and accordingly periodically restricted emigration through a series of legislative measures curtailing both the number of emigrants and the activities of recruitment agents, although concern was voiced for the plight of poor whites, the disenfranchised and displaced descendants of the indentured servants, who both drained the Parish reserves, and were considered unsuitable for agricultural labour.

By the 1860s, however, the problems generated through poverty began to assume an urgency. The cholera epidemic of 1854, in which 18,000 people died, and a series of droughts in the 1860s caused some members of the House of Assembly to consider seriously for the first time the notion that the island could not adequately sustain its population. Rather than look at raising wage rates, or reallocating land distribution, or generating alternative employment, or releasing the plantation labourers from the restrictive workings of the Contract Law, it turned to the possibility of emigration as an easy solution to the poverty and social problems of Barbados. An Act was passed in 1864 which, it was hoped, would encourage emigration. The encouragement was more in the letter than the spirit of the law, for although the House of Assembly may have been unanimous in fearing the disruptive consequences of poverty, they were not entirely convinced by the argument equating over-population with poverty nor with emigration as a solution. It was still only thirty years since the abolition of slavery, less since the ending of apprenticeship, and access to an unlimited supply of labour was still perceived as essential for the profitable production of sugar. Recruiting agents were, therefore, again restricted in advertising or touting for recruits, and little practical help was provided for potential emigrants. As a result, although 3,500 Barbadians (many of whom were white) left for St. Croix in 1863, and a further 1,500 left for Suriname between 1864 and 1870, the numbers were relatively small. The poverty remained. Nevertheless, the notion that the island was over-populated, that this was the sole cause of the poverty, and that emigration could be the solution, and perhaps the only solution to both over-population and poverty, had taken hold at least in the mind of the Colonial Office. By 1871 Governor Rawson, in a biting report, laid out the future in terms of stark Malthusian alternatives, 'Pestilence or Emigration,' he argued, 'is apparently the only alternative as an escape from starvation.'[8] Emigration, in his view, was the most 'humane' way of reducing population pressure on resources and stability and in 1873 an Act was passed to facilitate migration and in some limited cases to sponsor potential migrants.

Two years later, the proposed integration of Barbados within a confederation of the Windward Islands triggered a week of riots.[9] Although the ostensible cause was the Colonial Office proposal, the vehemence of the response from the black labourers, for the most part both disenfranchised and poor, indicated a significant level of discontent and prompted a Commission of Enquiry to investigate poverty in the island. Its report, too, put emigration forward as a possible solution although its recommendations were not endorsed. The House of Assembly remained ambivalent. As representatives of the planter interests, a strong lobby remained within the House of Assembly who could still argue (and win) the case that since, in crop time, there was sufficient employment for all, emigration was neither necessary nor desirable.

Two decades later, however, the decline in profits from sugar – a trend which had accelerated in the latter half of the nineteenth century – made it clear that the labour reserves were not only surplus to requirements but would substantially threaten the profits of the plantation economy and, more particularly, the stability of plantation society. By 1891, the population had reached 182,900, with a density of 1,096 per square mile. The implications of this for expenditure on the Poor Law were dire. A new direction was required and in that year the Barbadian Government appointed a commission specifically to review the possibility of emigration as a means of resolving the crisis. Its report, published in 1895, not only recommended emigration as a solution,[10] but suggested that a loan be offered to prospective emigrants, ideally to be made as a 'Poor Relief Test', whereby 'applicants (would be) given a chance of going away and thus helping themselves, instead of being given aid here.'[11] Emigration – which was to include the family of the applicant, to prevent them remaining or becoming dependent on the Poor Law – would, it was argued, be considerably cheaper than Poor Relief,[12] with the advantage that the loans, when repaid could then be recycled to assist further migration. Although emigration was not finally make a condition of Poor Relief, the post of Superintendent of emigration was merged with the Clerkship of the Poor Law Board, with the duties of promoting emigration, primarily among the 'poorer classes.'[13]

The commissioners were careful to distinguish casual from permanent migration, insisting that the real 'object' of any emigration scheme should be to establish *permanent* settlements rather than find *casual* employment for the 'surplus' population. Besides paupers as a potential pool for emigrants, there were others who, it was argued, were too proud to apply for Poor Relief, but who nevertheless should be encouraged to emigrate, among whom would be included poor white women 'physically unable to work in the fields under the blaze of a tropical sun.'[14] This group in particular, should be encouraged to 'get to a colder climate ... the emigration of this class to Canada and the United States which has been carried out to a limited extent during the past few years by private enterprise has proved a complete success.'[15] For the rest, the preferred destinations remained within the Caribbean. Those who should be denied assistance were those 'casual' labourers who were migrating for the purposes of 'betterment.'

Ideally, then, the potential emigrant would be poor, desperate and honest. With his (sic) dependents, he would be prepared to leave Barbados, repay the government loan and not return. The figure calculated as the ideal was set at 3,000 individuals, or 600 families. Since the yearly excess of births over deaths was between two and three thousand, and since in 1893 2,000 paupers were dependent on Poor Relief[16] (a figure lower than that at the time of the Federation Riots of 1875, when 3,600 individuals, out of a population of 162,000 were on Poor Relief,) the figure set would, it was thought, maintain the population equilibrium, reduce the actual and anticipated demands on the Poor Law, and continue to satisfy the seasonal employment demands of the sugar industry. Encouraging emigration was, in the Commission's opinion, an easy and painless remedy to a problem increasingly perceived within the terms of Malthusian logic.

> It is obvious ... that unless the question how the increasing population of this island can be satisfactorily aided to maintain themselves is solved by forethought and well directed effort, the question will solve itself at the cost of much pain, disease and death.[17]

The obstacle, however, as the Commissioners saw it, was that Barbadians were 'reluctant' to emigrate. Yet throughout the nineteenth century Barbadians *had*, in fact, migrated. Between 1838 and 1846 substantial numbers of Barbadians left for British Guiana and Trinidad, a movement repeated in the 1860s and 1870s. Between 1863 and 1870 nearly 5,000 Barbadians went to Suriname and St. Croix.[18] The 1873 Emigration Act lists as existing migrant destinations Antigua, Demerara, Dominica, Grenada, Nevis, Nickerie, St. Kitts, St. Lucia, St. Vincent, Surinam, Tobago and Trinidad.[19] Although statistics on migration were not kept in the nineteenth century, census returns from the British West Indian Territories indicate that between 1861 and 1891 approximately 30,000 Barbadians were resident there, principally in British Guiana and Trinidad. The 1891 census for Trinidad registers 14,000 resident Barbadians.[20] Moreover, and significantly, at least a third and sometimes as much as a half of the emigrants from Barbados between 1861 and 1891 were women.[21] This data excludes Barbadians resident elsewhere in the Caribbean, such as the Dominican Republic, or on the South and North American mainlands.

The difficulty for the Barbados Government was not that Barbadians were reluctant to migrate, but that the wrong people migrated, for the wrong reasons, for the wrong period of time. Given that the government comprised the planter elite, the entrepreneurs and landowners, whose views of black migration had been shaped by centuries of labour importation, primarily to their estates, the notion that emigrants could have agency or an agenda was beyond their imaginative scope. Yet the features of migration which had emerged in the nineteenth century, were of 'casual' migrations by *individuals* to and from the island, with the express purpose of 'betterment'. These individuals sent home remittances,[22] and they returned.[23] Barbadians *as families* – or at least families as defined by the planters, autonomous conjugal units, calculated in clusters of five – were reluctant to migrate. Such a pattern clearly did not reduce the population significantly or permanently. Migrant behaviour and motivation was clearly at odds with government desire. The Commission's disapproval however, is our enlightenment, for it provides a clear indication of migration patterns and an insight into nineteenth century migrant motivation, which have remained as a feature of migration ever since.

The source for such patterns can be found in the structure of Barbadian families and in the controls in Barbados on social and economic mobility. The most prevalent form of family and household structure which emerged in Barbados after slavery privileged consanguineal rather than conjugal units. The longevity of creolisation had enabled lineages and networks to be established which contributed to family cohesion, stability and loyalty. At the same time, individual autonomy for men *and* women had emerged as a significant feature of family life to an extent which the anthropologist Sidney Mintz remarks was:

> still quite unheard of in Western societies, for all their vaunting of individual freedom ... where individual prerogatives are commonly seen as flowing from individual *male* wealth, embedded in a nuclear family organisation.[24] (original emphasis)

At the same time, restrictions on internal migration, and the limited alternatives to agricultural employment, had not only closed opportunities for social mobility, but also the avenues for achieving independence from the plantations. Giving the population density and the planter monopoly over land, migration away from the island, though both dramatic and difficult given the dangers of nineteenth century sea travel, was perceived as one possible – perhaps the only possible – route towards both mobility and independence.[25] Indeed, as early as 1840 a petition had been presented to the House of Assembly in Barbados complaining of 'unjustifiable attempts to prevent migration.'[26] That emigration was viewed by black Barbadians as an alternative to plantation discipline and by the House of Assembly as a real threat to the labour supply is born out by, on the one hand, the repeated attempts throughout the nineteenth century to strengthen the restrictions on emigration, particularly of agricultural labourers and on the other, the failure of attempts to assist migration through loans and contracts. In 1873, 1876 and 1885 limited emigration under contract (to selected locations) was available, but was unsuccessful. Given Barbadians experience of contracts, this was hardly surprising. 'The labouring people of this island', Governor Brewster of Barbados wrote in a letter to the Governor of Trinidad, 'are unwilling to emigrate to any place under indenture.'[27] Assistance and contract labour, in other words, was perceived as 'location' by another name. Migration was to be on terms set by the migrants, not conditions imposed by recruiters, employers or the government.

The concerns of the 1895 Commission that emigrants include their families in their travels, and earlier legislation which penalised the 'destitute' families of migrants,[28] suggests that many of those who did migrate, went alone. Given the scale of remittances returned, they went alone to minimise expenditure and maximise profit, leaving the family in Barbados to save sufficient from the remittances to purchase where possible either a 'house spot' and release for themselves from the Contract Law,[29] thus easing the way for the future migrations of family members, or to consolidate and increase existing family holdings. Either way, 'casual' migrations for 'betterment' undermined the plantation discipline and for that reason assumed a symbolic as well as a practical significance within the culture of Barbados. Taking dependent family members would have defeated the purpose by increasing the costs of travel and sustenance abroad. While the potential migrant (and more likely his or her family) may have been able to raise the money to pay for travel for one, it is unlikely that they could have raised sufficient for them all to travel and even if they could, there would be no point in incurring that expense when return was imminent and the money could be put to better uses back home. Given the rates of return, and from evidence which suggests that migrant labour could be found for short-term (i.e. six-month) contracts[30] Barbadian migrants clearly came back to reap the benefits of their labour abroad. The whole family was embroiled in the migration effort by providing and maintaining support while the migrant was away. Individual men and women migrated; but the rewards were experienced by all. Migration had become a short-term, *individual* endeavour, albeit for the sake of the long-term *family* enterprise.

The years immediately following the Commission's report saw a slow increase in the rate of emigration. By 1901 there had been a net migration of 6,000, of which 2,000 were women encouraged by the Victorian Emigration Society founded in 1897 to support out-migration of (primarily) poor white women. But in 1904, the Americans renewed their project to construct a canal through the Panama Isthmus and in the following year set up a recruiting office in Bridgetown, their work eased by the passing of the 1904 Emigration Act. Between 1904 and 1914 an estimated 45,000 Barbadians migrated to Panama.[31]

The 'Panama' migrants, for the most part, went alone; they went to 'better their position'; they intended to – and many did – return, although some travelled on from Panama to Cuba and the United States. It was a migration exodus of casual, self-seeking, individual labourers, many of whom, though by no means all, came from the 'poorer classes,'[32]

⸌cisely the opposite to that envisaged in the Commission report of 1895 and far beyond the scales – of between two and three thousand, or 400 to 600 families per year – which the Report proposed as 'desirable.' Panama was the catalyst which revealed, more than anything else, the centrality of migration within the ethos or culture of the island and the extent to which it was poised to establish itself as a response to the predominant plantation regimen.

It had profound political repercussions. The period between the turn of the century and up to the Second World War was politically and economically dynamic, beginning with the migration of labourers to Panama and ending with the riots of 1937, events which are not disconnected. Indeed, those two decades saw dramatic changes in the political infrastructure of Barbados, and the development of political consciousness which incorporated, in its analysis, a growing awareness of race as well as class. Panama money enabled the growth of 'buy lands', small settlements independent of the plantations and of the Contract Law, and helped generally to establish an economic and emotional independence and patterns of co-operation and organisation which created political aspirations, confidence and, finally, change. Although the abolition of the Contract Law preceded the riots of 1937, agricultural poverty and resentment, and the fear of the consequences of that combination, were not far from the minds of the legislators. At the same time, the growth of independent small landowners and the significance of the gradual and piecemeal extension of the franchise to black people[33] was not lost in the calculations of those who began, in this period, to agitate for change.

The motive for migration may have had as much to do with maintenance of the family and its livelihoods, with the enhancement of status and experience, within a culture which prized migration *per se* and historically perceived it as a statement of independence, as to do with individual economic self-advancement. Migrants, in other words, had their own agenda which ran parallel with, but did not necessarily conform to, the demands of international capital and the pressures of domestic policy. There was scarcely a Barbadian family who was not touched by the migration to Panama, or the re-migrations to Cuba and North America. It became an active ingredient in the culture of Barbados, and entered into the dynamics of family and neighbourhood. It was not necessarily Panama *per se*, but what Panama represented – resistance, independence, mobility – which enabled it to retain its imaginative hold and pivotal role in shaping the narratives – these alternative narratives – of migration.

Between 1920 and 1940 there was a steady, though smaller, migration (at around 4,000 a year[34]) from Barbados to the Caribbean, Central and South America, particularly Brazil.[35] The 1924 Immigration Act in the United States imposed quotas on Caribbean immigrants and temporarily closed America as a destination, although the Second World War reopened opportunities on American bases within the Caribbean and for seasonal work within the United States, which continued after the war until the McCarran-Walter Act of 1952 again closed the doors. By then the population of Barbados had risen to 219,015. The sugar industry was still the major employer, but the work was seasonal and the pay low and fluctuating. The service industry, tourism in particular, remained in its infancy and other industry was either small or for the most part uncompetitive, depending heavily on the import of raw materials.

Although the Contract Law was taken off the statute book in 1937, it was too late to avert the riots which occurred in 1937 in Barbados, as elsewhere in the Caribbean. The economic and social stresses were undoubtedly one contributory factor of those riots; but many migrants had also returned from Panama, Cuba and the United States, bringing with them fresh expectations and political impulses, impatience with a system of political and economic privilege, experiences of political and labour organisation. The personal independence won from plantation discipline, via migration, began to be translated into the wider political arena. Migration came to symbolise a collective, as well as a personal, autonomy.

Migration raises the spectre of movement and uncertainty which, ironically, is now the antithesis of the modern nation-state with its nineteenth century legacy of immutable borders and its twentieth century legacy of ethnic homogeneity. The contemporary story of migration sits uncomfortably within international relations.

Why this is so raises fundamental historical, cultural and political issues. It brings us back to the essence of citizenship and imperialism, to issues of identity and ideology, to the oppositional heart of transnational and multinational migration, to the globalisation of both capital and social space, to the contemporary problematic of the nation-state. Yet, as Anthony Giddens reminds us, 'modernity is inherently globalizing.'[36] The culture in which the nation-state now lives is one in which communications and capital operate through as well as within national borders; its boundaries have become permeable. Arguably they always were. Nomad capital, like nomad labour, is not a new phenomenon. Trade, labour and migration have stalked hand in hand since at least the sixteenth century. But the fiction – the grand narrative – of unification and homogeneity persists. The migration narratives of the Caribbean ran parallel with the rhetorical metaphors of nation-state and Empire, and have helped shape, and continue to shape, the culture of the Caribbean at home and abroad. Indeed, the story of modernity is one of several, *unfinished* migrations, which began in the Caribbean, and which continue.

At the same time, the globalisation of modernity is not the sole prerogative of metropolitan states or of metropolitan capital. Imperialism, whether historic or contemporary, economic or cultural, is not a one-way traffic. It is appropriated as much as it appropriates, incorporated as much as resisted, mocked as much as enjoyed, inverted and subverted, exploited as much as exploiting. What unsettles about international migration is that it has internationalised the nation-state and globalised identity. It has appropriated modernity for itself. International migrants are by definition international people with allegiances and loyalties which transcend the nation-state, and no people are more international, more transnational, more migratory than those from the Caribbean. That is why the story of migration, in its infinity, is not a comfortable one, and that is why the history of Caribbean migration in particular does not sit easily within conventional explanations of labour movement, whose models more often than not originate in the (often reluctant) host society, and which doggedly resists the complexities of migration, of migration history, and a migratory history of the Caribbean whose actors, for most of the time, did not and could not recognise frontiers.

References

1   GA, born 1910, St. Philip, Barbados. Tape 1, side 1, p. 56. From Mary Chamberlain Barbados Plantation Tenantry System tapes, Dept. of History, University of the West Indies, Cave Hill, Barbados.
2   Thomas Hobbes, *Leviathan*, part 1, chapter 13. Oxford, 1909.
3   Alexis de Tocqueville, *Democracy in America*, 1835. Chapter 1. Oxford, Oxford University Press, 1965.
4   Lord Elton, *Imperial Commonwealth*, London, Collins, 1945, p. 239.
5   For a variant on this theme, see Michel-Rolph Trouillot, 'The Caribbean Region: An Open Frontier in Anthropological Theory', *Annual Review of Anthropology*, 1992, 21 pp. 19–42.
6   Sidney Mintz, Introduction to Walton Look Lai, *Indentured Labour, Caribbean Sugar: Chinese and Indian Migrants to the British West Indies, 1838–1918*, Baltimore and London, Johns Hopkins Press, 1993.
7   Mary Chamberlain, 'Renters and Farmers: The Barbadian Plantation Tenantry System, 1917–1937', *Journal of Caribbean History*, 1990, 24(2).
8   Quoted in *Barbados Emigration Commission Report 1895*, BDA. Pam C676.
9   In 1875 Britain appointed Governor John Pope Hennessey to implement proposals to integrate Barbados in a confederation with the Windward Islands and institute Crown Colony rule. The Barbados House of Assembly adopted a variety of 'dirty tricks' tactics to resist the proposals, including the sugges-

tion that Crown Colony rule was a means of reinstating slavery. Supporters of Confederation, however, campaigned among the black working class implying that Confederation would result in a more equitable distribution of power and wealth. The political impasse was broken by riots which in turn were quelled by the British Navy. Crown Colony rule was not imposed, and a compromise constitution was drawn up.

10   *The Barbados Emigration Commission Report 1895*, BDA. Pam C676.
11   *Ibid.*
12   The Commissioners calculated that the cost of passage, housing and land for 600 families of 3,000 individuals would amount to £19,000; the cost of maintaining them on Poor Relief would be £24,787/10/-. *Ibid.*
13   *Ibid.*
14   *Ibid.*
15   *Ibid.*
16   G.W. Roberts, 'Emigration from the Island of Barbados', *Social and Economic Studies*, 4(3), 1955.
17   *Barbados Emigration Commission Report 1895*, Barbados, Department of Archives. Pam C676.
18   Governor R.W. Rawson, *Report on the Population of Barbados 1851–1871*, Barbados, 1871, Department of Archives.
19   *Rules and Regulations Framed and Passed by the Governor in Council under the Authority of the Emigration Act 1873*, 23 September 1873. Barbados, Department of Archives, Pam A45.
20   Census returns for the British West Indies, 1891. BDA.
21   Quoted in G.W. Roberts, op. cit.
22   By 1895, it was estimated from the returns of the Colonial Postmaster that £16,446 had been sent home by Barbadians from the British West Indies, and £2,001 from the United States. *Barbados Emigration Commission Report 1895*. However, Dr. Elsie Payne argues that this figure is a gross underestimate and suggests a sum of £516,000 to be more accurate. *UWI/University of Sussex, Centre for Multi-Racial Studies*, 1968. Similarly, G.W. Roberts suggests that between 1865 and 1900 remittances totalled £355,000. G.W. Roberts, op. cit.
23   Calculations for migration and return migration are difficult to make throughout the nineteenth century due to the inadequacy of appropriate statistics. Given, however, the rate of growth of the population and the estimates of migration, the two could not be sustained without a substantial movement of return migration. The intercensal rate of population growth between 1844 and 1851 is 1.53 per cent which implies no emigration but a high rate of return migration by those who left Barbados (principally for British Guiana) after 1838. Quoted in G.W. Roberts, op. cit.
24   Sidney Mintz, 'Black women, economic roles and cultural traditions' in Hilary Beckles and Verene Shepherd, *Caribbean Freedom: Economy and Society from Emancipation to the Present*, Kingston, Ian Randle Publishers/London, James Currey, 1993.
25   The British Secretary of State to the Colonies, in disallowing the Masters & Servants Act of 1838, stated firmly 'the right of the free labourer to seek employment wherever he can find the best market for his labour.' Quoted in Dr. Elsie Payne, op. cit.
26   G.W. Roberts, op. cit.
27   *Ibid.*

28   In particular, 'An Act for the governing and better ordering of the poor of this island and the prevention of bastardy', 1838.

29   See Dr. Elsie Payne, op. cit. This trend, of purchasing land and hence release from the contract law, was reinforced dramatically after the migration to Panama. Bonham Richardson, *Panama Money in Barbados 1900–1920*, 1985.

30   G.W. Roberts, op. cit, p. 260.

31   Exact figures are not available, though Hilary Beckles estimates the total at 45,000. Hilary Beckles, *A History of Barbados*, Cambridge, Cambridge University Press, 1990.

32   Velma Newton, 'The Panama Question: Barbadian Emigration to Panama 1880–1914' in Woodville Marshall, (ed.), *Emancipation II*, National Cultural Foundation/Department of History, UWI, Cave Hill, Bridgetown, Barbados, 1987.

33   The franchise was based on a property qualification.

34   *West Indian Census 1946*, BDA.

35   For an interesting study of Barbadians in Brazil see Sydney Greenfield, 'Barbadians in the Brazilian Amazon', *Luso-Brazilian Review*, 20(1), 1983. There is also a Barbadian song which dates from the 1920s which immortalises the explanation given by a man for the disappearance of his wife, who claimed 'Millie gone to Brazil', when he had, in fact, murdered her. For a version of this song see Trevor Marshall, Peggy McGeary and Grace Thompson, *Folk Songs of Barbados*, Bridgetown, Barbados, 1981. Also B21/1/1/15.

36   Anthony Giddens, *The Consequences of Modernity*, Cambridge, Polity Press, 1990.

2 | From the Panama Canal to the Regent's Canal

Although the migrations to and from the Caribbean may be linked, and while there may be parallels in migrant experiences, the history of migration is not a continuum, nor is it homogenous. It is an episodic history. Each of those migratory movements occurred within a particular pocket of time, or historical duration, closely related to the past, but distinguished from it. Each migration episode, to, from or within the Caribbean, had its material causes and ideological justifications, to which migrants had to reconcile themselves in complicated and sometimes contradictory ways. While, as Andor Skotnes reminds us, most migration (to the Americas) took place within, and was the result of, 'a kind of internally complex, ever-changing grand master narrative of colour',[1] there are nevertheless specific differences between the responses of generations of migrants and between epochs.

Those periodic differences, as Raymond Williams suggests 'are the most difficult things to get hold of ... this felt sense of the quality of life at a particular place and time',[2] which he describes as a 'structure of feeling', 'a sense of the ways in which the particular activities combined into a way of thinking and living ... a common element that we cannot easily place ....'[3]

Each period has peculiarities which distinguish it and shape and inform the generations within it, marked by diverse (sometimes contradictory) but related activities, reflected in cultural and social, industrial and judicial enterprise. Most of the debate surrounding his model has focussed on its applicability to English history. Migration, on the other hand, is about international history. It is the social history of international relations. It may be mediated by governments and capital, from the 'top', reflected by the rationalist models, Marxist or otherwise, of migration theory. It is also a grass roots movement, a history from below, reflected by those models which emphasise the social and cultural character of migrant societies. But somewhere in between are the migrants themselves, moving and manoeuvring within and through cultures at moments in time specific to them and their generation and to the societies which they enter, responding in particular ways to particular circumstances at a particular time, in much the same way as the 'host' societies, though from a different historical duration, respond to them.

Nevertheless, adapting Williams notion of a 'structure of feeling' may offer some insights, for it highlights the historical dimension of culture and period in ways which sociological or anthropological models of cultural dissonance and adaptation, or economic models of rationalitity and calculus, do not. In particular, the notion recognises any one 'period' contains three or more generations, who bring with them both a past and a future, tensions which drive and explain change, and give it contemporary meaning and which do

> not seem to be, in any formal sense, learned. One generation may train its successor, with reasonable success, in the social character or the general cultural pattern, but the new generation will have its own structure of feeling, which will not appear to have come 'from' anywhere. For here, most distinctly, the changing organisation is enacted in the organism: the new generation responds in its own ways to the unique world it is inheriting, taking up many continuities, that can be traced, and reproducing many aspects of the organisation, which can be separately described, yet feeling its whole life in certain ways differently, and shaping its creative response into a new structure of feeling.[4]

Between 1955 and 1971, some 27,000 Barbadians migrated to Britain.[5] It was a migration whose dimensions paralleled that to Panama at the turn of the century. Most of those who came to Britain had memories of the earlier migrations of their relatives, not only to Panama, but also to Cuba and North America. But those migrants to Britain came at a particular historical moment. Most were born in the 1930s, a time of economic depression in the Caribbean as elsewhere. They grew up during the war, the stories their fathers told of working on the American bases, or in America, supplementing the stories of their grandparents and great-grandparents. These young men and women were eager to migrate, to travel and so pass through their *rite de passage*.

> Everybody write back, giving you encouragement to come over, to travel. I think, this word 'travel', I think that's it. They just want you to travel and see somewhere else.[6]

Between 1951 and 1954 some Barbadians had already left for Britain, though the numbers hovered around 300–400 per annum. In 1955, the numbers jumped dramatically to 3,143.[7] Hurricane Janet in

September of that year may have precipitated some departures; another impetus came from weekly advertisements in the press and on the radio, from mid-1955, by a shipping line announcing that there were 45,000 jobs vacant in Britain.[8]

A third impetus came from the Barbados Government itself. By 1952 the population of Barbados had risen to 219, 015. The government, acutely aware of the perils of insufficient employment and with the memory of 1937 still fresh, had been sufficiently exercised by the potential social problems facing Barbados that it had appointed a joint Committee in 1952 'to examine the question of over population in Barbados and to make recommendations for dealing with the problem.' Its report pointed to ways in which the economy could be revitalised and expanded to provide more opportunities for employment. It also argued that possible avenues for emigration be explored, though was pessimistic about their success. One member of the Committee, Dr. A. Cato went so far as to suggest that 'Her Majesty's Government should be asked to use its good offices to secure opportunities for emigration to other parts of the Commonwealth, viz., Canada and Australia.' The West Indies, he argued, had been loyal to both Crown and Commonwealth and this was 'a Commonwealth problem.'[9]

Britain, with its need for workers to assist in the programme of post war reconstruction, emerged as a possible destination and the Barbados Government seized the opportunity and began actively to promote migration to Britain, courting prospective employers in Britain and establishing a scheme to sponsor workers who wished to migrate.

From the beginning, however, there was tension between the political aims of the Barbados government – which it saw as relieving what were still seen as the pressures of over-population and under-employment – the individual trajectories of the migrants, their images of Britain, and the political and social climate of the Britain into which they arrived. This chapter focusses on two of those themes, the aims of the Barbados government, and the British response to West Indian migration. Later chapters look at the trajectories of the migrants themselves, although clearly what was happening in Barbados, as well as Britain, played a part in migrant response.

After the Second World War, Britain's postwar programme of reconstruction required more labour than it could supply at home, or find from Europe. Despite the shortage, and despite Colonial Office awareness of unemployment in the Caribbean, encouraging colonial workers to come to Britain was viewed initially with official abhorrence.[10] Moving colonial labour within the Empire was one thing; moving it to Britain another. For the British, the 'Mother Country', the central shrine of Empire, was a model of benefaction, not its altar.

Colonials (at least, non-white Colonials) should aspire to become like the Mother Country, but not to come to it.

Although Britain in the 1950s had been constructed in relation to Empire (a relationship which was always racialised), she was also embarking on another cultural and geopolitical exercise. The Cold War was imposing a rigidity on the global manoeuvrings of what had emerged in the post-Second World War order as the 'Superpowers.' It was a world far removed from the old certainties of *realpolitick* and of the security and autonomy of the nineteenth century and twentieth century nation-state and, by extension, its empire(s). Modernity itself was in crisis and the international response was to create, at the diplomatic and military level, alliances and spheres of influence which extended and secured the national boundaries and, at the intellectual level, a body of theory, based on an 'assumption of rational behaviour',[11] which attempted to analyse the new international world order and influence the behaviour of the actors within it, not because 'it is the one that evidently stays closest to the truth ... but that ... the premise of "rational behaviour" is a potent one for the production of theory.'[12]

The old nation-states of Europe, many of whom were still imperial powers, were juggling with the problem of retaining their identity as nation-states within a system of collective security *and* with awkward nationalist movements in their colonies which not only challenged the economic and ideological basis of that sovereignty, and presumed supremacy, but threatened to destabilise the new world order in which they were struggling to maintain a role. Whereas

> The Great Powers, by exercising *rational* self control, might keep the peace ... it is questionable ... whether the same can as confidently be said about conflicts provoked by ... elites inspired by nationalist or social ideas ... (who) destroyed the British and French empires ...[13] (emphasis added).

The mood of rationality was not confined to the international arena. British postwar domestic reconstruction was also based on principles of rational calculation which guided Beveridge's transformations of social inequality as much as the programme of nationalisation or the planning of new towns and the rebuilding of old ones. There was a domestic emphasis on social unity within an international emphasis on order, both of which became increasingly premised on principles of rationality. Coupled with this was the rhetoric of domestic homogeneity. The class war, as Macmillan declared, was over. The British had never had it so good. Despite forays onto the global stage, it was a time of political retrenchment into the borders of Britain and a wariness of foreigners, not least in Europe.

The colonials were rocking the boat, both abroad and, from 1949, at home. The entry of West Indians into Britain challenged visibly the assumptions of homogeneity, exposed the vulnerability of Britain's national boundaries, and the ethnocentric fallacy of the Commonwealth. The 'structure of feeling' of Britain in the 1950s and early 1960s figured both rationalism and nationalism. The welfare state and the 1962 Immigration Act were both manifestations of it, as was the attempt to recolonise the West Indians, to 'civilise' them by imputing them with irrefutable rational motives which conformed to models of acceptable national and international behaviour. Migration, internal or international, was seen as an individual rational response to a macroeconomic dilemma: unemployment and over population at home, opportunity and mobility abroad. 'The general low level of wages and the lack of opportunity have caused West Indians to look outside their islands for economic improvement.'[14]

Moreover, it was assumed that the immigrants were here to stay and would assimilate with (be domesticated into) the dominant domestic culture. Autonomy was undesirable and unthinkable. Integration was the goal.[15] The migrant, in other words, was rational and *stable*. The problem was not to understand migration, but to change the migrants. They must 'become like us.'[16] Indeed, why else had they come?

> It's precisely the immigrants' intention not to live like pigs,
> but like middle-class people, that forms their main incentive
> to move. They want to adopt British standards, to be accepted,
> to become inconspicuous.[17]

The response was to couch migration, and the solution to the migrant 'problem' in terms of domestic order. 'A job and a roof over his head – these are the main immediate needs of the newcomer in Britain.'[18] Modelled on the patriarchal middle-class family, such an order, in which discrete family housing and male employment were key, had been the organising principle of stability since the nineteenth century. It had been as central to the 'civilising' missionary endeavour in the Empire, as it had to reforming the slums of Britain. The language of the nineteenth century sanitary reformers at home mirrored that of Evangelical missionaries abroad, while nineteenth and twentieth century chroniclers of the London poor considered themselves as 'travellers' among the 'lost tribes' of Britain. The Empire had long since come home. The principle of *Pax Britannica* guided colonial governments as much as social reform in Britain. The natives, like the poor, needed to become 'like us', by reforming their domestic procedures. The 'Mother Country' was not merely the metropolitan heart of Empire; it embodied a concept of domesticity of which the postwar welfare state in Britain was the natural extension.

The arrival of the West Indians dovetailed with nascent fears and prejudices on the future of the 'black' colonies. It fed into an ignorance of both the West Indies and West Indians, an ignorance which created an easy stereotype – West Indians were native, and poor, labourers who 'lack skills ... (and) enter our society at the bottom of the status scale.'[19] Nevertheless, it was assumed, 'most of them are better off than they would be at home in the West Indies and they are not, therefore, so conscious of their deprivations.'[20] It stripped West Indians of a history and culture. Unlike India or, though in different ways, Africa, where the British Imperial Government had invented or reinvented indigenous 'tradition',[21] in Imperial eyes the British West Indies owed their existence and history exclusively to Britain. It was Britain which had 'founded' the West Indies, and which had subsequently liberated it from slavery. There was, in this view, no autonomous, indigenous tradition or identity to restore or reinvent. Whatever culture existed within the Caribbean was considered to have been borrowed, adopted or distorted. In more senses than one, Britain was the 'Mother Country' and commanded an intellectual, cultural and moral authority:

> Unlike the Chinese, Moslem and Hindu communities ... the West Indians lack any (such) distinctive and exclusive social organisation and culture which might serve as a basis for group cohesion.[22]

West Indians arrived in the 'Mother Country' whose axis was turning north rather than south and, if it focussed on empire at all, it was both as a sentimental vision of past Imperial greatness, and as a threatening vision of disruption to the domestic order and ideology at home. Competition for work and housing are 'the two main areas of competition and possible conflict between migrants and the local population, and therefore areas in which accommodation, though essential, is often difficult to reach on both sides.'[23]

In such a context, West Indians were not seen as welcome, above all, not *indoors*, not to cross the thresholds of either the front door or the factory door. British pride in her superior 'social values' of tolerance and liberty were conveniently forgotten, a point neatly made by Ralf Dahrendorf, himself an European immigrant, when he wrote in 1982 that one of the greatest changes in Britain has been

> the immigration of *unskilled* West Indians and Asians by the million .... The new immigrants remain, even if they succeed economically, a painful reminder of national failure rather

than a part of society once so proud of its inclusive sense of oneness and solidarity ...[24] (emphasis added)

Such was the climate into which Arthur Pickwoad, the Labour Commissioner for Barbados entered. He had made several attempts during 1954 to secure employment for Barbadians in Britain, focussing his attention on the health, the service and the transport sectors and emphasising the superior moral virtues and educational proficiency of the Barbadian worker. He wrote to individual hospitals asking if they would be 'willing to accept girls from Barbados'[25] and assuring them of rigorous selection procedures. Although the response was initially luke-warm, between June and December 1955 fourteen men and fifty-five women left to train in Britain as mental nurses, student nurses and pupil assistant nurses. By the end of that year, 361 sponsored workers went to Britain, 113 of them to train as nurses,[26] and many of the others to work in hotels and restaurants.

In November 1955 the Barbados Immigrants and Welfare Liaison Service was established in London in temporary premises in Little Smith Street, and Harold Brewster, a master at Combermere School, was appointed as the assistant Liaison Officer, working assiduously to promote employment for Barbadians and continuing to present them as the 'elite' of Caribbean workers.[27] 'The Barbadian', the *Bulletin of the British Hotels and Restaurants Association* announced to its members as it commenced employment of Barbadians in August 1955, 'is gener-ally hardworking, reliable and honest, with a high sense of moral re-sponsibility. They are British in outlook.'[28]

Along with the National Health Service, and the hotel industry, the London Transport Executive was targetted for the employment of Bar-badians. Despite LTE's labour shortage, they were, as Pickwoad re-ported, 'most selective in the recruitment of drivers and conductors.' Nevertheless, he continued, 'there are, however, other types of workers required such as stationmen, permanent way workers, women canteen-workers etc. ... as the population problem in Barbados is recurrent, it may well be that there could be an annual recruitment for the LTE ...'[29] By January 1956 the LTE's recruiting officer, Mr. Gomm, and Dr Fyfe, the Medical Officer, had arrived in Barbados to select the first recruits. An announcement was made in the press, potential recruits were inter-viewed and tested and in April 1956 the first recruits – 'a likely looking lot'[30] – arrived in London.

The major concern of the Barbadian government was to keep open the avenues of employment and recruit as far as possible only those likely to enhance the reputation of Barbadians abroad as reliable and educated workers. A clear decision was made to recruit for London

Transport only skilled male workers as the ones most likely to be of the 'right calibre' and behave responsibility. 'Barbadian conductors (on London Transport) are now well known among their colleagues for their courtesy, co-operation and, of course, cricket.'[31]

Almost from the beginning, however, the refrain of both Barbadian and British duplicity could be heard. Many of the nurses, for instance, were unhappy at receiving a training as a State Enrolled Nurse, when they had been led to believe they would be trained for the superior qualification (and the only one recognised in Barbados) of State Registered Nurse.

The hospitals, on the other hand, complained that the girls were leaving to have babies or get married. 'It seems to me', wrote one Matron, 'that they have no conscience about their intentions and that they have wasted a good deal of everybody's time and sympathy,'[32] and the men were leaving for the higher wages promised by industry. Further complaints were registered about those who came as domestics or nursing auxiliaries who regarded it 'as a backdoor to nursing,'[33] and who disregarded hospital hierarchy.

Although the Labour Commissioner protested that the misunderstanding and high wastage was due to those who came under their own, rather than government, sponsorship and in the case of the nurses insisted that all government sponsored trainees were fully informed of the difference in qualifications, the confusion over training remained a constant thorn. Nevertheless,

> They did not specify ... the correct qualifications ... you've got SEN and you've got SRN ... they didn't tell you, properly, the difference between SEN and SRN. You only knew when you came and you've started, then it was a bit difficult to get out of it ... (then) when I passed out my SEN and ... was applying to do my SRN ... there was a lot of prejudice when you applied, you know ... a lot of prejudice in trying to get through to a hospital to do my SRN.'[34]

That some Barbadians were behaving 'irresponsibly' and ungratefully by leaving their employment was a source of anxiety to the Liaison Officer. Nurses, and other women workers, left to have babies, join boyfriends, or marry. Some were simply unhappy. Others, like those in the hotel industry, (despite the initial fanfare from the Hotel Association which greeted their arrival), felt 'kitchen portering is beneath them ... (they) must understand that they owe this discomfort for the help they received from the Government of Barbados in getting to England.'[35] 'I, for one of the many British hoteliers who joined in the scheme,' wrote one hotelier,

really wanted to do something for the coloured British subjects. My view now, however, is that we were wrong in
getting so sentimental, particularly as we had no idea we were
dealing with such irresponsible people ... public money would
be better spent in finding means of their earning their living in
their own homeland rather than foist them on us.'[36]

Others 'knew' that they were 'not going to be a bus conductor for
life or for very long,' and 'left after about four months.'[37] This particular
recruit, who had been a school teacher in Barbados, left to study economics at the (then) Regent Street Polytechnic and fulfil an ambition not
available at that time in Barbados. He had chosen London Transport
deliberately as an entry route into Britain. 'I don't think I could con-
vince anybody that I really want to do nursing.'[38]

The problem was so acute that the Liaison Officer wrote, in exasperated terms, how,

In my talks with people this end, I have found that there is
only one reaction to their irresponsibility, that they would not
like it to be known in Barbados that they have behaved badly.
You say ... that 'everything possible is already done' in
Barbados 'to minimise desertions.' Frankly ... I am afraid I do
not agree since to my mind what is required, and this was
endorsed by the Honorable Premier, is a good straight talk in
each Parish by somebody who can speak intimately of the
conditions in this country and who can tell the people in each
Parish of such of the workers in that Parish who have done
their bit or otherwise in building up the good name of
Barbadians as workers.[39]

The problem of 'wastage' and 'irresponsibility' continued to haunt
the endeavours of the Liaison Officer as he continued to negotiate
throughout the 1950s not only with the London Transport Executive,
(who offered to pay off the last third of the government loan as an
inducement for workers who stayed for a year) but the British Transport
Commission, British Rail, the Health Service, Lyons Tea Shops, the
confectionery industry, the spinning and weaving industry, foundries,
laundries and coopers, with all and every avenue of potential employers.
In 1961 Brewster was still writing

Perhaps it will be useful to warn all recruits that this Service
will on no account extend help to anyone who wilfully refuses
to honour his or her obligation and so bring discredit to the
fair name of Barbados and the excellent reputation of Barbadians.[40]

Adding that workers who 'failed to honour their obligations both to British Rail and the Barbados Government ... can mean "curtains" to Barbadian recruitment as far as BTC is concerned.'[41]

But the pressure of population was not an easy bedfellow of either personal ambition or government policy. Repayment of loans was difficult to enforce. While London Transport deducted repayments from wages, for the most part the government had to rely on the honesty of the workers and their ability to repay the loan from their wages. For some workers, low wages, high rents and the need to return remittances home left little each week for regular repayments. However much the Liaison Officer may have considered calling in 'the Bondsmen ... for having received a loan under false pretences'[42] there was also evidence of hardship, coupled with the practice of deferring payment on the grounds, as Brewster described, that 'the government has money.'[43] At the same time, while the government was able to select and target its skilled workers towards certain employers such as London Transport, it had far less control over others such as hoteliers or hospitals where vacancies were plentiful and employers prepared to recruit sight unseen. Although Brewster might lament that 'it might be as well to eschew the too-learned'[44] for hotel work, nevertheless many used the opportunity of such work to secure a government loan or sponsorship as a means of coming to Britain. Once there they sought work that was either better paid or closer to friends and relatives elsewhere.

Indeed, the conditions which many Barbadians found in Britain were intolerable. Menial jobs in hotels and hospitals were poorly paid, and often in isolated areas. In the cities, the postwar housing shortage meant that accommodation was limited, a situation aggravated by the refusal of many British to let to black tenants. The initial pace of sponsored recruitment was determined not by the numbers of workers prepared to come, or the numbers employers wished to recruit, but by the housing available. Despite Brewster's considerable efforts, there was simply not sufficient accommodation to meet the needs of recruits. Sharing rooms was commonplace, and the source of considerable grievance. At the same time, there was pressure from employers to produce regular cohorts of recruits, with the fear in the government's mind that failure to do so would drive employers to search for labour elsewhere. The pressure to export labour led to suggestions in Barbados that the early recruits were arriving insufficiently prepared, and the scheme itself had been hurriedly implemented. Passages to Britain were secured by the cheapest route, on the Italian Sorriento or Grimaldi lines. Conditions on board ship were crowded, the food was poor and 'the arrangements for landing in this country are primitive in the extreme.'[45] The Sorriento docked in Genoa and recruits had to travel by train and ferry, often with little or no food, from there to Britain, 'a most unpleasant and strenuous experience'.[46]

> The worst part about it (according to one informant) you sitting down, like four in this compartment ... and the shoes. Everybody feet was swollen when we come, we had to cut, you had to cut the shoes right across to get your feet in ... you could imagine, two days sitting down ... nowhere to walk around, train went backwards ... you got to try to sleep in there so. It was like carting animals, animals really.'[47]

There were frequent charges of lost luggage and delays and although Pickwoad 'strongly advised that they ("our specially recruited workers") be not sent that way in the future',[48] the line continued to be used, principally to secure passages for the increasing numbers required by both London Transport and British Rail. There were other problems. In the shipment of London Transport recruits there were, as Pickwoad wrote,

> not wanting to be found men who claimed to have been told that they would get a room to themselves; also that the £10 sent for them was not to include accommodation. When I pointed out that they had signed an agreement before they left, they said this was pushed under their nose just before departure and they had no option but to sign. Admittedly, only a few made this claim ... on the subject of the £10 sent to me, frankly this is not enough ... many of them arrive with no money at all and the £3 remaining after the payment of two weeks lodging fees is not really sufficient.[49]

There were charges that the men had not received the full loan, and had arrived with insufficient clothing, for which the Permanent Secretary laid blame on 'the department (which) has failed to ensure that the men took enough warm clothing from here.'[50] He authorised Pickwoad to make *ad hoc* loans, admitting 'He is clearly in a bad hole and on no account must the scheme break down.'[51]

But the cost and standard of accommodation remained a problem, and many recruits left the lodgings prepared for them to find their own accommodation. This posed two further problems for the Liaison Officer – first, the need to fill the accommodation already committed, through further recruits,[52] while maintaining the high standards expected of those recruits. And second, to keep the lid on discontent, a discontent fuelled in part by 'militant and subversive union elements' who are quick to prey on new arrivals comparing what they pay for a subsidised unfurnished countil flat with the amount our workers pay for a room.[53]

and partly by the migrants themselves who, although

adequately informed about the problem of finding accommodation in London where there are thousands of homeless English people ... in order to save themselves a few shillings, they subject themselves to the most intolerable conditions ... misconduct and lack of proper hygeine on the part of some of our workers contribute to a large extent to their own discomfort.[54]

In order to alleviate the problem, the Barbadian government made loans available to Barbadians to buy property in London and Birmingham on condition that it be used solely to accommodate transport workers. It aroused some controversy and attracted some unscrupulous landlords. A tenant of one such complained that

The sheets were as dirty as if dogs were sleeping on them. Some of the boys had to sleep on top of something like a cart, one up and one down, in a room with four other boys ... the food is just sufficient for a cat (one dumpling and a piece of potato was all we had for the day that I was there) ... When I left Barbados I was living in a good home. I hadn't expected to find conditions the same over here as I was told by Mr. Jeremiah in Barbados, but certainly not so bad.[55]

The Liaison Officer had an impossible task. Most Barbadians, those who left the accommodation found for them, or independent arrivals, were forced into renting crowded accommodation from the few people prepared to rent to them – Jamaicans or other immigrants who had managed to purchase property and sublet in order to repay their own mortgages, or, as in London, landlords such as the notorious Rachman who had his own agenda in leasing out rooms. 'Necessity' was how Roy described his tenancy with Rachman.

People weren't letting you accommodation. One, because you were black and two, if you had children, and that was a double portion of prejudice and Peter Rachman saw this opportunity to do business ... people say he exploit it. I take care how I use the word because ... if it wasn't for him, lots of people would have sleep on the street ... necessity. I just couldn't get any place other than his place at the time.[56]

Nevertheless, the charges that the Barbadian government had 'misled' its workers remained. Wages, for instance, rarely met expectations, for the figures quoted were gross rather than net amounts. 'I am constantly being told that "I left a good job" because the Labour Department called me' commented Arthur Pickwoad.[57] 'I never lived that way before in such a hermit way,' wrote one young man explaining why he left his hotel employment, 'nobody to talk to ... washing pans and saucepans weren't my idea of coming to England ... I was disappointed but never complain until now, I was a shoemaker in my own country ...'[58]

Although an information booklet was provided to all prospective emigrants, and sponsored workers, particularly for London Transport, were given preliminary talks on what to expect, the consensus was that neither the booklet nor the talks addressed the real issues of discrimination, low wages and poor housing beyond a bland and general statement. As a result Barbadians arriving in Britain were ill prepared for the high costs of living, especially in housing, or for the climate of prejudice and discrimination. Yet the government was highly sensitive to charges being made by both Barbadians and the British that they had misled migrants, and denied that there was any 'question of irresponsible persuasion of West Indians to migrate to this country in order to relieve local unemployment problems.'[59]

In any case, government controls could only operate on those who were eligible for and were successful in securing a sponsored passage or a government loan. Sponsorship and loans required someone able to stand surety in Barbados, and many potential emigrants were turned down for failing to provide a guarantor. By far the majority of those who arrived in Britain came, however, under their own steam, raising the money themselves from their own resources, or from private loans, preferring to secure their own employment and their own accommodation. Over these migrants the government had no control and, as Pickwoad and Brewster frequently argued out, it was they who risked giving Barbadians a bad name for:

> The difficulty is that our people go with one object – to make as much money as possible as quickly as possible so as to be able to come home (to) re-establish themselves. They are not really interested in a job as a job in England.[60]

Finding work in London was difficult, especially work which was commensurate with status and skills, although there were more opportunities in regional centres such as Birmingham, Leeds or Reading. But most Barbadians coming to Britain found their qualifications discounted and their skills unrecognised and were forced to take on poorly paid manual or menial work. Out of those wages they were required to keep themselves in addition to sending home remittances to care for children, partners or parents and, in some cases, repay a private loan.

The pressures on the Liaison Service were formidable. In addition to finding work and housing, they were required to meet the sponsored emigrants at either the port or station, a problem compounded when in many cases they were not accurately informed of the numbers to be expected. They were expected to monitor loan repayments and chase up those who reneged. As the only liaison organisation for Barbadians, they were approached increasingly for help by Barbadians stranded in England, by families abandoned in Barbados, and berated by aggrieved employers. One exasperated Barbadian woman, the mother of three children, finally by-passed the Service and wrote directly to the Labour Department in Barbados, complaining that she had been ill and unable to work. She could not therefore repay the loan, and no one would send her home. 'It is not so bloody marvellous,' she wrote,

> coming to a strange country with people that don't care whether you live or die ... I can't fulfil my duties as a mother ... I shall finish myself for good for I am fed up Begging to Return Home ... I think it's about time I stop writing for your decision and leave my three children for you to support or find they fathers because you damn well know England is not so easy without being able to slave day in and day out ... get me out and you will get the balance of money or else I go mad or commit suicide ... Hurry for it's Bloody murder out here living on six pounds a week, £4.50 for Rent and the Rest to buy food, parrifin (sic) and the lot. Think, and think hard what it's like.[61]

The Caribbean Welfare Service was dissolved in 1958 with the ending of the Federation of the West Indies and the Barbados Immigrants Liaison Service found its resources further stretched as it became a *de facto* welfare agency for non-sponsored as well as sponsored Barbadians. 'There is more work in this office', Brewster complained in 1960 'than can be comfortably attended to by three men.'[62]

The migration momentum continued throughout the 1950s and was given a further boost in 1961 and 1962 when more Barbadians entered in time to 'beat' the Immigration Act of 1962. The existing problems of inadequate information and accommodation were compounded by rising unemployment in Britain and the new requirement of a work permit. The field was ripe for exploitation. Shifty operators such as the Italian Grimaldi line advertised passages and acted as employment agencies,[63] and in Britain bogus agencies advertised jobs for fees.[64] Most of the migrants were still arriving by ship, the Italian lines, Sorriento and Grimaldi, offering by far the cheapest, though least satisfactory, service. Flying was costly and although BOAC offered a special rate, this applied to sponsored workers only and was still expensive, although it was the preferred route for London Transport, the elite corps of sponsored workers. The Chicago Agreement of 1944 on cabotage bound the Barbadian authorities to the use of British planes only and as a result charter operators were prohibited from offering services. The Liaison Officer urged the Ministry of Transport and Labour to make representation to the Secretary of State for the Colonies to permit charter flights for 'it is vitally important to get people out of Barbados whether they are sponsored or not.'[65] The restrictions on flights provoked one operator, Richard Williams, (who was also the agent for the Sorriento line) to charter a flight. Although the tickets were sold, the flight was refused permission to land in Barbados:

> To take bread out of the mouths of seventy one people – a letter to the *Barbados Advocate* argued – can be so serious as to bring about near riot conditions when the poverty of the people is taken into account and the fact that there is no work for them to do here ... I witnessed the teardrops falling from the eyes of a number of young women ... told they must live in misery and squalor longer ... the business of this no permission being granted to a charter plane ... makes me wonder if the runway want grease or ... if she is sticky.[66]

Williams eventually evaded the restrictions by airlifting passengers to Grenada first. The restrictions were relaxed in 1961 and although Williams continued to offer his services, the Permanent Secretary warned,

> I want to have as little as possible to do with Mr. Williams ... he is a most unprincipled fellow. Nor do I accept his apparent sympathy for emigrants ... His motive is to get business.[67]

Williams did not, however, give up so easily. By 1962 he was arguing stongly for the financial advantages to Barbados and Barbadians of sea travel. By then, however, the government was committed to advocating air travel as the most efficient means of transport.

By 1962 the rate of migration to Britain slowed down, rising again in 1965 before the Immigration Act of that year. By then, however, the United States and Canada had relaxed their immigrant policy and Barbadians wishing to migrate turned their attention north rather than east. Between 1960 and 1970 emigration – to Britain then Canada – accounted for 44,500 persons.[68]

From the perspective of the Barbadian government, the emigration to Britain was timely. It reduced the population, relieved pressure on employment, and enabled individual social mobility. 'The population pressure is such', wrote Brewster, 'that migration is the only solution ... the old and never ceasing movement of people in search of greater opportunities.'[69] It was an official perspective which had changed little in a century. Its novel feature was the active recruitment of workers and the engagement of employers, and the use of sponsorship and loans to facilitate migration, although the overall numbers of sponsored or assisted workers was relatively small. Despite the Liaison Officer's difficulty in reclaiming some loan payments, most loans were repaid and the scheme was judged a success.

The foreign exchange earnings from remittances from Britain made a significant contribution to the Barbadian economy. In 1961 – the year of the greatest migration to Britain – $4,180,623 in money and postal orders were issued and paid from Britain.[70] In the same year, however, there were reports of a shortage of skilled and semi-skilled labour in certain categories as a result of emigration,[71] of a growing incidence of child employment in agriculture, and of the disruption caused to family life as a result of migration.[72]

The agenda of the Barbadian migrants seems, as we shall see, more haphazard. Earning money was clearly on that agenda, as was travel. The 'wastage' reported by the Liaison Officer is clear testimony to that. 'It is obvious,' Brewster wrote, in relation to two men, that they 'used our scheme to get into this country and had absolutely no intention of honouring their obligation.'[73] Most migrants arrived alone, and there were equal numbers of men and women migrating. Many women came to join husbands or boyfriends, but many travelled independently. For the most part, Barbadians anticipated that their stay in Britain would be short term, as it had been in earlier migrations. Invariably it proved longer than anticipated, and families were eventually sent for, or started, in Britain, complicating the prospects of return. And yet Barbadians have returned, and are returning. The Barbadian-born population of Britain has declined in the last decade by 17 per cent,[74] some of it the result of re-migration, partly to North America or Europe, but principally to Barbados. Although the migration to Britain proved less 'casual' than other migrations, nevertheless there was retained a mentality of casualness on the part of the migrants which has in part been transmitted to the children of those migrants and which was reflected in the family structures which supported the migrant in his or her absence, and in those which have evolved in Britain to retain family flexibility.

Above all, however, the independent nature of the early migrants and the relatively low take-up rate of government assistance suggest that the migration to Britain conformed to patterns established in the nineteenth century, of individual, casual migrations free of the obligations of contract. The tradition of migration, and its particular characteristic of migrations by individuals on a temporary basis led also to particular patterns of settlement. The importance of networks in encouraging migration and in easing the settlement in Britain was crucial. Few migrants arrived in Britain without having made some provision for accommodation with a relative or close neighbour from home. Advice, housing and work were all to be found 'on the grapevine', which also provided leisure contacts and social support and proved a vital source of socialisation for the children born, or reared, in Britain.

References

1   Andor Skotnes, 'Some Reflections on Migration and Identity' in *International Yearbook of Oral History and Life Stories*, Vol III, Rina Benmayor and Andor Skotnes (eds), Migration and Identity, Oxford, Oxford Univeristy Press, 1994.
2   Raymond Williams, *The Long Revolution*, London, Pelican, 1975 (pp. 63–64).
3   *Ibid.*
4   Raymond Williams, *ibid.* p. 65.
5   UK census 1971, OPCS.
6   Barbados Migration Project (M. Chamberlain). Tapes and transcripts deposited at the National Life Story Collection of the National Sound Archive of the British Library. References refer to the interview number, tape number, side and page references. BB39 1/1/17.
7   Statistical Service *Abstract of Statistics*, Government of Barbados, Bridgetown, Barbados, quoted in G. Ebanks, P.M. George and C.E. Nobbe, 'Emigration from Barbados', *Social and Economic Studies*, 1979, 28(2). These figures refer to net migration losses and do not differentiate destinations. Nevertheless, it is likely that Britain received most of these migrants.
8   As quoted in *Barbados Advocate*, 29 January 1957, reviewing work of Barbados Immigrants Liaison Service.
9   *Report of the Joint Committee appointed by the two Houses of the Legislature to examine the question of over population in Barbados and to make recommendations for dealing with this problem, 1953*. Barbados, Advocate Co. Ltd. 1954. BDA. Pam C28.
10 Clive Harris, 'Britishism, Racism and Migration', paper presented at 25th Annual Conference of the Association of Caribbean Historians, Jamaica 1993. Lydia Lindsey 'Halting the Tide: Responses to West Indian Immigration to Britain, 1946–1952', *Journal of Caribbean History*, Vol 26:1.
11 Thomas Schelling, *The Strategy of Conflict*, Cambridge, Mass, Harvard University Press, 1960. This was a collection of essays which were first published, variously, in the 1950s.
12 *Ibid.*
13 M. Howard, 'Problems of a Disarmed World', in Herbert Butterfield and Martin Wight (eds), *Diplomatic Investigations*, London, George Allen & Unwin, 1966.

14   Ruth Glass, *London's Newcomers*, Cambridge, Mass, Harvard University Press, 1961.
15   Sheila Patterson, *Dark Strangers: A Study of West Indians in London*, London, Penguin, 1964; R.B. Davison, *Black British*, London, Oxford University Press, 1966.
16   Elspeth Huxley, *Back Street, New Worlds*, London, Chatto & Windus, 1964, p. 151.
17   *Ibid.*
18   Sheila Patterson, op. cit., p. 61.
19   Elspeth Huxley, op. cit.
20   R.B. Davison, op. cit.
21   See for instance Terence Ranger, 'The Invention of Tradition in Colonial Africa' in Eric Hobsbawn and Terence Ranger (eds), *The Invention of Tradition*, Cambridge, Cambridge University Press, 1983.
22   Sheila Patterson, op. cit., 1964.
23   Sheila Patterson, op. cit., p. 61.
24   Ralf Dahrendorf, *On Britain*, London, British Broadcasting Corporation, 1982.
25   Letter from Labour Commissioner 14 June 1954. E 5010/1 (b). Barbados, Department of Archives.
26   *Annual Report of the Labour Department*, 1955, SRL 9, BDA.
27   Report of the *Barbados Immigrants Liaison Service*, 1959, L10/23, Vol II, MTIL.
28   Report 10 August 1955. *Employment of Barbadians in the United Kingdom: Hotel Workers*, L10/11, Vol I, MTIL.
29   Pickwoad to Secchi, 23 August 1955. *Employment of Barbadians in the UK – recruitment for LTE*. L10/19, Vol I, MTIL.
30   Memo, Assistant Secretary, Ministry of Transport & Labour. *ibid.*
31   July 1958, Harold Brewster, *Monthly Reports, Welfare Liaison Service*, E5010/B(1), BDA.
32   E5010/1, Vol II. BDA.
33   *Ibid.*
34   BB39 1/1/A/20.
35   *Employment of Barbadians in the United Kingdom – Recruitment for LTE*, L10/19 Vol. I, MTIL.
36   Letter to Pickwoad, 6 January 1956. L10/11, Vol II. MTIL.
37   BB28 1/A/26.
38   *Ibid.*
39   Letter, Pickwoad to Secchi, 18 May 1956. *Employment of Barbadians in the United Kingdom – recruitment for LTE*. L10/19, Vol I. MTIL.
40   Brewster to the Labour Commissioner, 27 October 1961. E5010/8/IV. BDA.
41   Brewster to the Labour Commissioner, 16 November 1961. E5010/8/IV. BDA.
42   Pickwoad, 16 November 1955. L10/11, Vol II. MTIL.
43   Brewster to Labour Commissioner, 16 February 1962. L10/21, Vol III, MTIL.
44   Report from Pickwoad, 2 November 1955. L10/11, Vol II. MTIL.
45   *Ibid.*
46   Pickwoad to Jack, 11 April 1956. L10/19 Vol I. MTIL.
47   BB81/2/2/1/30.
48   Pickwoad to Jack, L10/19, Vol I. MTIL.
49   *Ibid.*

50   Reply from Secchi to Pickwoad, 18 April 1956. *ibid.*
51   *Ibid.*
52   Liaison Officer Pickwoad to Labour Commissioner Jack, 20 April 1956. L10/19, Vol I op. cit.
53   Confidential memo from Brewster to Labour Commissioner, 1961. Ministry of Labour, National Insurance and Housing – Emigration to the UK, Housing of Emigrants in UK. L10/21, Vol III. MTIL.
54   *Ibid.*
55   Letter to Brewster, January 1962. L10/21, Vol III. MTIL.
56   B34 1/2/2/42.
57   Pickwoad to Jack, November 1955. L10/11, Vol II. MTIL.
58   Letter, November/December 1955, L10/11, Vol II.
59   *Monthly Report, Welfare Liason Service*, September 1958. E501/B (1). BDA.
60   Memo, 22 July 1956. *Barbados Immigrants Liaison Service UK Reports*, L10/23, Vol I, MTIL.
61   E5010/29/3a, BDA.
62   Brewster to Labour Commissioner, 13 June 1960. E5010/14/II, BDA.
63   E. Hartley, British High Commissioner designate, Trinidad and Tobago to Pedro Welch, 28 August 1962. E5010/29. BDA.
64   *Ibid.*
65   Memo, 23 June 1960. E5010/18. BDA.
66   *Barbados Advocate*, 6 August 1960.
67   Permanent Secretary, Ministry of Transport and Labour, 10 April 1961. E5010/20. BDA.
68   B. Zaba, *1980 Caribbean Census.*
69   Harold Brewster to the Permanent Secretary, Ministry of Transport and Labour, 22 June 1960. L10/19, Vol II, MTIL.
70   *Annual Report of the Post Office Department, 1963–4*, SRL 49. BDA.
71   Darnley Lewis, Labour Commission to Secretary of State for Colonies, 13 July 1961. E5010/29. BDA.
72   Report of meeting of the Chairman of the Managers, Teachers, Education Officers, Welfare Officers at Turner's Hall Primary School. 12 March 1962. L10/35. MTIL.
73   Brewster to Labour Commissioner, 27 October 1961, E5010/8/IV. BDA.
74   Figures computed from UK census 1971, 1981, 1991. OPCS.

3 | Family Narratives and Migration Dynamics

The aim of the Barbadian government in encouraging and sponsoring migration was to reduce the level of its population at home. It was an aim which coincided with the private goals of individual migrants. Coincidence is not, however, the same as conformity and over-population cannot be equated with 'cause' in migration, although problems created by over-population may have contributed to individual decisions to leave. At the same time, although 'casual' migration for 'betterment' had become a feature of nineteenth and twentieth century migration, what that meant, or became, for the families concerned may not be as venial, as simple, or as disruptive as the authorities, from the 1895 to 1965, had suggested. Neither can it be considered in isolation from either the history of the families concerned, or from the historical duration in which it occurred.

Let me introduce you to some families. By tracing a detailed lineage within these families, it is possible to identify some of the ways in which family memory creates an ethos which shapes the lives of its members. In this case, the primary ethos is that of migration. In all the families, members of the previous generation had migrated in the early decades of the twentieth century, where some of the influences of the nineteenth century could be expected to resonate. In all families there is clearly a 'migration dynamic' whose meaning differs as it engages with other predominant cultural motifs of both class and colour. Migration, even within families, is never that simple. It probably never was.

The first family illustrates how independence from plantation discipline became a precondition for the family's migration, and continued as a theme of social mobility throughout the continuing migrations of family members. Jasper's father had migrated to Britain in 1954, his mother in 1956. Jasper himself migrated to join his parents in Britain in 1961, at the age of fifteen and returned, a successful restauranteur, in 1987 with his mother and family. Jasper's father, at the time he migrated, was employed in Barbados, and economic improvement was only one consideration in his decision to migrate. Social influences also played some part. 'It was an exciting time,' Jasper recalled, 'because

everyone on the island ... was talking about emigration to Britain ...'[1]
Talk which was placed, significantly, within a broader historical
context.

> I loved listening ... to the old fellas ... telling stories ... about
> how they went off to Curaçao and they went off to Panama
> and they was building the canal, and they went off to Cuba
> and Aruba and they found the oil ... the new place on stream
> then was Britain ... the big talk back in the 1950s was emigrat-
> ing to Britain ... these men were talking about emigration to
> Britain, it was the new thing.[2]

and played also into a particular domestic context. Jasper's mother
Olive, (born in 1926) describes how

> My grandfather ... was in Cuba and send for my two uncles ...
> then after my mother could get grown up, then she went to
> Trinidad ... and leave me very small, as a baby ... (My mother)
> was working ... then she leave Trinidad and went on to Panama,
> and meet her husband there ... he took her from Panama to
> Jamaica ... *Our family love to travel* ... (emphasis added)[3]

Olive, an only child, had been reared by her grandmother, a cook
in a plantation house, by her great-grandmother, Lola, and by her aunt,
while her own mother was away in Trinidad. Olive's mother had also
been reared by Lola, while *her* father was away in Cuba and her mother
had worked. When Olive and her husband migrated to England, Jasper
was cared for by his maternal great-grandparents; his siblings were
reared by his grandmother who was still in Jamaica. The importance of
other families members, in particular grandmothers, in child care is a
characteristic of many Barbadian families.[4] In this case, it facilitated and
enabled the migration of two generations of one family. For three
generations (including Jasper's great-grandfather's migration to Cuba) a
parent had been absent through migration. In terms of family models
and historical continuities, this had resulted in the youngest generation
being brought up by grandparents whose own historical reference points
were a generation removed. Models of migration were part of the family
lore, and migration was the norm.

The family facilitated migration in other ways. Although, as Olive
pointed out the family was not 'very big' principally because they 'was
away' nevertheless both she and Jasper maintained they were 'very
close.' The extended family, of cousins and aunts, included Jasper's
grandfather's 'outside' families. All provided mutual support for each
other, in terms of exchanging and sharing provisions,

... relatives used to travel for miles to bring ... provisions ... breadfruit, sweet potatoes, yams ... when one of the old cousins ... were growing things like sweet potatoes, we'd probably be growing cassavas and eddoes, so we'd do a swap ... back in that period ... for a woman to bring up a family completely on her own would have been difficult ...[5]

Mutual support was 'all part of the family thing' and applied, in this case, whether a partner was absent as the result of migration or for other reasons.

Second, Jasper's great-grandfather had sent the money for his sons to join him in Cuba. When Jasper's father decided to emigrate

... he didn't have the fifty pounds (for the passage) ... so my grandmother from Jamaica sent the money to my father ... she was instrumental in helping him get to Britain so that, in turn, he could help us to get to Britain ...[6]

Third, throughout the travels of the various members, regular remittances were sent back home;

... the boys (Olive's uncles) went and send back to their mum. My mother went too, and my mum send back to her Mum and they're always sending ... thereafter then ... my uncle (in Curaçao) used to send out a lot of clothes, pretty bath towels and powder, and everything you could think of, panties, everything.[7]

Clearly, with each remittance, contact was maintained. Just as family support enabled the migrants to leave, so migration assisted in the maintenance of the family at home, ensuring family loyalty and identity across the generations, and across the seas. This may account for the ultimate return of family members to Barbados which, in turn, became incorporated in the family model of migration. The family demonstrated a positive disposition to migration, and a determination to maintain family links and unity throughout migration. This was a family which, as Olive said, 'love to travel.'

But how did it start? Both Jasper and his mother emphasised that they were not 'plantation' people, that is, agricultural labourers. Olive's maternal grandmother who brought her up, was 'a cook. She never worked *in* a plantation ... She used to work *at* Wiltshire's plantation ...'(emphasis added).[8] Her grandfather was a fisherman. Jasper's father worked as a butler and chauffeur for a plantation owner. This pride of independence can be traced to Lola, who, although originally a 'located' plantation labourer, (that is, a labourer *in* a plantation) baked bread, and by working

> very, very hard ... was able to buy the land from Wiltshire's
> Plantation ... that cost her just over ten dollars. But ten dollars
> in the late 1800s was a fortune, you know.[9]

Lola, in other words, had raised sufficient money, by baking and selling bread, to buy her family land and therefore release from the Contract Law. She – and her descendants – were therefore free to sell their labour, and to migrate without constraints.[10] Olive, Lola's great grand-daughter, was still carefully distinguishing between working *at*, rather than *in* a plantation. Jasper, his mother, and grandmother had lived on this land and,

> attached to the kitchen was a lovely large oven ... that was my
> great-great-grandmother's oven, ... she used to bake as well.
> Our whole family's always been in cooking or catering ... in
> fact, today ... there is a corner ... known as Lola Corner ...
> because that's where she baked ... everyone converged there
> every Friday and Saturday ... there's nothing there now, just
> the piece of land ... which has been handed down from the
> family, from Lola to her daughter, which was my great-grand-
> mother, to my grandmother, to my mother, and I suppose my
> mother pass it on to me ...[11]

The land was at once both a symbol of individuality, and of resistance to the plantation.[12] In this family there is a clear recollection of genealogy, and a clear recognition of the role of their ancestor in differentiating and demarcating the family route away from direct dependence on the plantation. Lola's independence, and success, became incorporated into a family dynamic which was as much a part of the family inheritance as Lola's Corner. It pervades the accounts of her family, whether descended by blood or marriage. Olive's grandfather returned from Cuba. He was a fisherman who owned three boats, (and supported an 'outside family') and 'was considered fairly wealthy.' Olive's uncles returned from their travels, and built 'a lovely bunga-low.' Olive's mother has a restaurant in Jamaica. It may be to this that Jasper's final entrepreneurial success (in food) may be attributed. It is possible, too, that the fact, as well as the sense, of long-established independence from plantation control may have been a contributory factor in the ability and the willingness to migrate. The decision of Jasper's family to migrate appears to have been prompted by a simple and time-specific economic expedient, but in fact contains within it a far more complex history of *family* social mobility and geographic migration. It is a history which confirms the patterns of migration identified in the nineteenth century: of individual 'casual' migrations of both men and women.[13]

In the second family, although migration has been a consistent pattern, it is not migration *per se*, but another powerful family legend, (and one which in Barbados has a particular resonance) which can be used to explain and understand motives. Ursula was born in 1938, left Barbados in 1959, and returned in 1976. Ursula's father, a carpenter, emigrated to Curaçao, visiting home every three years. Although he was absent throughout most of her childhood, his remittances from Curaçao paid for her secondary education, and a range of private tuition which she enjoyed as a child.

Ursula's interview contained one agenda item: that of difference. Her childhood was 'different', she married a man 'completely different', her own migration pattern – and her return – was 'different' to the majority of those who migrated in the 1950s. The family circumstances which eased her settlement in England were 'different.' Ursula had been brought up to believe she was 'different,' by her mother and, particularly, maternal grandmother, with whom she lived, and 'gradually it's instilled in me up to the day, and I'm still that sort of person.'[14]

Her father's migration, her status as a singleton child, (her mother's only child) provide one explanation for her 'special' status. It is not, however, sufficient, for the strong sense of difference derives not from the material comforts resulting from her father's migration, but from the fact that:

> My mother was mulatto ... my grandmother remembers her father was white ... So naturally my mother still had a very strong high colour ... so I was of a lighter complexion. People tell me that I still have features that show I am (partly white) ... my grandmother ... had actually grown up on the plantation ... (and) looked more to the white race than the coloured ...[15]

Although her grandmother's sister had 'married back into white',[16] her grandmother had 'married to a coloured person,' which 'created a stir ... so ... she used to more or less stay to herself.'[17] Ursula's grandfather, a tailor, migrated to Panama.

> My grandmother said that ... he did not stay for long because he was not the labourer type of person ... being very soft ... he couldn't work as hard as the others, he was not used to it.[18]

Race was the leitmotif of her life. The story of her ancestry was told in the opening stages of the interview. It continued to dominate her narrative. She was the child, and the grandchild, of migrant workers. What appeared to be important was not the absence of her father (in other interviews, this is often given priority) but that her father provided the means for the family – and Ursula in particular – to live out a life of difference which it was felt, as light-skinned people, was their entitled inheritance and which her grandmother, in particular, wished to convey by stressing, and practicing, difference. 'I suppose having all this for me I was special.'[19] This was something her grandfather had failed to achieve for her grandmother, and mother, in Panama. He was too 'soft.' In one stroke – repeating her grandmother's story – she both dismissed his attempts, and explained it by elevating his status. He was not a natural labourer, unlike other Panama migrants. For, unlike her grandmother's sister who had married a white man, it was her grandmother's 'lot'[20] to marry someone who was 'a coloured person and brought here, on this very estate.'[21]

Ursula went to the Modern High School. She wanted to be a nurse but,

> I didn't want to really go to England with the people that were going at the time ... my mother used to say (if) there were too many people rushing anywhere, it can't be (for you) ... she brought me up that way too ... it's funny, I didn't want to go (to England.)[22]

Ursula left in 1959 to train in Canada. After two years, however, she returned to Barbados to marry 'somebody completely different.' They returned to Canada, but in 1963 migrated to England, in order for Ursula to complete her training, and for her husband to begin his. In England, Ursula experienced neither discrimination nor prejudice. Everyone was always friendly; they were treated as 'special'. 'Especially me coming from Canada.'[23] 'We have always integrated'[24] '... but then everybody's not like me, you see. Having mixed and travelled, I suppose it made a difference.'[25] England, moreover, 'felt like home.'[26]

When their second child was born, Ursula's mother came over from Barbados to help look after the baby, an 'arrangement ... *different* to other people.'[27]

> This baby was light in complexion ... And she used to always say, 'if anybody sees me outside they'll think he's my child.'... she didn't even want my husband to do much for him. She wanted to do everything with him ... She said, 'If anybody sees him outside they'll think he's white.'[28]

Her mother died in England, and was buried there. '... I suppose it's *more usual* for people to fly bodies backwards and forwards ...' (emphasis added).[29] At the time, they had no plans to return to Barbados. England was 'special.' In 1976, however, the family returned. Ursula's daughter, Rosamond, recalls that in England 'Mum and Dad ... never had any coloured friends at all.'[30] She was eleven when the family returned. England, she felt, offered

> an easier life than here ... a better life than here .... It was a shock when I first came ... Mum and Dad didn't talk that much about it (Barbados) ... we knew they were not born in England ... that they came from Barbados, but we hadn't a clue about what it was like, nothing ...
> ... (Barbados) felt really strange ... at first I said, 'Dad, look at all these black people' ... That was really strange at first ... it was a bit of a shock ...[31]

Rosamond was sent to a private girls school on the island. In her opinion, 'The best schools, the private schools, are more white than black ... the schools that you find low in standard, you'll find more black people.'[32] Rosamond works as a clerk in a department store in Bridgetown. She admits that her GCE results were not 'really too good ...' but is nevertheless determined to send her own child to the same school when she is of age. Her brother, the 'light skinned' child, however, 'didn't seem to like it (Barbados) and never settled,' and has returned to England to live.

Ursula returned to Barbados on the death of her father who left her some property and a small grocery business (described by Rosamond as a 'rum shop'). In the course of the interview with Rosamond, it emerged that Ursula had not been her father's only child. She had a half-sister, (an 'outside' child) who had migrated to Trinidad, and who also inherited some land from their father, which she then sold to Ursula. Whether Ursula, as a child, knew about the existence of this half-sister or not is almost immaterial. She did not mention her in the interview. The value she inherited, cherished and nurtured was that of racial difference which was offered as an explanation for a life which she perceived to be radically different from those around her. This was a 'specialness' which would not have been shared by her half-sister, was not shared by her father, nor her grandfather. It is, however, a characteristic still sung by Rosamond, and repeated in Rosamond's aspirations for her own daughter. That single white ancestor is now six generations removed from Ursula's granddaughter. Migration, for Ursula, enabled a perception of difference to be materialised, initially through her father, secondly through her own migration to England. It is still reflected by her daughter.

The model of migration offered in the third family is more ambivalent. Here, the theme which emerges is one of struggle and resistance, and a reshaping of the family migration model. It is a theme consistent through two generations, although it assumes a different form. Charles was born in 1913 in St. George, Barbados. He has two children of whom Irene, the eldest, migrated to Britain in 1960.

Charles' father migrated to Panama before he was born. He sent no remittances and made no contact. Charles never knew his father. Although his mother remained in Barbados, Charles was raised by his maternal grandparents. One maternal uncle who had also gone to Panama did, however, send remittances which proved the leitmotif of Charles' life:

> When I were at the age of twelve years old, my uncle ... said he want me to go to Secondary School because the people in Panama who is educated gets the best job .... My grandmother had a brother and he worked on an estate as the bookkeeper. The white half could work there[33] .... So I was to go to Combermere.[34] I had my money, my books, my khaki suit, everything ready. The money ... that my uncle send to pay for the school fees, it was eight dollars and eight cents. I will never forget this as long as I live .... I was home on evening ... and my grandmother sister came very dressed. Two sisters came, two aunts, and my grandmother get dress. I saw her boots, her umbrella, and they leave. I do not know where they were going. But the next thing I heard, my uncle that was the bookkeeper ... they ship him to Canada .... My grandmother took the money, with my two aunts, and ship my uncle to Canada ...[35]

This uncle had got 'heself in trouble', through gambling with 'all these white fellas.'[36] Unlike Olive's family, this model of migration is confusing. Charles' father migrates and abandons him. One uncle migrates, and promises him a better future. Another uncle 'robs' him of that future, by himself leaving on the money destined for Charles' education. The story of the 'robbery' occurred within the first few minutes of the interview. It was all Charles wished to tell. The interview concluded:

> I made a oath .... If I walk the road, pick paper bag, bottles and sell, my children got to get a secondary education .... I've made that vow, for what my family did me .... But my other two friends (who went to Combermere) ... ent as successful as me. I came out successful. My children will get education. I have a roof over my head and I am not hungry ... I don't owe nobody nothing. Nothing.[37]

How did that success come about? Charles himself migrated shortly after his marriage to Muriel in 1941. He went first to Trinidad, then to St. Lucia. After the war, he migrated to America, then returned to St. Lucia where he stayed until 1978 when he retired and came home to Barbados. Charles was a master tailor by trade. He secured work, however, as a clerk on the American bases in St. Lucia, even though 'I were not educated ... I didn't went to Combermere but ... I was really bright, man.'[38] His wife helped him in his work. 'And I thank she .... First thing she made me do, bought a dictionary and I got ... a small book ... algebras, different arithmetic ... how to make up accounts, reports, all different things ...[39]

He worked as a clerk all his life, supplementing his income with tailoring. On each migration, Charles insisted that his family accompany him. 'No where I go to live and ... there's no way my family can't come .... I have seen too many homes broken up.'[40] It was a story which his daughter, Irene, reflected upon.

> My mother said that when my father sent for her, everybody says, 'You're not going to St. Lucia?' They thought it was bush and forest and snakes and donkeys .... They said ... 'that's no place to take a child.' And so my father said, 'But now we're a family' ... that's as he saw it, that we were a family and you don't split a family up .... He's always kept and maintained that .... They say black men don't have that kind of responsibility, the women are usually left to do every-thing ... they blame slavery, they blame the ... economic set up in the West Indies. Well, it certainly wasn't the case in my family. I don't know where my father got his ideas from.[41]

On one level, Charles' own migration enabled him to fulfil the oath he made for himself when 'robbed' of his education. Throughout his narrative, the notion of being 'robbed' was frequently portrayed. Migration became synonymous with theft, and absence. His motivation appeared to be to restore what he perceived as a lost inheritance – of education, success, and family. Charles paid for his two children to go to secondary school. Both now have university degrees.

This was a family that was 'together', but where, because of migration, the extended family did not function in an active or support-ive role. In order to understand Irene's motivation for migrating to England in 1960, we need also to look at her mother, Muriel. She came from a family who 'felt we was a different breed, more elaborate in that neighbourhood (in Barbados).'[42] Muriel's grandfather owned a 'big, upstairs house. Thirty, forty acres of land. He was a rich man.'[43] Like Lola, in the first story, he had amassed his fortune and secured the family's independence. Unlike her, this was the result of remittances sent by his children who had migrated (to Panama and the United States).

The family employed servants in the house, and hired labour to work the land. Muriel passed through seventh standard at elementary school and was sent to learn dressmaking. She wanted to be a nurse.

> I was very bright too ... [but] I believe my parents were a bit ... backward ... not that they didn't have the money to pay .... They would look out for the boys more than the girls, because [they say] a woman role in the house .... If I had my life to live over ... I would be a brilliant woman some part of the world.[44]

In St. Lucia, Muriel and Charles had servants in the house and, like Muriel's mother, hired labour to work the land. She engaged in voluntary work. Her friends were 'doctors and lawyers.' She helped Charles become a white-collar worker. For her, migration created both her family's wealth, and enabled her to maintain her status. Her only regret was her lack of further education.

For their daughter, Irene, the perspective on migration synthesised the complexities of class and struggle which was her familial inheritance. According to Irene, her father, Charles, migrated 'because he married my mother. It sounds silly, but for some reason he wasn't accepted by the family. Then he thought he was going to ... make a life for himself and come back to Barbados and ... prove his worth, so to speak.'[45] Irene grew up in St. Lucia, 'and that was awful .... St. Lucians tended not to like the Barbadians very much .... It was always, "You're from Barbados, why don't you go back where you came from?" .... I wanted to belong and to be accepted, so I learned to speak patois .... I joined the Catholic religion, all that ...'[46]

Irene felt an outsider in St. Lucia, distanced by nationality, culture and by class, 'I wouldn't say that we were wealthy, but ... we had servants ... and the best of everything ... beautiful hand-made leather shoes ... music lessons, all that sort of thing ... and that created a lot of envy in people.'[47] She also felt an outsider in her own family in Barbados, 'I missed out on all this sort of grandma, grandad, aunts, uncles, cousins, all that sort of thing .... When I met them I always felt somehow an outsider.'[48] The whole thing came to a head for me,' she explained, in 1956 when 'I won a scholarship to go to Puerto Rico to train as a nurse .... My father ... thought it wasn't good enough ... if you were privileged enough to go to a grammar school, well, they thought teaching, or working in a bank, anything like that would be better than nursing. Nursing ... just didn't have that kind of status.'[49]

The scholarship was subsequently withdrawn when it was discovered that Irene was not St. Lucian. 'I realised, yes, I am a stranger ...'[50] According to her father, she was 'robbed.' After this, Irene was sent to stay with an aunt in Barbados. She remained there for two years, then migrated to England, to train as a nurse, this time with her parent's support. Within a year of arriving in England, however, Irene gave up her training to marry. Her husband was Barbadian, but

> life was rough .... I was living in a working-class area, being a working-class mum with working-class children and had middle-class values and expectations .... That was an awful time in my life ... a very big mistake ...[51]

At the time, class differences, she felt, were not important. 'This was England, and we were both young .... In the West Indies, he didn't have the opportunity ...'[52] Migration had been the source of the family's social mobility. For Irene, it resulted in downward mobility. 'I didn't even correspond with my parents. I felt such a failure.'[53] Irene struggled to complete her training and study for a degree. She divorced her husband and remarried. Her second husband had gone to Combermere.

For Charles, migration implied absence. For his wife, it implied mobility. For Irene, it implied class and cultural distance. Paradoxically, however, for all of them it also implied opportunity. Like her father, Irene had to struggle and, like her father, she had won against the odds. More, she had become the professional woman her *mother* had aspired to be. Education was a dynamic, but it was a recent one. Irene lived her life as an outsider – in St. Lucia, with her family in Barbados, with her first husband in England. The identity originates in the act of migration itself, and in the success deriving from that. 'To get here, ' Irene says, 'it's not been easy.' 'I have a roof over my head and I am not hungry,' Charles insists, 'I don't owe nobody nothing. Nothing.' Charles and his wife returned to Barbados. Irene and her husband have made plans to return.

In the final family the ethos concerns again the role of migration in social mobility, although it was given a fresh twist as perceptions were interpreted to conform to genre. Jeffrey came to England in 1962. He was twenty years old.

> My plans was to start out five years in England ... from England go to America, Canada, do a bit of travelling ... get a lot of money, and go back to Barbados ... and build a right, nice house ...[54]

He was a carpenter and joiner. Like many other informants, economic hardship was not the primary reason for leaving Barbados. Indeed, most of those who came to England were young, skilled and employed.[55] Like Dick Wittington, he came for adventure and hoped to find fortune.

Jeffrey nearly made his fortune. Soon after he arrived, he formed a rock group in which he was the lead singer. In time, they turned professional and were due to cut their first record, when Jeffrey left the group. Nevertheless, the group 'got the nerve to do the recording, and they got the worst singer in the group, he ended up singing the record.'[56] The record made the charts. If he had been the singer, Jasper believes, 'it would have got to number one.'[57] 'I do regret it, when I talk about all that money we could have made ... thousands, millions of pounds.'[58]

Fortune had eluded him, fate was against him. Even small opportunities were lost, 'if I was as wise as I am today, I would have buy a house in the sixties, probably I'd be in a better position ...'[59] Although Jeffrey went to Germany to work for a while, the big opportunity never returned again. 'Unless you're a gambling man that win the money all the time, or have a crooked mind to get money other ways.'[60] But what was the context for this? Jeffrey's father, Garfield, was born in 1920. His mother left him when he was four months old, and went to Guyana. In them days, he says, 'boats come and pick them up alongside the wharf and carry them away to Guyana ...'[61]

His mother never returned. Unlike Olive, whose mother also left her as a baby, or Ursula, who lived without her father, Garfield's experiences were not so fortunate. Under the regime of his father and stepmother, he 'had to do everything around the house ... I couldn't leave home and go out and play when I got work to do.'[62] During the school vacation, he had to work for eight cents a day, 'picking grass' on a plantation. He gave the wages to his father and stepmother. He left school at fourth standard, working full-time at the plantation for eighteen cents a day. The work was 'hard', so he went to learn the mason's trade. As an apprentice, his wages were less than agricultural work, and he was exploited by his boss who required him to work at the weekends with the horses.

'It wasn't easy,' Garfield said, 'not for me.' His life he characterised by bad luck, and hard work. When he was eighteen he went to the United States as a migrant worker and continued going for the next twenty-five years. Jeffrey remembers his father, 'was always travelling ... Cuba ... Panama ... America, for two, and three years at a time.'[63] Garfield went to harvest his fortune. However, 'I wasn't lucky.' One time, for instance,

> ... went to Florida to pick oranges. When I get there, last year enough oranges, last year. Oh Lord, ... but not when I get there! Oranges gone! ... The American people would get the

best bearing tree, and you, a contract man ... you never get the best.[64]

Although Garfield used to write, Jeffrey recalls that 'he never used to get enough money to send ... home ...'[65] As a result, with eight children at home, Jeffrey's mother worked as a domestic. His maternal grandmother, with whom they lived, helped with the child care. She died when Jeffrey was twelve, 'so that's when I had to finish school ... early ... because I had to help the other kids ... I had no choice.'[66]

At fourteen Jeffrey began his apprenticeship as a carpenter. A few years later, Garfield managed to make sufficient money in America to buy some land. He built the house himself, 'because I didn't able to pay.' The children helped by fetching water to mix the mortar; nobody else helped. 'Friends? Ha! Friends help if you got money.'[67]

Despite these interpretations, Jeffrey's perception of his father is that he 'done well.' Indeed, the contradictions in their perceptions and narratives is striking. According to Jeffrey, when it came to building the house,

> ... I (did) the laying out, the foundation work and all that ... and some of the lads that I was learning trade with, my father says to me, 'tell them to come and help me build indoors, ' he says, 'I'll pay them.'... so they came one evening, straight from work ... they used to come on Saturdays and Sundays ... they got it all finished.[68]

When Jeffrey migrated to Britain, he sent money home, with a letter, every two weeks. Garfield remembers,

> He never send back nothing ... I can remember, oh, help me Lord ... I can remember. I ask him one time ... if he had anything to send, and help me to progress. I think he send twenty pounds ... and told me, remember, he has a wife and children now. And as soon as I catch myself, I send back his twenty pounds. So he never send nothing, ever. Never. Ever.[69]

Garfield, however, believes Jeffrey has 'done well' in England and it is parsimony which prevents him sending money. According to Jeffrey, his father believes,

> You should be working all the time and you're making, you're earning about three times the wage that you're earning in Barbados. He always think like that, you know? ... His thing is 'Well, you're in England, and you're earning three or four hundred pounds a week, and you could save three hundred pounds a week.' That's his thinking all the way.[70]

A sense of exploitation, grievance and lack of control pervades Garfield's narrative, commencing with his mother, who was 'carried away,' continuing through his father, his boss, American workers, the failure of the harvests, the friends who would not help and finally his son who sent no money. His life was a series of misfortunes; his agenda was one of perceived failure. Garfield went regularly to America. Now, however, his life had been conflated into a shortage of luck and money and an abundance of fruitless labour. Migration had failed to give him the rewards he expected. Rather, it had left him as poor, and as abandoned, as he was as a four-month old baby, when his mother departed to seek her fortune in Guyana.

The contradictions between their narrative accounts reflect and reinforce a mutual, though different, sense of grievance and failure. Both father and son explain their lives in terms of failed opportunity – *if only* the bumper orange harvest had been a year earlier; *if only* the pop group had made their record two months before. Like seasoned gamblers, both father and son were waiting for the big win. Even though Garfield had clearly failed to make a fortune, Jeffrey had perceived migration as the chance to do so. The themes which pervade Jeffrey's own narrative – his failure to make his fortune, his entrapment in England – are as obsessive as that of his father. Yet both maintain that the other 'done well.'

Looking at families across generations identifies the role of the family in enabling and permitting migration. In the families presented here, the importance of grandparents in the raising of grandchildren is clear. The wider sample confirms the resilience and role of the 'transnational' family where examples are presented of first and second generation British-born children being sent home to grandparents, or family, in Barbados. Indeed, the sample begins to suggest a link between the role of the family in other areas such as the creation of cultural identity in Britain, and professional success.[71] The maintenance of links throughout migration through, in particular, remittances suggest a primary loyalty to the family, made all the more remarkable precisely when it fails to occur. It suggests also that while economic advancement, or social mobility, may have been a consideration in the desire to migrate, its locus was directed not towards metropolitan contrived notions of success, but towards home-island rewards, and a maintenance of social and family structures. It accounts also for an expectation and, in two of the cases here, realisation, of return migration. It may help account for the relatively large decline in the last two decades of the Barbadian community in Britain, and suggest that the much vaunted 'myth of return' may in fact have more grounding in reality than is commonly acknowledged.

The strength of family organisation in supporting migration suggests, clearly, a willingness to sanction it, and a positive disposition towards it. What may appear to be a personal economic motive to migrate, often involves a *family history* of social and geographical mobility. This history, moreover, links back directly to the migration movements of the nineteenth and early twentieth centuries and the particular form which such movements assumed – the conjunction of the role of the individual within the broader framework and long-term perspectives of the family, the primacy of the family in establishing a sense of independence and identity, and the flexibility of the family as an essential mechanism for so doing. Migration could perhaps be seen as an extension of what Sidney Mintz described as 'liquid capital' and the use it could be put to 'escape the plantation regimen in order to define their lives outside its iron order.'[72]

In the case of Barbados where 'free labour' was effectively curtailed by the Contract Law, and where the opportunity for exploiting other skills were also limited, the notion of 'liquid capital' as the mechanism of establishing both freedom and identity through family lines, was vital in the shaping of both family and culture, and remains a dominant, if obscured, dynamic in migration.

The importance, therefore, of a family model in creating an ethos which shapes expectations, behaviour and allegiances, and the importance of migration within this, is one which cannot be ignored. Neither can the links between family and culture. It is, therefore, reasonable to extend the notion of a migration ethos from the family and into the broader culture, and to look at ways in which the two interrelate.

Although the detail of the family histories outlined here differ, the narratives are organised around a particular theme, a genre of improvement or 'betterment', which has been transmitted across generations and transformed by them. These were individuals, specific families. At the same time, the stories conformed, or were recounted and interpreted so as to conform, to what had emerged as a wider migration narrative. From the nineteenth century, migration from Barbados was perceived as a mechanism of both asserting and achieving independence. The symbolic value and material rewards of migration were one and the same. They tended to be reinforced with each migratory movement[73] and, as such, entered into a mythology of success. Three of the four families delineated here perceived themselves and, by any material measure, can be perceived as 'successful.' Migration did its job; it enabled a 'better life.' Disparate though the stories and motives are, they all conform to a broader consensus: migration equates with opportunity. This is the stuff of narrative, the mechanism by which collective experience is expressed and explained. For the final family, migration, by the same measurable standard, has been unsuccessful. Garfield made no money; Jeffrey has had periods of unemployment. Yet both father and son not only persisted with their migrations but, more importantly, perceived each other to have succeeded, even though the reality suggested the opposite. This particular genre had become the means by which they interpreted, and made sense of, their own and each other's lives. The contradictions and the omissions are not so much evidence of 'faulty' memory, but clues to unrealised dreams, to lives which require reconstruction, and as evidence of genre under construction and transformation.

This suggests the need to perpetuate, and reinforce, the particular notions of success surrounding migration, by suppressing individual anxieties and hardships both for the greater family good, and to maintain the family reputation if, as seems the case, that reputation and status was largely built on the successful migration of individual members. Evidence from the interviews confirms a reluctance to return to Barbados unless substantial material improvements can be shown.

This particular notion – of improvement and mobility – has been highlighted here because components of it were appropriated by government agencies, and find echoes in models of migration. It is not, however, the only dynamic. It may, finally, not be the most important one. In Ursula's family, for instance, the relationship between colour and mobility is well articulated and engages directly with the rewards of migration. In Jasper's family, the connection between land, independence and mobility suggests more than a material connection. The theme of abandonment also figures centrally. All the families, though in very different ways, were shaped by it. Equally, the motif of denial and exclusion – of opportunity, of parental love – recurs throughout the narratives. In many ways these may be the melodies of the universal migrant. But they may also be specific to the Caribbean, and a cultural history shaped by slavery – whose resonances found easy analogy between Bible myths of liberation and movement, Emancipation and mobility, diaspora and return on the one hand,[74] and on the other, in Bible teachings of stoicism, patience and deferred rewards in the final migratory destination of Heaven.

References

1   B9/1/A/19. All extracts from the Barbados Migration Project (M. Chamberlain). Tapes and transcripts deposited with the National Life Story Collection of the National Sound Archive at the British Library. References refer to interview number, tape number, side, and transcript page number.

2   B9/1/A/20.
3   B5/1/A/48.
4   See Christine Barrow, 'Migration from a Barbados village: effects on family life', (1977) *New Community*, Vol 5(4).
5   B9/1/A/9.
6   B9/1/A/20.
7   B5/1/A/11.
8   B5/1/A/3.
9   *Ibid.*
10 For a fuller exposition of this argument see Sidney Greenfield, 'Barbadians in the Brazilian Amazon', *Luso-Brazilian Review*, 20(1) 1983.
11 B9/1/A/16.
12 Sidney Mintz, 'The origins of reconstituted peasantries' and Woodville Marshall, 'Peasant development in the West Indies' in H. Beckles and V. Shepherd (eds), *Caribbean Freedom: Economy and Society from Emancipation to the Present*, Kingston, Ian Randle Publishers/London, James Currey Publishers, 1993; J. Besson and J. Momsen, *Land and Development in the Caribbean* London, Macmillan, 1987.
13 See for instance *The Barbados Emigration Commission Report 1895*, BDA. Pam C676.
14 B18/1/A/10–11.
15 B18/1/A/3–4.
16 B18/1/A/13.
17 B18/1/A/14.
18 B18/1/A/5–6.
19 B18/1/A/7.
20 B18/1/A/13.
21 B18/1/A/4.
22 B18/1/A/17.
23 B18/1/B27.
24 B18/1/B/34.
25. B18/1/B/27.
26 B18/1/A/2.
27 B18/1/B/29. In other families from the sample, children were sent back to their grandmothers in Barbados. Ursula's was the only family where the grandmother came to England to look after the children.
28 B18/1/B/28.
29 B18/1/B/31. Winston James, 'A Long Way from Home: On Black Identity in Britain', *Immigrants and Minorities*, 5(3), 1984, p. 258–84.
30 B19/1/A/4.
31 B19/1/A/3,9.
32 B19/1/A/10.
33 A great-grandparent had been white. At that time, black Barbadians were not given management positions on the plantations. This uncle, however, was sufficiently light-skinned to secure work as a plantation bookkeeper.
34 Combermere was one of the leading secondary schools in Barbados. It was fee paying. Free secondary school education was not provided until 1962. Until then, the majority of black Barbadians had an elementary education only.
35 B3/1/A/3.
36 B3/1/A/4.
37 B3/1/B/17.

38   B3/1/A/8.
39   *Ibid.*
40   B3/1/A/10.
41   BB1/1/A/16.
42   B2/1/A/5.
43   B2/1/A/2.
44   B2/1/A/8–9.
45   BB1/1/A/3.
46   BB1/1/A/5.
47   BB1/1/A/7.
48   BB1/1/A/5.
49   BB1/1/A/10.
50   BB1/1/A/7.
51   BB1/1/B/34–37.
52.   *Ibid.*
53.   BB1/1/B/38.
54   BB2/1/A/12, 50.
55   This characteristic was referred to frequently in correspondence between the Barbados Immigrants Liaison Office in London and the Labour Commissioner in Barbados, correspondence 1957–63. It was, of course, a double-edged sword for skilled laborers maintained the high 'calibre' and 'reputation' of Barbadians in Britain, while draining Barbados of scarce resources.
56   BB2/1/A/20.
57   BB2/1/A/21.
58   BB2/1/A/28.
59   BB2/2/A/61.
60   BB2/2/A/67.
61   B6/1/A/1.
62   B6/1/A/3.
63   BB2/1/A/3.
64   B6/1/A/7–9.
65   BB2/1/B/31.
66   BB2/1/B/36.
67   B6/1/A/11.
68   BB2/1/A/8.
69   B6/1/A/12.
70   BB2/2/A/66.
71   Mary Chamberlain, 'Family and identity: Barbadian migrants to Britain' in Migration and Identity, *The International Yearbook of Oral History and Life Stories*, Vol. III, Oxford, Oxford University Press, 1994.
72   Sidney Mintz, op. cit.
73   Bonham Richardson, *Panama Money in Barbados 1900–1920*, Knoxville, University of Tennessee Press, 1985. A similar theme is also explored by him in *Caribbean Migrants: Environment and Human Survival on St. Kitts and Nevis*, Knoxville, University of Tennessee Press, 1983.
74   My thanks to Catherine Hall for pointing out this connection. The different historical experiences of slavery and post-slavery in Jamaica and Barbados may also be reflected in religious experience and practice. While Biblical myths of liberation were more powerful in Jamaica, where they conformed more readily to actual experience and to a pronounced history of overt slave

resistance, in Barbados the religious emphasis most readily adopted was on stoicism and deferred reward.

4 | Narratives of Exile and Return

Barbados. It was like, you came home from school, and you came ... through your front door and you were ... in Barbados. You were very much in Barbados. In fact, we all referred to Barbados as home, and it's always home, and yet we were (born and) raised here ... Even now, my husband says, 'Barbados is not your home. Britain's your home.' But yet, I still say, 'home', you know, 'I'm going home.'[1]

We really believed that we're going home to a Mother Country, a place that's going to be loving and nice ... we were told that the place and everybody in it was nice, virtually angels.[2]

I want to focus on the concept of 'home'. First, because as the two opening quotations suggest, 'home', as symbol of both place and belonging, features in the narratives, and in their transmission and plays a key role in the construction of British–Barbadian identities. Second, 'home' as a mechanism for social control, and a metaphor of imperial loyalty, featured in the ideology of Empire and it was this ideology which was one of the distinguishing features of the postwar migration from the Caribbean to Britain.

For Sharon, whose extract opens the chapter, 'home', is an inherited memory, remembered space. She was born in Britain and has never lived in Barbados, though she has visited. For Roy, in the second extract, 'home', was an imagined space, the 'Mother Country.' For him, and others of his generation, migrating to England was a move into the heartland of imperial patronage. In more senses that one, Britain was the 'Mother Country' and commanded an intellectual, cultural and moral authority. As Roy explained,

So much was taught down our throats about the Mother Country and so forth ... from the time we were training school from Britannia, raise the flag on Jubilee day and drink your lemonade, you know, we think of England. The Union Jack and the National Anthem ... we were virtually told that everybody up there was a Christian. And that's true and we believed it.[3]

Euline, another informant, told how,

> We did things like the history, so you knew all about the kings
> and queens ... I think we knew more about the history of
> England than we did about the history of Barbados ... And all
> about the geography of England .... Not a lot about the people
> ... themselves ... because ... the way of life in Barbados ... and
> the way of life in England ... there's not a lot of difference ....
> I didn't know a lot about the people themselves, but about the
> history of ... the Royal Family and all that.[4]

Sharon's father, Orville, suggested that,

> I knew a lot about England, although I never saw it ... because
> we had a radio in the (tailor) shop and all the programmes in
> Barbados coming through was basically English ... there was
> always the English news ... 'This is London calling ...' .... And
> you heard John Arlott and Rex Alston speaking from Lords ...
> and you hear Raymond Glendenning describing boxing and
> horse racing. And you heard ... the boat race ... these sort of
> commentators were household names ... you hear about
> Regent Street and Charing Cross, those things you knew ... I
> had a very good understanding of England ... every aspect of
> English life ... the Festival of Britain ... the Coronation ...
> Everest ... he started with that, he says, 'with the news that the
> British expedition have conquered Everest.'[5]

As a result, although the topography of the 'Mother Country' had
a familiar ring, most of the migrants had 'no idea. None whatsoever' of
what the reality of England was like. Coming to Britain was coming to
an imagined country, mythological territory, what Raphael Samuel described as 'mnemonic landscape':

> Sacred geography, secularized in the service of the state (which)
> was to play an even more vital part in nation-building and the
> geopolitics of colonial expansion.[6]

It was a landscape constructed by the British, to pursue and justify
their own imperatives of Empire, and to secure the loyalty of her
colonial subjects by fixing it in time and space. The migrants who came
from the Caribbean including, from 1955, Barbados came with particular expectations of Britain. Although most had experienced the migration of previous generations and many – like Roy – had already
migrated to North America, Britain was *not* just another destination in
the migratory sequence.

> I had already travelled ... considerably throughout the United States ... I was working for the government (in Barbados) in a job which was considered very reasonable ... I was happy. I was married ... My mother was here, a mother I loved very much so it would have to be *something* to make me feel I would want to go abroad again .... The main thing that attracted me was to see Britain ... despite the fact that I had travelled before, (I) was very, very keen to come to England more than any place else. That was my first motivation, my first attraction.[7]

As we have seen, the arrival of West Indians in Britain was perceived as a threat to the domestic order and stability of a society whose own identity and role was profoundly challenged by the dissolution of Empire, and the new world order. West Indians were not welcome, above all, not *indoors*. As Orville recalled,

> You go to the newsvendor shop and you look on the board and you see the various advertisements ... and then you'll see 'No Irish, no coloured'. Some you see 'No coloured' ... so there might be as much as fifty on one little board ... and you would find that is narrowed down to about ... five, that were willing to take blacks.[8]

Yet the imperial mythology, the 'sacred geography' of empire, remained unpunctured within the Caribbean. With the exception of the weather, – 'the few that had gone up said that ... they didn't die from the cold ... you don't drop dead as it were, from the cold.'[9] – letters home excluded mention of the problems encountered. On the contrary, they contained missives of encouragement. Estelle recalled how

> Emigration was on, and most of your friends have gone, and they'd be writing you letters, you know, 'Things are good. Why don't you come up and see the place?'[10]

As a result, for those who arrived in Britain between 1955 and 1962, the 'reality' of England, the problems – of employment, accommodation, racism and loneliness – were unexpected and compounded by a sense of outrage at what many considered the moral and physical degeneracy of the British. Byron described how,

> When I got to Southampton, I was shocked ... because the people working on the docks appeared to be underfed, they were, they appeared to be very, very poor and the Immigration Officers ... seemed totally and utterly disillusion, and there wasn't an air of happiness around. Everything seemed dead.[11]

And Beryl,

> I thought it was horrible ... the buildings dirty and the streets
> with the dog mess ... it didn't really seem to be the right place
> for me ... and people kissing in the street. Oh, that was very,
> very nasty to me ... they were very discreet with their kissing
> and thing in Barbados ... but here is people kissing and cud-
> dling up and thing, under trees, on the buses ... it looked really
> rude, you know ... the way of life ... I felt it was ... a bit more,
> a bit primitive ... those kinds of things we never did ... things
> that you would respect yourself for ... I have to stop and think
> ...'Was this made for me?' I have to say, it was dreadful.[12]

Such detail was concealed in letters home, and replaced by a bland
and universal endorsement of the migration. The letters remained silent
on the central problems which confronted the new migrants. Estelle
remembers,

> ... They didn't let you know that they didn't have much place
> to live, you know, finding somewhere to live was difficult.
> They didn't let you know any of that.[13]

And, as Leroy explains,

> Well, actually, a lot of them didn't tell the truth ... they told
> you ... they earn so much and things like that. But they didn't
> tell you how difficult it was to get a job, and things like that.[14]

Why? There were practical reasons to conceal experiences in Britain from those at home. First, most of the migrants were young men and
women in their late teens and early twenties.[15] Some were married, or
had families of their own. Recounting problems may have caused worry
to parents or partners. The kindest and simplest solution was, as Leroy
admitted, to keep quiet,

> It was only when you come here you realise that you would
> upset your parents and your friends down there if you told
> them that things were so difficult. So you always tried to cheer
> them up, you know, just say, well, you're doing fine, ... or
> you're alright.[16]

A view reinforced by Beryl,

> I didn't make her (mother) feel bad, 'cos I knew that she
> would worry and so we (she and her brother) wrote the usual
> and 'we okay' and 'we both fine' and 'it's cold' and things
> like that. But we never really told her that it was that bad ... we
> never did, because she would pine and worry ...[17]

Second, the migrants considered that their stay in Britain would be temporary, from three to five years. Difficulties could be tolerated on a temporary basis, and would not be resolved through grumblings sent home. Third, most had borrowed money to come – from family, from the government – and needed to repay the debt; others sent remittances home. If there was little to save, there was even less to be gained by admitting that money was short. Finally, there are also more abstract explanations which can be located in a home-grown tradition of migration itself. It would seem, as Byron suggests, that other migrations (to North and Central America) had been similarly characterised by muteness.

> It was very difficult in my day to find out what people do abroad, because you find that people don't talk about it. I now gather that it (migration to North America) was exactly like black people going to Britain, that it wasn't what you could offer ... it was the fact that you were an immigrant and ... all immigrants are treated alike.[18]

No one – at least from my sample – appeared to blow the whistle on Britain. This silence became one of the expressive modes of migration. How can we account for the consensus of silence, this collective, pervasive muteness which characterised the primary years of migration?

The first clue may lie in a form of cognitive dissonance, an inability to assimilate and interpret new experience within existing experiential structures. Mel Thompson suggests that in Jamaica stories of racism in Britain,

> like the many cups of tea ... was put down to the quaintness of the English and to their ignorance. The majority of West Indians did not associate racism with Britain. [As a result, Jamaicans may have listened but] whether those listening would have been able to interpret the meaning, however, was a different matter.[19]

It is an interpretation supported by a number of informants. Roy, for instance, argued that,

> Prior to then, you was getting nothing. Whether people was up there and didn't want to say what they were going through, or there wasn't sufficient people to speak enough about it, *or people, even if they hear it down here, say they wrote their family and tell them things, they probably won't believe it, they probably don't tell it to anybody else.* But I can assure you that up to when I left England in 1956 I had nothing but

a hundred per cent good picture of England and everybody else that is in England. I felt I was going to a place which would be second to heaven, and that is true ... they gave us a lot of advice. We weren't short of advice at all. What to expect about the weather. They were very honest about that ... (emphasis added)[20]

By 1961, however, there were reports, in the newspapers and elsewhere, which indicated the prevalence of racial tensions, poor social conditions, and employment difficulties in England. Certainly, as Sutton and Makiesky-Barrow suggest, news of the Notting Hill Riots was widespread,[21] but, as Byron, who migrated in 1961, insists,

people had written home about it, *but you couldn't understand it*. You couldn't believe that the Britain who you were taught so much of, were going to, was not going to represent you ... you heard of these things, but you couldn't really imagine it. You couldn't believe it. (emphasis added)[22]

Cognitive dissonance may provide one explanation. Another may come from the notion of alienation, not so much in the Marxist or sociological sense, of people divorced from, and deformed by, their relations to labour, but in Barthian notion of mythological alienation. In this case, two mythologies ran concurrently. One was the mythology of migration as improvement; but the other was the larger mythology of the 'Mother Country', alienated, as Barthes might argue, from itself and its historical origins. 'Myth is a word which has been stolen and given back. Only that the word was not exactly the same when it was returned.'[23] More particularly, it was not the same when its meaning was put to the test. What had been 'read' as truth proved to be perfidy, duplicity. Roy told me,

I can assure you that up to when I left England in 1956 I had nothing but a hundred per cent good picture of England and everybody else that is in England. I felt I was going to a place which would be second to heaven, and that is true.[24]

What he found was that '... in short, the English could teach hypocrisy better than anybody else on earth.'[25]

The 'Mother Country' proved empty of all meaning. It was an artifice. Many of the narratives allude to the 'Mother Country' as the 'land of milk and honey', peopled by 'angels', its streets 'paved with gold.' Such descriptions were a response to the question, *'What did you imagine England to be like?'* The imperial myth had been translated into concepts of sanctuary and salvation, and had been memorised in the mnemotics of food and colour. The myths of England and the imaginings it encouraged echoed biblical phrases and motifs. Docking at South-ampton, or alighting from the train at Waterloo, dispelled instantly the primary colours of the image. However well prepared for the cold, migrants had not been immunised against England's 'dull', 'dead', 'gloomy' appearance, nor from their subsequent experiences.

A third explanation may be found in the confrontation with urban modernity. The majority of Barbadians originated from rural or semi-rural communities, country villages or the suburbs of Bridgetown, neighbourhoods characterised by kinship networks, neighbourhood in-volvement and by an occupational framework which with the exception of white-collar workers such as teachers, was small-scale, personal and often required the ability to shift between areas of work or to assume more than one job. With the exception of a few – mainly nurses and hotel workers – most Barbadians (and West Indians) who came to Britain gravitated towards major urban centres, London, Birmingham, Leeds, Reading or Liverpool, a built environment seemingly far differ-ent from that which, with the exception of those who had travelled to North America, they had experienced previously. Misreading the sign-posts in that urban landscape – as, for instance, did Estelle.

> Well, I first look at the house, and I wonder, what's these things on the roof for? And I said, 'All these factories!' Cor I only knew factories had chimneys, you know, and I says ... 'they must got a big shortage here for labour, with all these factories.'[26]

– Or social convention, like Cedric who, on his first morning in London,

> got up, I walk, bare feet, to Albany Road, from Beatty Road to Albany Road, bare feet, and everybody was watching me. I didn't know why everybody watching that, so when I get up my cousin, she said ... 'where's your shoes?' I say, 'Home.' She say, 'Nobody walk here bare feet.'[27]

– Or like Victor who 'rambled' a lot rather than ask directions

> (because) it's always the thought in your mind, whether they will laugh at you, or whatever ... there's no doubt, there's a strange feeling. And loneliness is one of the first feeling that counteract a person who travel for the first time, because you were just home with friends and families, all in your small corner, cosy, warm and all this kind of thing and suddenly you are into a big, cold country with no friends, no relatives, just you alone.[28]

were at once symptomatic of a confrontation with a particular modern social and urban environment, characterised by Durkheim as *anomie*, or Simmel through his concept of the *stranger*, in which the newcomer was both ignored and the object of intense scrutiny, if not hostility, particularly in the twin areas of housing and work, a particular industrial environment which was regimented by time and negated any notion of occupational multiplicity, a particular concept of urban power and domestic organisation which was built into the fabric of the houses, the workplaces and the street, and also a concept of sophistication which incorporated the possibility for both opportunity or suffocation. It was a confrontation implicit in a critique of the 'Mother Country', but one which also went beyond it. It was not a simple confrontation between the rural dweller and the city, but a clash between two aspects of modernity, between the needs and aspirations of a migrant Caribbean population, and the social rules which attempted to regulate, incorporate or exclude them.

The first response, – the first solution – at least in letters home, was silence. Another response, was to insist on the temporary nature of the migration, and within that to emphasise the casualness of the decision to come, (a response analysed in greater detail in Chapter 5) as if so doing minimised their culpability in their actions. Although some, (like Orville) came with a calculated agenda to provide for his family, others, like Euline came to escape an overstrict parent,

> My mother was very strict ... and I thought ... it might be a good idea, just to leave the country, because I couldn't see my mother really letting go if I'd stayed at home in Barbados.[29]

Many – and there is a gender dimension here, for it involved only the men – described their decision as isolated and as an act of impulse, or foolhardiness. Leroy says, 'I just made up my mind to go.'[30] Byron says the time between deciding to go and departure took 'seven days ... Once I decided to do something, there was no hanging about ... I had my passport and I just went on the first available boat.'[31] Speed was emphasised by Lloyd, another informant, 'I get my passport Monday ... I booked my trip and I left on the next week ... and I said (to my wife), "You know me. If I can do something, I don't talk about it, I just go ahead and do it." I went. I bought a grip, the same time we went to get my pictures and get the passport.'[32]

The consistent patterns of dismissal within the narratives suggest that the adoption of such a devil-may-care approach has been a response to, rather than a description of, the actual process and experience of migration. The framework of silence had other manifestations, too, in a pattern of denial of racism, or downgrading its importance. Leroy suggests that he did not

> really go around looking to see who don't accept me. I look to see the ones that accept me. So I don't really notice the others ... I heard of people slamming doors in your face and things like that, but I didn't experience that ... with finding jobs, I moved from one job to the next, because it was only in the first stage that you didn't know what type of job to apply for, because you didn't know what it involved, you know.[33]

And Euline insists there was no problem,

> Everybody around was rather nice to us ... I didn't think there was anyone who was ... really prejudiced or anything like that, or actually didn't show it anyway if they were ... no problems with the patients.[34]

When pressed, however, the incidences of prejudice or discrimination trickle through. And yet, as Byron argued, it

> has never really affected me, because I can speak out for myself. I can tell people where to get off ... I once had an interview ... where they were choosing some of the brighter chaps who will go forward to be top managers. And the interviewer said to me '... How do you feel supervising white people?' And I was able to say to him, 'Did you ask previous white people how did they feel supervising black people?' And he said, 'No.' I said, 'I'm not going to answer your question.' And I found, by having that particular approach, it has benefitted me ... I think the whole structure of British society and people really think, and ... feel, to some extent, that they're superior. I don't think they are. I think they're totally and utterly lacking in ambition.[35]

Darnley dismissed it as

> Ignorance. Through ignorance ... I happened to know a chap who automatically sacked himself ... he refuse to take the bus any further with a coloured conductor ... they had some people did drop the money in your hand, it was dirty! You know, that sort of thing ... I personally didn't have a lot of problems with them because I would treat such people as, you know, poor fella, you know. You need not to get in their argument with them, but again everybody don't have the patience.[36]

Roy explained it through the fact that

> ... they suffer with, the indigenous population (of England) as
> a whole, suffer with an inferiority complex in the sense that
> they've got to have somebody one step above them, and they
> accept that ... and if they think that you're a step beneath them,
> you got no right coming up to their level.[37]

The coincidence in the responses may reflect the coincidence of
experience; but it also suggests another narrative genre, of retrenchment
or cultural autonomy. Narratives are the memories of a community.
They reflect social action and interaction. At the same time, they are
subject to revision, to choice. They are never stable. West Indians came
to Britain with expectations about migration and the 'Mother Country'
which was at total variance with what the 'Mother Country' thought
about migration and West Indians. The illusion of the 'Mother Country'
was punctured at the point of arrival. Darnley, synthesising the casual
and the temporary, describes how

> ... I just said, I'll go, come to England, see what it was. And
> when I come here I was very, very disappointed, very dis-
> appointed indeed because I thought, well, I looked at my grip
> and I said, well, I'm not unpacking my grip ... I'll be going
> back home.[38]

Some migrants did, indeed, turn back. Those who stayed sought a
creative solution, finding support and sustenance in collective action.
First, through building social networks, or adapting existing networks,
to provide a range of support within an alien society. Many of the
networks were built on kinship relationships. Victor walked barefoot to
meet his cousin. Estelle joined her brother, sharing his room. Darnley
went to his brother also. Beryl similarly

> was coming to family, so I felt I had a little bit of protection
> there ... but then most of the people ... they was coming to
> people, anyway, so it wasn't too bad for them. For people, in
> particular, they always make sure they was coming to some-
> body.[39]

They were also built on neighbourhood and friendship patterns which
originated in Barbados. Vernon left Barbados in 1955 when he was
eighteen years old. His father wrote to a former neighbour and friend
who was in England and 'ask him to receive him and ... see to him in
those early days ... so he didn't have to wander about nor nothing.'[40]
Households in Britain were created from such kin and friendship networks. At the same time, there was an element of random camaraderie,

of chance meetings which could extend the networks. In December, shortly after Vernon had arrived,

> me and my friend ... we were walking down Mitcham Lane ... and we met a West Indian gentleman, (a Barbadian) ... he saw us just walking, you know, in the cold. We had nothing on. We had no coats ... we just had like little pullovers on ... we used to call them lumberjacks in Barbados ... and this man noticed us and so he, straight away, and of course we had on the old style West Indian felt hats that we used to import from England and ... he could see us and our trousers, in the old Zoot fashion, that ... American fashion ... and he noticed this and he realised that we were West Indians and he stopped and talked to us, he made friends with us, and he invited us over to his home ... and we spent that Christmas with him and his family.[41]

Vernon and his friend eventually moved into this household, where they lived for 'about three years, amongst other West Indians that came there. He had a very big house ... and other West Indians from different parts of the West Indies came and stayed. We had like a *big family* there.' (emphasis added).[42] His description is indicative. Far from causing a breakdown of the household, or kinship and family organisation, a feature commonly associated with industrialisation and urbanisation, (although recent empirical research has qualified this assumption, pointing to ways in which neighbourhoods and households have been strengthened by the process of urbanisation)[43] migrants from the Caribbean to Britain rapidly constituted or reconstituted households which acted like 'a family', providing similar support and constraints. Rules for cohabitation needed to be put in place; infringement could be a cause of grievance; conformity a source of strength. For Barbadians this was particularly so as communal living within a single house was a new experience, and many of the houses in which they rented rooms were owned by Jamaicans who

> understood the room section. But you see, in Barbados, we never did. Regardless of how small the little house was, it was yours. There was no rooms. But the Jamaicans ... could face a lot of things that the Barbadians couldn't face. They were tough. So they themselves, when they got a house ... well, they rent it out in rooms because they were accustomed to such a situation. But we were not ... then again, the Barbadians came with an idea that after five years ... they would return home. The Jamaicans never came with that idea. They

came with the idea to settle ... so they were more prepared for the migration than we were.[44]

Nevertheless, it was an adaptive response as much to the conditions of material deprivation experienced in Britain as from the flexibility of household and networks which had characterised life in Barbados, where support and exchange, often as a result of the migration of one family or household member, ensured collective survival, and where return migrants themselves shared experiences of survival abroad, pointing particularly to ways in which, even in the labour camps of the United States, the system could be subverted and negotiated to advantage. Some of these households divided responsibilities as well as pooling resources. Darnley and his brother were living in Birmingham in a house that

> was all West Indians and ... I decided that ... it doesn't make much sense if we all got to be here cooking together, so there were at least two girls that was there working and I suggested well, look, why not stop one of them working, let them prepare the dinners and so forth and pay them a wage ... we discuss this and this was a pretty good idea and it was working very well.[45]

The households were linked into micro-neighbourhoods, existing within, though independent from, the broader neighbourhoods. In those days, as Estelle says,

> I knew everybody who was here, 'cos everybody I knew from Reading had come from where I come from, you know. All the black people knew one another. So this is how we all mucked in, visited one another ... we were like a little close-knit neighbourhood again, in Reading.[46]

As such, they provided social support and help. Estelle, again, recalled how

> If anybody was sick ... you would always be one of us to go and look after them, make sure they're all right, you know? You would actually bring them in your room till they were better, and care for them. And we were happy ... we'd eat together, and drink together, and laugh and talk together, and you meet at this one this Sunday and they'll have, pool the drinks ... you always kept together.[47]

They were also fluid. The boundaries may be defined geographically, but this was not their defining feature. The neighbourhood was internal, rather than external. As Victor described it:

> There's always grapevines. There was always grapevines. I live ... in North London and some of my mates that went to school with me was living in South East ... it was quite a fine group of vines ... (I found through that) everything that was good ... work, accommodation, friends, cricket, pack up one job if it wasn't good ... know that these friends will always say, well, there's a job going here, or there, or wherever ... (I met my wife) through the grapevines again.[48]

Using networks, and the neighbourhoods built up around them, it was possible to bargain with their white neighbours. Estelle, for instance, furnished her first house through

> this little furniture shop in the town, that used to supply all the blacks. And this man had good business, too, by the blacks, 'cos one introduce the next. And he would come ... and furnish it for you, and you pay him every week. But I suppose that was good business for him.[49]

While Vernon, who

> had this commitment to send money back to them (parents) and ... had to keep yourself in clothes, because the clothes you brought ... were not up to the standard of this country because of the cold ... there was a firm in Brixton ... the older members of the staff were very familiar with West Indians so they used to do a kind of credit thing. They had salesmen who used to like visit all these West Indians on Saturday mornings ... they would bring around some of the stock and you ... would select at home and they would take ... maybe two shillings or whatever it was, 2/6, and that way you were able to buy clothes ... shoes. Things of that sort and that was very helpful, you see. Eventually then, say if you got a flat, you could buy furnitures from them ... that's the way I had to live.[50]

Local 'meeting turns', a Barbadian form of savings, were also established through the 'grapevine' as were, at another level, church communities or Saturday schools, where teachers like Victor, trained in Barbados, who had come to Britain 'before we get too settled into it (teaching), ... (to) just enjoy a bit of fun and see somewhere else',[51] found themselves caught in low-scale, low-paid clerical jobs, but provided their services voluntarily to provide for 'additional coaching, additional teaching' for

> West Indian parents (who) were disappointed with the progress their children were making in the state schools ... the West

> Indians kids at the time were too easily classified as no-hopers
> ... no one would convince me that there are not children in
> Brixton who are capable of going to Oxford or Cambridge and
> getting a first. I am sure they are, given the right push.[52]

Indeed, the racism experienced in the education system was a major
source of anxiety for Barbadian parents and for many was the first time
that they had to confront authority on behalf of their children.

The concentration of the West Indian community within particular
city areas has been well documented.[53] Accommodation was overcrowded
and often sub-standard, reflecting a general shortage of housing which,
despite the slum-clearance programmes of the previous four decades,
remained acute and had been exacerbated by the Second World War, a
resistance on the part of white landlords to let or sub-let properties to
black tenants, and a propensity for the migrant community to create
'safe' city spaces through their own networks, which provided material
and psychological support and ensured a continuing contact with the
values and culture of 'home'. Far from 'traditional' culture disintegrat-
ing in contact with the modern, urban, industrialised world, it proved a
highly adaptive structure through which, and from which, Barbadian
migrants were able to operate. It was also a fruitful market for the
enterprising.

Many Barbadians took on more than one job. Estelle, for instance,
supplemented her factory wages by dressmaking for her friends within
the community. Roy became an electrician and used those skills in the
neighbourhood to supplement his wages. Indeed, Roy at one time had
four jobs. He worked as a station foreman for London Transport, and in
addition was

> selling washing machines and vacuum cleaners on a team ... I
> was doing the electrical wiring for my landlord, who was then
> the famous Peter Rachman ... and then I realised that there
> was a big demand for light removals, and I managed to get a
> deposit and put on a van, and went doing light removals ... but
> then over the years, I have always made do with four hours
> sleep or less but at that time, the first concern was about how
> to keep your family in house, how to keep them in food and
> clothes.[54]

Others utilised skills – such as tailoring or carpentry – learnt in
Barbados for the benefit of their Barbadian and West Indian neighbours.
It was a means of supplementing wages, as well as keeping the cost of
such services within reach. Although taking on a number of jobs simul-
taneously was clearly one way of making money, making ends meet and

returning remittances home in order to maintain the household of origin, and retain membership within it, also reflected a culture and tradition of occupational mobility. Consistent unemployment and underemployment – which had been a feature of the Barbadian economy since Emancipation – encouraged a pattern of employment which was flexible and variable, as workers moved between seasonal or temporary work, between waged and self-employed labour, all of which could include migration as part of an occupational strategy. Thus Estelle, prior to coming to Britain, alternated working for the government and working on her own as a seamstress. Vernon's father moved between agricultural labour and road building. Many Barbadians, particularly though not exclusively women, supplemented the family income through growing vegetables and rearing stock, and selling or exchanging the surplus. It was an occupational pattern which was transported by the migrant community, transposed into a migrant lifestyle and became a component in a strategy of survival.

There was a belief in the value of return, even though the commitment to going 'home' was deferred. Nevertheless it supported the notion of transience, gave a piquancy to the social networks (which was to have a particular value for the children of migrants) and ensured a qualitative membership of the household 'back home'. Where return has happened, or is about to take place, it is not presented as a spontaneous, autonomous act but as a carefully planned and organised manoeuvre which necessarily involves the entire family. Orville planned to stay for five years but within that time his wife, Selma, joined him. Selma left their three children with her mother in Barbados. She had three more children in Britain, two of whom she sent back to her mother in Barbados. She worked the night shift as a nursing auxiliary and she and Orville juggled the child care for their last child.

'You hadn't really consolidated yourself', Orville explained,

> ... the bills were round your neck and you were just hanging on and working and hoping that you'll get off this one ... everything was about three years. Because the furniture you took, that was about three years, the gas stove ... was about the same, the second mortgage that you had was around the same, three years. So everything was tied up around the three basis.[55]

Nevertheless, in 1963, seven years after arriving in Britain, Orville, prompted by Selma and her desire to reunite the family, bought his first house. Three years later the children came over from Barbados. Five years later, he remortgaged that house to build another on Selma's father's land in Barbados. By 1975 the house in Barbados was completed, and rented out. 'We had our goal in view,' he said. By 1980

> we had three of the children ... working ... our own finance
> had risen ... the mortgage was down ... with the savings from
> the rent ... we were increasing all the time. And then we took
> a chance then to start the other house ... and that was rented
> too ... and then we were planning then now on the exodus.[56]

Six years later, they sold their house in London, bought another
one for the children to live in, and returned in 1987 to Barbados. 'It was
just perfect planning.'[57]

Buying property in Britain to use as collateral for Barbados was a
sound financial strategy. But it is also significant that Orville, for instance, built on family land, implying not merely a commitment to
return, but a commitment to return to *that* family. Ties with household
and kin in Barbados had not, in other words, been severed but confirmed
through migration.

But Barbadian migration to Britain in the 1950s did not originate
out of a historical or cultural vacuum. Part of that space had been
occupied by the experience of colonialism in which the 'Mother Country' as an organising narrative had played a role. But if Britain could use
that narrative selectively so, arguably, could Barbadians. It did not have
the same meaning or uses, intentional or otherwise, in Britain as in the
colonies. What had been historical watersheds for Britain did not always
have the same echoes or meanings in the Caribbean, and vice versa. The
1937 riots, or the Second World War, were seen very differently within
the Caribbean and from Britain, and the shockwaves from both had very
different effects. Communications theory suggests that people do not
absorb messages passively; they select what is appropriate, useful or
relevant at any one time. The ideology of the 'Mother Country' may
have enjoyed an hegemony in education and the media. It is doubtful
whether it enjoyed it so decisively elsewhere or was much considered.
Indeed, anti-colonial sentiments, nationalism, the move for independence, an articulation of social inequality, trade unionism and demands
for enfranchisement had been gathering momentum from the 1930s.
Although engineered by a generation born in the 1920s, its effects
would have been felt by that born in the 1930s. In addition, the negotiations towards the Federation of the West Indies, in which Barbados,
under Sir Grantley Adams, was a key player enabled an ideological, if
not a constitutional link, to be established with other (and, arguably,
more radical) nationalist movements such as that of Eric Williams in
Trinidad or socialist movements such as that led by Norman Manley in
Jamaica. At the same time, the Caribbean was far from immune to the
posturings of the Cold War; America had long since declared the Carib-

bean as within her 'sphere'; Britain's central position in the region implied a potentially active involvement. The independence movement has also to be seen within this light. Anti-communism may have been an issue but I am not sure, from the perspective of the Caribbean, whether the theme of international rationality and national stability meant quite the same in the Caribbean as it did for Britain and America. There was, in other words, a sense of cultural autonomy which enabled a specific, credible space to be created by Barbadians abroad, and one which was highlighted by the focus given to West Indians in Britain in the 1950s and 1960s. Such were some elements of the 'structure of feeling' in Barbados in the 1950s.

The migration to Britain was another. Within a decade, 27,000 Barbadians migrated, facilitated, as we have seen, by the Barbadian government anxious to remove the threat of social unrest by removing the 'surplus' population.[58] But that migration took place within a tradition of migration when, at any one time, Panama, Cuba, the United States, Brazil, Trinidad or Curaçao could have been the preferred destination, around which specific mythologies evolved within a broader ideology which stressed migration as an improving strategy. All of which necessarily influenced the organisation of and meaning for the Barbadian (and Caribbean) communities in Britain.

In that sense, Britain *was* one stop in a sequence. It was different from the others in that, as the 'Mother Country', it had a tailor-made rational. But the 'message' from the 'Mother Country' was selective and selected. The 'Mother Country' was perceived as welcoming, as the 'home' of a 'family of nations', who had 'invited' Barbadians to come. It represented more than the simple cash culture of the United States, and the searing racism associated with migration there. Attitudes to Britain were from the start complicated and ambivalent.

From my sample, the majority of migrants had seen members of previous generations migrate. Many still had family members abroad, and had been abroad themselves. Barbadian migrants to Britain held memories and models of earlier migration experiences, of their own, or of an earlier generation. As migrants, they knew what behaviour was expected of them 'back home'. They also had a grander migration narrative in which their own particular experiences could be organised and made sense of, which enabled survival networks and a surviving ideology to evolve. Byron's suggestion that, ultimately, the migration to Britain was no different from that to the United States is, in this sense, significant and a clue.

Another clue is suggested by Roy who returned to Barbados in 1987, after thirty years in Britain. 'I am a patriot,' he declared,

A real patriot. A real Bajan ... I am the only person, and my wife will bear me out, that whatever I am doing in here, when the national anthem strikes on that television or this radio, I leave from wherever I am and ... stand to attention and salute, and I don't take my hands down till it stop ... if many people knew, they would think I am mad. I'm not. I'm a real patriot. A real Bajan ... and I'll tell you another thing. When we got Independence, after crying actual tears for joy that we had receive Independence, I then sent off a telegram to the Prime Minister, who was then Errol Barrow, and I send one off to the Colonial Secretary ... so my patriotism is there, it's been, it's intact.[59]

Roy had been particularly enthusiastic about coming to England precisely because it was 'home.' He had already travelled in the United States. He had a good job in Barbados. He was reluctant to leave his wife and his mother. He neither wanted nor 'needed' to migrate. It was England, and only England, which attracted him. He compares the situation of people like himself who returned from Britain to those of his parent's generation who returned from Panama and Cuba.

People who, in their eyes and their heart, they had wiped Barbados off the face of the earth ... it wasn't anything for them at all. If they didn't throw them out, they wouldn't remember there's such a thing as Barbados ... they didn't come out of Panama because they wanted to. They were thrown out.[60]

It is an important statement, for it stresses the practical, as well as the emotional, need to maintain contacts with 'home', indeed to have a 'home.' If migration is represented as unstable, then the place and role of migrants is equally unstable, and provision has to be made.

Imagine me in Britain. I'm not writing to my brother. I'm not writing to my neice ... should I be surprised if when I come here now, they resent me? ... (or, imagine) that (I) going to be in England forever, in the English way of life, then ... circumstances dictate and ... (I) have to be back here.[61]

The experiences of Britain forced an urgent reappraisal of migrant position in line with the precarious tenure of all migrations. Far from being relegated to a secondary role, Barbados emerged as a symbol of stability, and a focus of identity, but always in relation to Britain. Barbados as home displayed a resilience and Barbadian migrants a resistance to assimilate and integrate with British culture. Contact with family in Barbados, and the growth of family structures in Britain, have ensured that the idea of Barbados continues to be transmitted to the generation born in Britain. Thus Sharon, Orville and Selma's youngest daughter who was born in Britain in 1960, talks of Barbados and intends to go there to live.

> I always plan to go back to Barbados ... to live ... it's a better place to bring up children ... I ... want to build there, and all the things that I remember my parents saying, you know ... always planning ... I've been raised in that atmosphere of Barbados being home, and of going back to Barbados ... and I would like to give my children ... an identity ... I had an identity, even though half an identity, but I had an identity and that gave me a sense of who I was, and where I was from ... I'm a British Barbadian.[62]

One of Roy's daughters has since returned to live in Barbados.

The sustaining narrative of migration stressed transience and return. It suggested an 'instability' in regard to national boundaries, and an implicit challenge to the idea of the nation-state (and the 'British' way of life) as the natural and only form of political and social organisation. Attitudes to Britain before migration were ambivalent. Britain, as a destination, was always contingent. When the dust had settled, the bags unpacked, the migrants got on with living in Britain. The ideology of survival derived from and sustained many features of Caribbean living. It continues to be reflected in the children of Barbadian (and Caribbean) migrants whose family structures and work profiles, life styles and loyalties, remains the focus of official and governmental concern. It is part of their 'structure of feeling'.

Migrant responses are neither simple nor linear, but reflect a complicated process of negotiation and reevaluation between two different national and political perspectives in which identity is not multiple but mobile, ambivalent and contradictory, what Homi Bhabha describes as a 'negotiated phenomenon, in relation to a number of models, priorities and norms, (which) at any one point ... is not multiply poised, but ... ambivalently structured in relation to itself ... It is the doubleness of the subject, rather than its multiplicity, that is at issue.'[63]

More particularly, the responses of Barbadians in Britain were historically conditioned, reflecting and creating a 'structure of feeling' which was essentially international, and represented one resolution of a set of contradictory relationships. The narratives – of exile and return – are essentially stories of a journey, which is always a process, and always relational.

References

1 Barbados Migration Project (M. Chamberlain). Tapes and transcripts deposited at the National Life Story Collection of the National Sound Archive of the British Library. References refer to interview number, tape number, side and page reference. BB76/1/1/1/5.
2 B34/1/2/1/30.
3 B34/1/1/2/30.
4 BB40/1/1/1/23.
5 B20/1/2/1/45.
6 Raphael Samuel, *Theatres of Memory*, London, Verso, 1994, p. viii.
7 B34/1/1/1/30.
8 B20/2/3/1/64.
9 B20/1/1/2/37.
10 BB29/1/1/2/22.
11 B12/1/1/2/35.
12 B65/1/2/1/51–53.
13 BB29/1/1/2/32.
14 BB3/1/1/2/17.
15 G. Ebanks, P.M. George and C.E. Nobbe, 'Emigration from Barbados,' *Social and Economic Studies*, 28(2), 1979.
16 BB3/1/1/2/29.
17 B65/1/2/1/53.
18 B12/1/1/1/25.
19 Mel Thompson, 'Forty-and-one years on: an overview of Afro-Caribbean Migration to the United Kingdom' in Ransford W. Palmer (ed.), *In Search of a Better Life: Perspectives on Migration from the Caribbean*, New York, Praeger, 1990.
20 B34/1/1/2/31.
21 Constance Sutton and Susan Makiesky-Barrow, 'Migration and West Indian Consciousness' in Constance Sutton and Elsa Chaney (eds.), *Caribbean Life in New York City*, New York, Centre for Migration Studies of New York, 1987.
22 B12/1/1/2/40.
23 Raymond Barthes, *Mythologies*, Paris, Editions du Seuil, 1957.
24 B34/1/1/2/38.
25 *Ibid.*
26 BB29/1/2/36.
27 B26/1/1/17.
28 B24/1/2/33.
29 BB40/1/1/1/30.
30 BB3/1/1/1/18.
31 B12/1/1/2/31.
32 BB5/1/B/2/31.
33 BB3/1/1/2/25–6.
34 BB40/1/1/2/33.
35 B12/1/1/2/42.
36 BB13/1/1/2/24.
37 B34/1/2/2/38.
38 BB13/1/1/2/14.
39 B65/1/2/1/59.

40   B4/1/1/2/22.
41   BB48/1/1/1/8.
42   BB48/1/1/1/9.
43   Jerry White, *The Worst Street in North London: Campbell Bunk*, London, Routledge, 1986; Mary Chamberlain, *Growing Up in Lambeth*, London, Virago, 1989; Ellen Ross, *Love and Toil: Motherhood in Outcast London, 1870–1918*, Oxford, Oxford University Press, 1994.
44   B20/1/3/1/76.
45   BB13/1/1/2/20.
46   BB29/1/1/2/39.
47   BB29/1/1/2/44.
48   B26/1/2/20.
49   BB29/1/1/2/52.
50   BB48/1/1/1/15.
51   BB27/2/1/22.
52   BB27/2/1/1/8/, 2/2/1/2.
53   Nancy Foner, *Jamaica Farewell: Jamaican Migrants in London*, London, Routledge and Kegan Paul, 1979; R.B. Davison, *West Indian Migrants*, London, Oxford University Press, 1962; Sheila Patterson, *Dark Strangers: A Study of West Indians in London*, London, Penguin, 1964; Ruth Glass, *London's Newcomers*, Cambridge, Mass., Harvard University Press, 1961.
54   B34/1/2/2/42.
55   B20/1/3/1/70.
56   B20/1/3/1/77.
57   *Ibid.* p. 79.
58   See, for instance, reports of Barbados Immigrant Liaison Officer, L10/19 Vol I, MTIL.
59   B34/2/1/2/20.
60   *Ibid.* p. 21.
61   B34/2/1/2/22.
62   BB76/1/1/2/38–9.
63   Homi Bhabha, 'Between Identities', *International Yearbook of Oral History and Life Stories*, Vol III, Migration and Identity, Oxford, Oxford University Press, 1994.

5 | Gender and the Narratives of Migration

Let me set the scene:

MURIEL: My mother died now, a long time ago, she died about –
CHARLES: – 1946.
MURIEL: – we went to St. Lucia, when I first gone, she die about a year after, 1946....

MURIEL: ... he had to write to my father for me. In those days, you had to write home, write a letter to the girl father, what not –
CHARLES: – I will explain it better than she, because she can't explain nothing.
MURIEL: ... I had a big wedding in church. It was a four o'clock wedding or something, and when did you marry, he had in those days –
CHARLES: – twenty two cars....

MURIEL: ... when he went away then to other places like Curaçao or America, then I went with him –
CHARLES: – I work for the American, she can't tell you, she don't know nothing for me.[1]

Muriel's account was frustrated by, and clearly frustrated, her husband. He complained that she was inaccurate. She 'mix up' time. She did not stick to the point. '... if you're going to ask her,' Charles explained, 'I think you will spend from now till tomorrow, cause she got so many things she will ... tell you the same thing again, till you will run over the same thing.'[2]

Charles recalled precisely the date his mother-in-law died. So did Muriel. Her recollection of the date of her mother's death was, however, calculated around a significant moment in her life: the year that she first emigrated. Charles continued to correct his wife's account throughout her interview. In his own interview, he went back over his wife's agenda, recounting (and correcting) it, describing his first meeting and his courtship with her, the conversations and negotiations he had with

91

her, with her parents, and with his own grandmother, with whom he had been living. In this extract, he concludes the story,

> ... we married, six months time ... how old I was? Twenty-three, my birthday will be the next month. I marry the 21st April, my birthday would be the fifth May, to make me twenty-four. You hear? .... Well, we left for St. Lucia. When I went for St. Lucia, I went to St. Lucia after we married, get a home rent in St. Lucia and went to St. Lucia and they had the American bases in 1941. Well, my ambition, I rent a place, I rent and get two machines, and I open a tailoring department, myself and four other people, boys, in Vieux Fort. I went to Vieux Fort, I land in, I land in September, the 11th September, and in September month I get a place and open up a tailors.[3]

He steps from his marriage to his migration to St. Lucia where, within a few weeks, he achieves his ambition, and opens a tailor's shop. Compare his account of that period with Muriel's.

> Well, when I got married, well, at first, we didn't, we got married so early that we, I had married in the home at my mothers, because the house was so big, she could rent then. The others had married and gone, the other two brothers had married and gone, so I was the only girl then, so I married and live there, and then, only we were living there for six months, then we bought our own home and move out, and we stood in it till we went away (to St. Lucia) and when we went away, we leave it for rent.[4]

The emphases are very different. Charles presents himself as the sole player. He talks in the first person, his command reinforced by a precise recall of dates and sequence. He interlaces his account of his courtship and marriage with the chronology of his career. Most of his narrative is taken up by his career, the tailor's shop, his work as a clerk first on the American base in St. Lucia, then for the fire department. His sense of self, the agenda out of which his identity emerges, is rooted within his work and the achievements of his working life. 'All I own,' he concluded, 'all I is .... Praise God, I see what I work for.'[5]

Muriel talks more commonly in the collective 'we'; she describes where they were married, and recounts their early life in her mother's house by accounting for the circumstances under which they came to live there: they married early, her brothers had left, her mother had room to rent. She locates herself in relation to others: to husband, to her family, and finally to herself. Unlike her husband, she does not perceive herself primarily as an autonomous agent, nor defines herself by her own agency. 'What going on outside,' she said, 'don't worry me. That have nothing to do with me what going on outside.'[6]

Although the questions and the interviewing approach for this research remained the same for men and women, and although each account had its unique imprint of style and presentation, important similarities and distinctions emerged in the narrative structure of the responses of the men and women. It is these differences which I now wish to explore.

The popular image presents the Caribbean migrant as single, male and lonely. It is an image reinforced through literature. Selvon's., *The Lonely Londoners*, opens with Moses, homesick and single, going to Waterloo to meet the boat-train. The novel ends with him standing alone by the River Thames,

> It was a summer night: laughter fell softly: it was the sort of night that if you wasn't making love to a woman you feel you was the only person in the world like that.[7]

Yet women as well as men migrated. And male or female, the decision to go, the logistics of leaving were not isolated, individual events but the result of collective action. The family, for instance, through loans, through material support, through child care, enabled and supported the migration of its individual members. At the same time, migrants reciprocated by returning remittances to help or maintain the family left behind. Equally, few migrants arrived in the country of destination alone. Most came to join friends, neighbours and relatives already there. Support networks were created and strengthened. Their motives and decisions were influenced by, in the case of Barbados, a culture of migration. Many families, through the migrations of family members over the generations, fostered a migration ethos, a powerful dynamic in determining who migrates and why and with what effect, which in turn engaged with other family dynamics, of colour, class, mobility, or adventure. At the same time there existed a presumption of household, family and neighbourhood support which permitted and encouraged the autonomy of individual men and women. Broadly speaking those circumstances were similar for men and women. There are, nevertheless, significant differences in how men and women migrants explained and recounted their experiences.

Many of the men who migrated had already experienced migration, principally to the United States. Roy, for instance, had spent some years in North America. Darnley went to America as a young man straight out of school. Migration, for them, was not a new experience. None of the women I interviewed had migrated prior to coming to England. Nevertheless, the men who had migrated and those for whom this was a first experience, stressed equally the impulsive nature of the decision to come to England, and the influence of friends in that decision. Darnley, for instance, described how

> I just got up like that, just like that, and decide, because I had some friends coming along ... all of a sudden, seeing people, because that was the norm then, everybody wants to try to go to England, get out ... that sort of way and I just decided, well, okay, I'll go ... to England.[8]

Lloyd, another informant, had also been to America,

> following the others. I was following other people, just like when I come up here ... because I adventurous, I want to see, I want to do something .... A good friend of mine, he came up here...and he tell me that if I want to come to England, I could come ... I said, 'Okay, I'll decide to come.' ... I went, I get my ping-pong, went and get a passport. I get passport Monday, and I booked ... my trip and I left on the next week.[9]

George described how

> I was a barman...and on a day's off ... we were ... having lunch ... and while we were there we started discussing this thing about going to England ... and we left there and went straight (to the Emigration Department) and sign on, you know? And when we came back (my friend) said, 'Wait! You know what we just did?' And we said, 'Yeah, man, why not?' ... we didn't plan it ...[10]

Neither Darnley nor Lloyd revealed that they left partners and children behind when they went to England, or that their decision to come had in any way been a family decision. Even those male informants who present their decision to come as a means of providing for their families nevertheless placed the emphasis on impulse and autonomy as well as, paradoxically, social conformity. Stanley, for instance, (who had previously been working in Antigua) confessed that

> I talk about it a little. I don't know if I talk about it sufficient with *her* ... because it happened so quick. I decided. I came and I talked to her. I said I would like to go to England to see if we can make things better. Because my outlook on life was to try to do the best I could, especially having children ...[11]

These men, whatever the actual circumstances, *present* their decision to migrate as autonomous. This is not to suggest that they were merely self-seeking and selfish, or to cement the stereotype of the

Caribbean male as marginal to the family. Roy, Darnley and Stanley sent home remittances and eventually a ticket to travel for their wives and, later, their children. Charles took his wife and children with him from the outset. Their statements do reveal insights into family relations and decision-making. These men (although they did not mention it) were able to leave their families of creation. Family and neighbourhood structures existed for the continuing support of their partners and children in their absence, revealing, or sustained by, an ideology of conjugal autonomy. Yet the genre through which they chose to narrate their decision highlights a sense of self articulated through an ability to make autonomous decisions, confirmed and reinforced, in many cases, by reference to their male peers. Given that recall takes place in the present and to a large extent makes sense of the past, how can we explain the tendency in the male narratives to focus on their personal trajectory, to catalogue (like Charles) experience in a linear fashion, to list their occupations as a defining feature of their lives, to place themselves as subjects in the drama? Is it merely a simple reflection of gender roles, or does it indicate a more complicated reflection of, in this case, the migration experience and responses to it? Is there, in other words, a master narrative of migration through which *all* experience is ordered?

Of course there is a paradox here, between autonomy and compliance, active agency and passivity, between choosing to go and following the crowd. Even Charles describes how, at the end of the Second World War, the 'Americans ... were going to Long Island *so they decide to carry me, so I go and went with them.*' (emphasis added)[12] Parallel with the emphasis on autonomy, spontaneity and fashion run casualness and transience as characteristics of the male migration narratives, as outlined in Chapter 4. All the male informants were in employment at the time of migration. Charles (of an earlier generation) and Stanley offered, as an explanation for why they migrated, the desire to improve their children's chances. The majority of informants, however, suggested that they came primarily for adventure, to travel, because their friends were going, sometimes to make money, and always to return within a few years. Jeffrey, (as was noted in Chapter 3), planned '... to start out five years in England ... from England go to America, Canada, do a bit of travelling ... get a lot of money, and go back to Barbados.'[13] Orville said, 'five years. I said that probably we will stay for five years and then go back.'[14]

Similar reasons were given by those who came over on the sponsorship scheme. British Rail or London Transport were means to a greater end, not the end in themselves. Contrary to economic models which present migrant motivation as the individual rational pursuit of improved employment opportunities, these informants offered a range of motivations, of which making money was only one. Indeed, most were deskilled on arrival in Britain. Byron, for instance, was a secondary school teacher in Barbados. The only work he could secure when he first came to England was that of postman. He eventually became a senior manager with the Royal Mail but

> Even ... when I got into management, and I go for higher jobs, people would say, 'But you started as a postman, and you're a manager, you've done very well.' And I would say, 'But I started as a postman not out of choice. I started as a postman because it's the only way I felt I could get entry into the system'.[15]

Although some of the migrants from Barbados (to Panama, to Cuba, and to North America) in the first four decades of the twentieth century remained in their host countries, many returned to the island. There was an expectation and a pattern of return, albeit one in many cases of coming and going. That my informants expected to come for three or five years had a specific explanation: it approximated to their own or other's experience of migration spans. Roy and Darnley, for instance, had already been to America and had returned. Stanley had been to Antigua. Other informants recalled the migrations of their fathers who returned home approximately every three years. Jeffrey's father, in the 1940s,

> travelled to Panama, and then he used to work in America, contract work ... he'd ... spend two years, sometimes three years, sometimes eighteen months before he returned to Barbados.[16]

Elaine's father migrated to Curaçao in 1942. 'He was away for a very long time, but he used to come, like, every three years or so.' She added, 'and it was like a great big Christmas every time.'[17]

These family models of migration conformed to, or were perceived as conforming to, patterns of migrant behaviour. Children in Barbados were not privy to the decisions of 'big people', nor were they entitled to ask about, much less question, those decisions. The behaviour of their elders was revealed rather than explained. Elise's grandfather migrated (to and from) Guyana but, as she says,

> In those days, you can't ask so many questions, you just take what they tell you or if you hear conversation, and you was not allowed to, like, sit and listen to big people having conversation. That wasn't allowed. You never even know your parent's age.[18]

To a child, the migratory behaviour of fathers or grandfathers may have appeared as impulsive, adventurous, a pattern of behaviour rather than a strategy, reinforcing a perception of male autonomy. Absent fathers were a regular feature of many children's memories. 'Lots of children,' said Beryl, 'grew up without their fathers ... their dads were dead, or away, or something.'[19]

Temporary migration as a feature of Barbadian migrant behaviour had already been noted, as we have seen, by the end of the nineteenth century. This model, of temporary (if regular) absences, also equated with geographic and social mobility. Remittances sustained families, and in some cases improved the family circumstances. It was her father's remittances which enabled Elaine to have a private, secondary education. The migration of Olive's grandfather and uncles (to Cuba and Curaçao) enabled them to build a house and, in the case of her grandfather, buy three fishing boats on their return. Muriel's grandfather built himself an 'upstairs house' with his Panama money.

Return migrants were expected to bring if not with wealth at least some indication of prosperity – a point made, somewhat ironically, in the song, *Panama Man*,

> When the Curaçao man come back to Bim
> He bring me a calico dress,
> When de Panama man come back to Bim
> All he bring is de Spanish caress.[20]

The migrants who came to Britain in the 1950s and 1960s stayed not three years but thirty. Barbados was a long way away; return was expensive; the financial rewards in Britain were, at least in the short term, meagre. They could not return within the time-scale they had set themselves. 'I managed to settle in the end,' Beryl said, 'But I had to, because I didn't have the fare to get back. There was no return fare, so I had to settle and get the fare if I want to go back.'[21] Migration to Britain did not conform to the model or mythology of migrant life. It was neither temporary nor lucrative. The open adventure which was England proved to be closed. What we hear is the displaced hopes, the struggle to transform a past into a constructive and useful enterprise, of order being imposed on this experience for it be to given meaning. If migration had not reaped the rewards expected, then that was because the expectations were limited in the first place. It was impulse; it was adventure; it was casual. Responsibility could be abdicated onto a youthful pursuit of fashion.

Perhaps it was always so. Jeffrey's father, Garfield, never made money from his sojourns to America, nor did Verona's grandfather in Panama. Perhaps part of the narrative of migration has always included an element of bravado, of devil-may-care, a built-in explanation for failure, if it comes. And if it doesn't? Over the years, remittances *were* sent home, work *was* secured, houses *were* bought. Migration did reap some material reward. The route to 'success' may have deviated but the attention to detail the concern with accuracy and chronology present a picture of progression, calculation and achievement, in which these men had been the significant players, and the decision to come finally vindicated. They arrived as autonomous agents and, like heroes, succeeded against the odds as they discovered them. Impulse and calculation may seem paradoxical, even contradictory. But like Anansi, curiosity led them into scrapes; cleverness allowed them to escape. It is a particular presentation of self, and one which ultimately conformed to and perpetuated a broader, historical narrative of migration. Given the circumstances of nineteenth and early twentieth century sea travel, migration from Barbados had been an adventure; it some cases it might be seen as heroic; it was perceived as a liberation (or at least a change) from the economic and social strictures of the plantation economy.

The women, however, presented their accounts in significantly different ways. In many ways, the women were as autonomous as the men. They, too, could presume family support – loans, guarantees, care for their children in their absence. Historically, women had also migrated. Between 1861 and 1891 at least a third, and sometimes as much as a half, of the emigrants from Barbados were women.[22] Although the age profile of these nineteenth century female migrants is not known it is unlikely that these women were childless. Someone was willing and able to keep the home fires burning while they sojourned abroad. But the women from my sample did not present *their* migration as an autonomous decision, nor did they stress spontaneity. Women migrants incorporate family members, and the context, when describing their decision to migrate. Some came to join their partners. Stanley, who left with little consultation, and describes his departure in spartan detail, eventually sent a ticket to his wife, Elise, to join him in England. Yet she describes how

> I was outside hanging out clothes one morning. Postman stop. He feeling proud. He send a ticket, without a penny. A ticket, without a cent in it. Yes. I drop clothes, everything and I rushed down to my mum. A ticket to come. It must have been two weeks time or something ... I bought a whole outfit. I want shoes. I want to look like somebody. And only a ticket! I was livid ... when I get to my mother's, I burst in a crying. And she say, 'Well, it's your husband. He mean business. You have to go.' Anyway, I borrow a few ... hundred dollars.

> I went to the grocery and leave quite a bit of groceries with my mum. The children have a lot of school clothes ... and I sort myself out and I went .... when I get to the airport, and the plane take off, is then I realise that I was up in the air, that I really leave my children, you know ... I burst out crying ... I was hysterical I can't jump from the plane, and I left my children behind.[23]

Estelle had two children. She was a seamstress by trade, though she worked for the government taking water and messages to the men building roads. She and her children lived with her grandmother. 'Emigration was on,' she said,

> and most of your friends have gone, and they'd be writing you letters, said ... 'things are good. Why don't you come up and see the place?' ... by then, I was living fairly comfortable ... you kind of think, 'well, instead of me coming to England, why don't I give my brother the fare and let him go?' So that's what I do. I paid my brother's fare and let him come ... and then when he say what he could work for and what he used to send for my mother, and I said, 'Well, I've got to go and have a try.' So I decide then to leave my job, pack up my dressmaking and come to England. So I brought my Singer machine with me ... I had a big Singer machine, and brought that ... they were very sad, especially my grandmother. The first words they said, 'I'll never see you again.' ... she was right. She didn't see me again.[24]

Estelle left the children with her grandmother, and joined her brother in England. Nevertheless, the decision to go was not phrased in terms of impulse, but calculation, and like Elise, her description is replete with detail. The material and emotional context is described, family relationships spelled out. Equally, the decision is not presented autonomously. Elise's mother and Estelle's grandmother are both brought into the picture, as are the arrangements they made for their children and their feelings on leaving the family behind.

What other motives were offered? Some women, like Elise, left to join a partner or husband. Some left to improve themselves, to follow a specific professional training, principally in nursing. Others migrated to escape, or rebel. Vivien had five children. Her marriage was failing. Her sister had migrated (to train as a nurse) in 1958 and had been encouraging her to come but,

> I didn't really want to come ... my parents didn't really want me to come ... nobody didn't really want me to come, and

that's the truth. Husband and things. None. They didn't want
me to come. And I decided, 'Well', strong head, 'I'm going.
I'm going.' ... I call it rebel, you know, I must admit. So I
rebelled ... I know I said I was strong-headed, but I come
because they didn't want me to come.[25]

She left the youngest three children with her mother, and the older
two with their father. Some women used professional advancement as a
means of leaving home. Euline, you recall, came to Britain to train as a
nurse, a decision which offered her both a career and an opportunity to
escape.

In some cases, the process was more duplicitous. Beryl had been
frustrated in her ambitions to become a secretary in Barbados by her
lack of education and the colour bar. She worked as a dressmaker, and
in her mother's rum shop. Her brother, and her boyfriend, of whom her
mother disapproved, had already migrated to England. Her mother was
due to marry and

she just asked me if I wanted to go, you know, 'cos there was
just a shop and there wasn't nothing there for me ... I wanted
to do, maybe a secretary, which would give me shorthand and
typing. She couldn't afford that. I couldn't even go to secondary school the way I wanted to ... but then, you know, when
she asked me if I wanted to come, I said, 'Oh yes, I'll come.'
Then I suppose because John was here, I thought, 'Well,
there's an ideal opportunity ....' Seeing the family again was
my first thought, and seeing John and them again, it was my
first thought and at least I felt that I'd come somewhere and,
you know, away from the mother, and the mother, and the
mother, and all that one restricted area ... I was glad for the
freedom. That was me.[26]

Her mother thought England 'a big place' where the chances of
reunion with her boyfriend were slim. Telling her mother she was going
to train as a nurse, Beryl left for England to join her boyfriend in Britain,
whom she subsequently married.

Sheila's mother, like Beryl's, disapproved of her boyfriend, and
disapproved even more when she became pregnant.

My mother nearly went mad! ... that was the whole problem of
it, you see. She got very, very, very cross and upset about that,
see ... she didn't want I slept with him as well.[27]

The boyfriend migrated to England. However, Sheila's father had
died (of tetanus) and 'after the way my father died, we always said one

of us should really have some knowledge of nursing.' Coming to England to train as a nurse

> ... was my mother idea, in the first place. She said I wasn't to stay, she wasn't going to have me here to do that sort of thing, you know, and if my father was alive, blah, blah, you know, he would shoot me and all this sort of lark. So an uncle I had in St. Lawrence, he was fairly well-off, and he said that he'll help my Mum to get me to England. So my Mum and him paid my fare ... (Mum) sold some sheep she had and she used that money ... to buy clothes for me, and then let me go.[28]

Her baby was two months old when Sheila left for Britain. She left him with her mother. Unlike Beryl, Sheila did enroll for her SEN. Shortly after arriving, however, she married her boyfriend. The Matron of the hospital

> call me to the office and she said, 'Well, in England, your husband comes before your parents.' And I said, 'Well, in the West Indies, we respect both. It was my mum that sent me here and ... with my education, I just can't work as an auxiliary.'[29]

Despite Matron's disapproval, Sheila completed her training.

Departure for many women was complicated by having to leave their children, and reunion with them became paramount in their thinking. Selma – who migrated in 1958 to join her husband, Orville – left her three children with her mother.

> I looked back at the children. Oh, my heart bled. And I said, 'Why didn't I take these children with me?' ... I cried many a night on the ship ... I always used to dream about them.[30]

Elise says,

> I didn't buy a lot of clothes. I just bought the immediate things to see me through, and I make do with them, as long as I was clean. Because my whole idea is to save money to get these children with me. And that is what I did.[31]

At this level, of the decision and motivation to migrate, the women integrate their narratives within a context. They get events and emotions 'mix up' and do not demarcate the personal, the domestic and the professional in the way that the men appear to do. On one level the differences may indicate gender roles: women, whether or not they live with the fathers of their children, express a primary responsibility for their children. They often share that responsibility with *their* mothers, to whom there is a continuing loyalty. Sheila, even after she had married, continued to abide by her mother's demands, defying the Matron in the process. They are not truly autonomous agents. Neither are the men. But whereas the men present themselves autonomously, the women present themselves within a set of family relationships, as part of a larger picture and process, where acting on impulse, pursuing an indeterminate goal, is neither compatible with, nor within the framework of, their points of reference and decision-making.

Ostensibly the net result may be the same. Estelle, Beryl, Elise, like Roy, Darnley and Stanley stayed with relatives on their arrival. They experienced similar difficulties in finding accommodation and employment. They planned to stay for three years. Yet their sense of self did not appear to be so acutely bound up with presenting themselves as autonomous, nor their lives in the shape of progression even in cases like that of Estelle, who was both provider as well as nurturer, whose remittances maintained her children and mother in Barbados. 'The outside', as Muriel indicated, 'have nothing to do with me.'

But if the men had a master narrative, of impulsive, casual migrations which could exonerate failure and highlight success, did the women have theirs? To what extent do the accounts of women (which include content and expression) conform to an historical experience of female migration, as much as to their roles and position within the family? In many ways the profile of women migrants is less public than that of men. Numerically, they have been a smaller proportion of migrants. Historically, they have been obscured. From my interviews, some precedents can be found. Mr. F. was born in 1909.

> I don't know my mother. My mother leave and been to Panama. So I raise by my grandmother. So I don't know my mother. I knew my father. But I didn't live with my father ... I have brothers and sisters here, from my father, and I have brothers and sisters and – my mother went to Panama and the children was in Panama.[32]

Jeffrey's paternal grandmother had migrated to Guyana in 1920 when Jeffrey's father, Garfield, was four months old. He never saw her again, although 'she correspond me, up to a period of time ... I had other brothers and sisters but they all been along with her to Guyana.'[33] Olive, who was born in 1926, and came to Britain in 1957, recalls how

> my mother leave me very small, as a baby ... her parents look after me from then until I was twenty. I never knew my mum, not until I had my second baby three months, and then she came home.[34]

Olive's mother first migrated to Trinidad as a domestic for 'some white lady there.' She then went to Panama, where she met her husband, following him to Jamaica, where she stayed. Olive, too, was unclear why her mother had migrated, explaining it in terms of her own, and her family's experience.

> Just like how young girls are going to Trinidad, or going to England ... our family love to travel. I do. I love to travel. You know, when you grow up, you go to a place, and you may get a job there. And that's it. Yes.[35]

Sheila's mother, Bethany, was born in 1894. She married when she was seventeen, and had her first child when she was eighteen. (Sheila was the eighth of her mother's eleven children). But at twenty-five, Bethany left her children with her mother in Barbados and migrated to Trinidad, to join an aunt already there, finding work as a seamstress. She left her family because her husband 'had a woman, you understand?' She stayed in Trinidad a year, returning to her husband in Barbados after he promised to leave the woman. Even then,

> If he didn't leave the woman, cor my aunt tell me come along back ... send and tell her, and she would send the passage money.[36]

In the absence of quantitative data, or supplementary qualitative data, we cannot be sure how representative these examples are. We do know that their children were left in the care of their grandmothers; we can presume that all four found work abroad; at least one migrated to escape domestic problems; three established new families abroad, and never returned. Bethany would have stayed in Trinidad had her husband refused to abandon his 'woman'. Bethany's aunt in Trinidad never returned, although she had in fact helped 'raise' Bethany, through the remittances she returned to her mother and sister. Roy's aunt had similarly migrated to the United States in the 1920s – never to return – sending home money and goods. At Christmas, for instance, she would

> make up a barrel, send stuff down to us and I think it is true to say we got our first saucepan off of her. All the modern things then she send down to us and so forth.[37]

Why they did not return is speculation: it could be that as women they earned less than men who migrated; saving for a return passage was therefore more difficult and, in the 1920s, the logistics of reuniting with children may have seemed insurmountable. If – as many appear to – they established new relationships and families abroad, the economic, social and possibly legal difficulties of migrant status may have led to, or compounded, a dependency on their new partners which may have militated against return. There may have been difficulties of leaving younger children in the host country with no family networks for support in their absence. Dependency and lack of a wider family support characterised the experience of many women who migrated to Britain in the 1950s and it is reasonable to speculate that those pressures would have been present – even exaggerated – in earlier migrations.

I shall stick my neck out and suggest that the 'mistress' narrative for women migrants was not one of temporary but permanent migration; that women did not, or could not, return, laden with goods and replete with adventure. There were no old women telling their stories of adventure and heroism, of building the canal, or finding oil, or working the foundries. There were no grandmothers returning from Panama to build the 'upstairs house' or buy a fleet of fishing boats, or like Verona to remember, as a 'good-looking old man' with 'he kerchief round he neck, and watch and a break.'[38]

Women's migration was likely to be a more permanent, more searing experience for those left behind, less likely to be thought of, much less articulated in, the casual tones of bravado and heroism, of building canals and finding oil – or setting up a tailor's shop, or rising to management in the Post Office, or driving the buses of Birmingham, or London, and then securing

> promotion as a driving instructor for London Transport ... I made a first, I was the first black man who ever done it ... I want to go higher now ... I'm after senior instructor now ... go for senior instructor ... I end up working there as a senior instructor, being a senior official ... and I'm the only one, up to this day, who made it. I retired as such. *That is my story.* (emphasis added)[39]

These were not the narrative genres of women's migration, this was not their 'master' narrative. They did not stress casualness as a hedge against disappointment, nor monitor their progress as a metaphor of achievement. Nor did women always have a clear model of return which would have lessened the pain of departure, however much they anticipated return. What they stressed in the style and content of their accounts was the enormity of the move, an implicit acknowledgement that migration contained the potential for permanent absence, stressing within this the emotional wrench of leaving children, the compulsion to be reunited with them. And reunion was not always possible. Vivien, as her 'two years' stretched into decades, tried to bring her children over but when I did get some money, they (the British Government) wouldn't let the children come, because they said their father wasn't here ... (I was) devastated. Oh, I didn't get over it ... I walk the ward, and I smile, and I churn but it really broke my heart ... they wouldn't even let the boy, the last boy, come for a holiday because they feel that I would want to keep him in the country. They didn't let him come for a holiday ... it's something you could never explain, because when I see some children turn their back on their parents, because their parents left them and go, you know, I really do shed a tear because it could've happened to me. But, lucky enough, they didn't do it ... they know that something went wrong along the line that they didn't come up here, but it really, really, really is heart-breaking, it is, you know, it is. It is. It is.[40]

Coming to Britain in the 1950s was to confront the modern city, its size, its bustle and, within its vast numbers of inhabitants, its anonymity. As Beryl recalled,

I used to walk, and I used to speak to these people, and they used to look at me because, I mean, it's a thing you do in Barbados, you speak to people, everybody ... everywhere you go and 'Hi!' or whatever. And I was just walking and I was speaking to these people, and they look and say, 'Is she crazy, or something?' You know, they're looking at me, and I thought, 'Well, maybe I'm something funny.' ... You have to break out of that habit as soon as possible, because you feel bad, especially if you speak to someone and they don't speak to you.[41]

But it was also to confront the city in its contradictions, for anonymity coexisted with an intimate personal focus, where instant judgements were made on sight alone. 'Going round looking for rooms,' as Beryl said,

or whatever to rent, or a flat ... you know, 'vacancy for room or flat to let', well, by the time you got there ... they just slammed the door ... they opened and slammed the door ... you will find it in the shops as well ... people didn't want to serve you, you have to put your money on the counter, they never touch your hand.'[42]

Within the city it was vital to carve out space, a physical and symbolic retreat, which set a distance from the anonymity of the city and its racialised gaze. A home, somewhere to live, somewhere to *be*, was one such retreat and for many women, in particular, the need for a home took on a peculiar urgency if they were not to live out the potential of permanent separation from their children.

'I am not impulsive, ' Lucia, a nurse who came to Britain in 1966, argued

> If I have an idea, I think it through and I try to look at it from as many different points of view as possible ... and if I can see that it can work, I will put my arguments to you, and I expect you to tell me, if you tell me it isn't going to work, to have arguments that can balance mine.[43]

The 'argument' in question was with her husband over buying a house in England, and the spur to house purchase was the birth of her first baby, a daughter, whom she had to take back to Barbados and leave in the care of her mother.

> Even though I may appear to drift along, at the back of my mind I give careful thought and consideration to most things and I knew nurses who had children and I knew what was happening to those children and I knew how the mums felt. They had to take them to childminders in the morning before they came to work ... and collect those babies after ten o'clock ... rain, snow, sleet, sun ... and I knew she would ... be properly looked after if she was in Barbados ... but it was very difficult ... it took me years before I actually got her to understand that I didn't take her back (to Barbados) because I didn't want her.[44]

Not only was Lucia working full-time, but she and her husband were living in a rented room which was unsuitable for bringing up a young child, and in Lucia's opinion a waste of money.

> I see rented accommodation as throwing water in the sea to make the ships run faster ... even though in Barbados, to outside people, it looks as though we live in shacks, the shacks are ours ... renting ... was quite a new situation for me.[45]

She told her husband that if

> he didn't look for somewhere for us to live, that I could get my daughter back, because there was no way I was going to bring her back to live in a room, I was going to leave him ...[46]

After six years, her husband eventually bought a house, and Lucia was reunited with her daughter. Selma had a similar experience. She had already left her three Barbados-born children with her mother in Barbados, and then sent the first two of her British-born children home. They lived in a single room, and Selma worked full-time, eventually persuading her husband, Orville, to buy a house so that the family could be united. It took her seven years.

A home of your own marked an autonomy and an independence, a place where the boundaries could be set by you and not be subject to the whims and demands of others, of landlords or co-tenants, where the money put into the gas meter would not be used by another, or the bathroom left uncleaned by the previous occupant. Estelle left her two children in Barbados when she came to Britain in 1956. She married in Britain and gave birth to four more children. She and her husband bought

> this dirty, bug-ridden, three-bedroom house, and that place was hell. There were bugs everywhere ... the Sanitary Inspector ... come along (and) ... Flit the place ... Never mind, *you were still more independent.* So that is how we actually got off the ground. Own your own house, you know?' (emphasis added)[47]

House purchase provided collateral which, as we have seen, could be converted into other uses, notably to buy property in Barbados. But it also suggested stability and permanence, *de facto* recognition that return was not imminent. This may explain why house purchase was pushed by women, with a recognition both that migration was unlikely to be temporary, at least for them and, within such a time-frame, contained the danger of the break-up of the family, and initially resisted by some men, whose model of temporary migrations demanded cash-savings and a quick return. Not everyone was in a position to buy a house. Beryl, her husband and four children were evicted from their privately rented accommodation and rehoused by the council in a series of substandard dwellings until, eleven years after the birth of their first child, they were allocated a new council house, but 'I had to make a lot of noise, though. I had to go up there everyday at the office ... we had to battle against that council ... that's where some of the prejudice that we felt came in as well.'[48] The importance of a home transcended the real and immediate needs of the family. 'When I got my own kitchen' Beryl said,

> ... that was like Heaven. I could then cook when I want, cook how I like and, you know, *it was like you were somebody now. You now become somebody. Before, you were just a person. You were nobody. You were just a bare frame of a person.* (emphasis added)[49]

Purchased or rented, carving out space was a resistance to the domination of the city and to the power of the streets which denied sanctuary. It was one way in which women could achieve personal autonomy in a society which homogenised and marginalised black migrants and where, through their families, a cultural autonomy could be sustained. As Sharon reminded us, 'you came through your front door and you were ... in Barbados.'

Becoming somebody. The structure of memory and its narratives appears to divide along the fault line of gender; but that fault line cannot be dislocated from masculinity and femininity, those powerful sexual directives, however culturally informed, which shape subjectivity and identity as well as propel sexual behaviour. The men project a sense of self bound up by autonomy and activity. Their manhood continues to be linked not with the home and family, however emotionally bound to it they are, but with the culture of the street, the city's anonymity which, while marking them as different, demands conformity. Through chronology and career, their space has been defined, and their place confirmed.

For women, reinstating the family reasserts one expression of autonomy (however much their role within the family may deny them that). But they also linger over the finer details, over an expression of their womanhood though projecting an image of self in terms of their external appearances. Estelle, for instance, recalls how,

> when I was leaving, I got a tailor to make me a nice jacket, and I made a skirt, so I had a nice outfit. And when I came to Victoria my brother bought me a lovely red coat, fitted one. And *I was this pretty young girl in this lovely red coat.* (emphasis added)[50]

Elise, in a similar fashion, described how

> My sister come over from Curaçao ... she brought over some stuff, and I bought it off her. It was a kind of tweed with a brown splash in it. And I had a bodice. I bought a blouse ... a nice one, with embroidery on both sides ... and a beige hat. And gloves. I looked quite nice, I must admit. *I didn't show I'm poor* at that time. (emphasis added)[51]

We can feel for Sheila whose mother, Bethany,

> spend so much money buying flannelette this and flannelette that, and even the lisle stockings! ... and when I got there, a good job that I put a couple of decent pair of knickers, you know, with me. When I got there, I see these girls with all the

ordinary clothes, and I with a caseful of flannelette pyjamas, suits and things like that, you know! The only thing I had nice was a blue satin housecoat ... and the slippers to go with that ... ready-made, nice. They were the best, the only things I had.[52]

We have no image of the men as they arrived at Victoria or Waterloo, no immediate sense of their masculinity. Yet appearances signal sexuality and represent identity. They indulge the imagination and the senses. They are a central statement, and presentation, of self. They are there to be 'read', to be interpreted. Estelle in her coat, Elise in her gloves, Sheila in her blue satin housecoat, 'ready-made, nice' – this is the iconography of womanhood, directing us towards their femininity. Time and again women refer to the clothes they wore, for dressing well places them in the centre, as subjects, as creators of an illusion. It is through iconography that women signalled their individuality, their difference. Could it be that men *expressed* their autonomy through migration; women *achieved* theirs through migration?

When you look back over their narratives, hear the circularity of their accounts, listen to the collectivity of their lives, what may appear as confusion, as time and detail all 'mix up', of an inability to demarcate the personal from the public, what you have, in aural form, is an image not an account, a unitary vision, rather than a linear measure.

Clothes may seem superficial and ephemeral, an unlikely focus for historical interpretation. Estelle's daughter, Beulah, recalls her mother's departure for England:

> I can remember her going ... I can remember my mother had on a white organza blouse the day she left. And I always remember thinking how pretty she looked. But I was devastated.[53]

Beulah was seven when her mother left. Four years later, Beulah joined her in England. The drama of Beulah's narrative is punctuated and highlighted by visual description of her mother. Her memory of her mother is of a woman 'smelling of perfume, with nail polish, wide skirts ... laughing.' When her father left for England, 'I can remember the dress my mother wore ...,' the visits to her paternal grandmother marked by 'my prettiest dress ... (which) would fan out.' After thirty years in England, Estelle left again to remigrate to Canada,

> I was devastated ... she has an old dressing gown that she left in the house the morning she left. And I picked it up and when I'm upset, I put it on, and I sleep with it. Sometimes I go and wrap it round my neck. I can smell her on this dressing gown, which is ridiculous. I am forty-two years old.[54]

In this mother–daughter relationship – one shaped by migration – clothes became an expression, and a symbol, of their relationship, with all the complexities of absence, of loss, of sexuality, of happiness and of love. They conveyed a set of meanings integral to the identities of mother and daughter, and to their experiences.[55] In the structuring narrative of women's migration, their experiences were expressed in images of who they wished to be and how they wished to be perceived, their life stories recounted not through individual progression, but through the cycle of the family where progress and time were marked by events, not dates. There were no heroic frameworks of return and glory, curiosity and cleverness. Rather there was a membrane through which emotions and heartbreak, dreams and reality flowed in and out.

It is a distinction which becomes mellowed with age, when the life cycle of the family and the working lives of those within in it enter into a later stage. With retirement comes the possibility, and the choice, of returning to Barbados, a decision which, however carefully taken and anticipated, means leaving children and grandchildren behind in England. Migrant's families walk the tightrope of material aspiration and emotional need. As we have seen, those who have returned achieved it after meticulous planning, for the strategy of survival incorporated the strategy for return, manoevers which not only involved the family, but have helped shape it. Sending children home to grandparents not only helped the parents, but ensured that the links with Barbados would continue for another generation. It also ensured that the model of the family was transgenerational and that even if the links with Barbados may not survive, the family culture would. Thus Selma, who returned to Barbados in 1987, is now bringing up two of her British-born grandchildren while her husband Orville takes time to reflect on some visual symbols.

> Those hats there ... all of them came in '87. And there were the hats that were bought ... To me it means a lot, those hats. When I see them – I always keep them there – I say, 'Well, those are the children's hats.' And they mean a lot to me. They mean a lot to me. It means a lot to me.[56]

References

1   Barbados Migration Project (M. Chamberlain). Tapes and transcripts deposited at the National Life Story Collection of the National Sound Archive of the British Library. References refer to interview number, tape number, side and page references. B2/1/1, various pages.
2   *Ibid.*

3   B3/1/1/7.
4   B2/1/1/11.
5   B3/1/1/17.
6   B2/1/1/19.
7   Sam Sevlon, *The Lonely Londoners*, London, Longman, 1956.
8   BB13/1/1/13.
9   BB5/1/1/27,30.
10   B35/1/1/2/22.
11   B23/1/1/28.
12   B3/1/1/8.
13   BB2/1/A/12,50.
14   B20/1/2/1/69.
15   B12/1/B/1/38.
16   BB2/1/1/3.
17   B18/1/1/7.
18   B22/1/1/6.
19   BB55/1/1/A.
20   Trevor Marshall, Peggy McGeary and Grace Thompson (eds), *Folk Songs of Barbados*, Bridgetown, 1981.
21   B65/1/2/43.
22   Figures quoted in G.W. Roberts, 'Emigration from the Island of Barbados', *Social and Economic Studies*, 1955, 4(3).
23   B22/1/2/29–30.
24   BB29/1/2/30, 32,37.
25   BB22/1/2/33–4.
26   B65/1/2/38, 39,49.
27   B39/1/1/24.
28   *Ibid.* p. 27.
29   *Ibid.* p. 30.
30   B27/1/2/25/34.
31   B22/1/2/33.
32   M. Chamberlain. Barbados Plantation Tenantry Tapes. RF, 1/1/7, 1990. Tapes deposited with the Department of History, University of the West Indies, Cave Hill, Barbados.
33   B6/1/1/1.
34   B5/1/1/2.
35   B5/1/A/9.
36   B40/1/1/9.
37   B34/1/1/9.
38   B28/1/1/3.
39   B34/1/2/2/51.
40   BB22/2/1/49.
41   B65/1/2/1/54.
42   *Ibid.* p. 59.
43   BB3/1/1/2/23.
44   BB3/1/1/2/23.
45   *Ibid.*
46   BB3/1/1/2/24.
47   BB29/1/1/2/59.
48   B65/1/2/2/71.
49   *Ibid.*

50   BB28/1/2/36.
51   B22/1/2/32.
52   BB39/1/1/27.
53   BB45/1/1/2/31.
54   *Ibid.*
55   For a fuller exploration see Mary Chamberlain, 'Gender and memory: oral history and women's history', in Verene Shepherd, Bridget Brereton and Barbara Bailey (eds), *Engendering History: Caribbean Women in Historical Perspective*, Kingston, Ian Randle, London, James Currey, 1994.
56.   B20/2/3/2/88.

6 | Absence and the 'Consolation of Freedom'

'Where you say my grandmother went?'
'To Panama, ' my mother answered ...
'And my grandfather who was your father?' I went on.
'Oh, he died, my child; he died before I was born.'
'And my uncle who was your brother?'
'My brother went to America,' my mother said ...
'And when my uncle who was your brother and my grand-
mother who was your mother, when they went away, how old
you wus?'
'Two.'
'Two years?'
'Yes, two,' my mother said.
My birth began with an almost absence of family relations.
My parents on almost all sides had been deposited in the bad
or uncertain accounts of all my future relationships, and lone-
liness from which had subsequently grown the consolation of
freedom which was the legacy with which my first year opened.
George Lamming, *In the castle of my skin*[1]

There has scarcely been a Barbadian family who has not been
touched, and shaped, by migration and its absences, at a literal, metaphysical, cultural and historical level. For those migrants to Britain, the
duration of their stay proved longer than anticipated. However frequent
the letters and the visits home, the family became characterised by
geographical and generational distancing, and an isolation from the
wider networks of kinship in Barbados. The children of migrants in
Britain experienced a mirror image of the absence of close kin which
characterised their parent's childhood in Barbados. This absence, of
family and home, have been an integral component of the dynamic of
diaspora, moulding the narratives and subjectivities of the migrants and
their children. Families themselves foster notions of roots and exile as
points of reference, explanation and survival in the host societies. For
the first migrants to Britain, 'home' was the physical space in which
they found their primary identity and Barbados became for most the site
of unambiguous allegiance, heightened by a resistance to be incorpo-

rated in Britain under a homogenous black ethnicity in which their old rivals, the Jamaicans, had hegemony.[2] Clearly, for this generation raised in Barbados, the cultural roots and family models had a direct, primary influence, establishing defined attitudes towards migration, its anticipated goals and patterns of survival behaviour. For them, their grandparents, other old 'ancestants', the proximity of an extended family, the village streets and family plots, had shaped their memories. But for their children born in Britain, those memories were not only at one remove, but foreign. Family continuities, which made sense of, and for, their parents have had to be reconstructed by their children within a context of mobility and movement not of their choosing and devoid of their parent's rationale. How they do this is the first theme of this chapter.

But for this generation, there is also another meaning to absence, located in Dereck Walcott's unresolved metaphor:

> I had no nation now but the imagination.
> After the white man, the nigger didn't want me....
> The first chain my hands and apologize 'History';
> the next said I wasn't black enough for their pride.[3]

The early generation of migrants, brought up (and migrating) under colonialism, considered themselves 'British', but its meaning for them cohabited with an alternative cultural and national allegiance. Barbados was a nation and, after 1966, a politically autonomous one. Choice was a possibility and, after the 1971 and 1981 (British) Nationality Acts, a requirement. Although familiar with hierarchies of class in the Caribbean which were formulated on race and colour, the blanket racism experienced in Britain, the 'Mother Country', which cut across class boundaries and social distinction fuelled a reluctance to identify with a country which in any case was only ever a means to an end. But many of the British born Barbadians express a sense of exclusion from Barbados citing, with irony, their 'Englishness' as its cause, and a more articulate sense of dislocation and displacement in Britain, of belonging to neither one side nor the other.

As the generation of British-born black Barbadians have children themselves, and as they experience their parents final return to Barbados, the family models are extending and, paradoxically, the links with Barbados are becoming closer. They move out of the role of cultural broker, which characterised their childhood, and into that of cultural transmitter, finding their 'consolation of freedom' within the traditions of the family and its values. Subjectivity, and identity, like memory, is never static and always in a process of creation and transformation. Now, it runs parallel with the changes in the shape and function of the family.

How do I identify myself? ... at school, you was black, West Indian, in England ... You see, it varies ... When it comes to music, reggae music, rap music, everybody's saying, 'Oh yeh, this is British, this is *our* English music.' When it comes to cricket, 'Oh, go on, West Indies! Give England a thrashing!' If England are playing a football match ... and if there's four or five black guys, 'Go on England!' How can I identify myself? Realistically I'm British, black British. I have no ambitions, at the end of the day to go back to the West Indies ... unless things get really bad here. I always see my future as being here, and for my kids, as here ... I'm trying to look for a final word to say what I am. I'm black, that's a fact. I suppose British West Indian. I don't know how you term that. I don't know how you sort it out.[4]

David was born in South London in 1966. His identity he defines as black; but his allegiances within and beyond that emerge as mobile and migratory. Within one statement, he moves between black British and British West Indian. David's dilemma is not unusual; most migrant children, of whatever ethnic origin, stay bound to the cultural reins of their parents and juggle with ambiguous and sometimes contradictory allegiances. What is relevant is how and why allegiances differ, to what extent and with what effect.

The culture of Barbadian migration is permeated with the expectation of return. Within that culture family structures have, and can, adapt to the demands of migration.[5] All of those I interviewed anticipated that their initial stay in Britain would be short term, between three and five years. Many, indeed, planned on that basis, leaving children in Barbados in the care of relatives and tolerating, as a temporary expedience, racism and poor social conditions. Children born and bred in Britain lived with the potential not only of their parents' return migration but also, by extension, their own migration. To this end, many parents consciously transferred a notion of Barbados to their British-born children, reinforcing it with visits 'home' and maintaining close ties with relatives there. In some instances, young children were returned 'home' to be reared by grandparents or other kin. Children were aware of a restlessness, a sense that 'home' was absent in this country, located elsewhere. The intensity of this culturation was, however, closely related to the feasibility of return,

David's mother was Beryl who migrated to Britain in 1961, intending to stay for five years. She was eighteen years old. She arrived in London and settled with her uncle, her brother and a cousin who had already 'gone down', in living conditions which she considered 'primitive'. She had migrated to join her boyfriend (of whom her mother disapproved) and to improve her education. Migration had shaped Beryl's childhood. Her grandfather had migrated to Panama, her uncle to Cuba and her father to Trinidad. Beryl, like her mother and grandmother, was brought up without a father but with the help and support of the extended family. Unlike her brother's father, who supported him, Beryl's father, however, returned no money to the family and as a result she suffered at key moments in her life when, for instance, she won a place at secondary school, but since her mother 'was on her own, she couldn't afford it, so I lost out there. My brother's father send him.'[6]

Her great-grandfather's migration and return had provided the family with land which helped sustain successive generations; but her father's migration, about which she felt 'angry' had left her with an emotional and material loss. Improvement, and absence, the goal and the reality of migration, were forceful family models for Beryl and a formative influence on her attitudes towards bringing up her own children in Britain.

> I feel very, very strong about children not having their parents
> with them, and not be there with them when they need them,
> and things like that. And I don't know if because that I did not
> have my father ... I felt that no way that my children be the
> same. They should have a father and all that kind of thing.[7]

Unlike many other women in the sample, Beryl did not work outside the home while her children were young, nor did she consider sending her children home to her mother in Barbados. They lived on her husband's wages as a Post Office driver. Both Beryl and her husband found life in England difficult: in addition to the problems of bringing up their family on poor wages, in often sub-standard accommodation, and without the support networks of an extended family, they experienced considerable personal prejudice and institutional discrimination. Unable to save, much less buy property, they were locked into a cycle of deferment, with the prospect of 'home' receding into the distance and the 'promise' of England crumbling like pie crust. Beryl felt displaced in, and entrapped by, England. With return no longer viable, neither Beryl nor her husband – as their son David recalled – spoke directly about Barbados though it encroached as a stern metaphysical presence. He considered his parents to be the 'strictest' in the neighbourhood. They emphasised education, and restricted when, where and with whom he could play. For David, this seemed both unfair and the explanation confusing:

They would draw a reference sometimes, like if we misbehave, 'If I was back home now, you wouldn't get away with
that.' They would draw a reference, but they wouldn't really
go into it deep ... (It was only) when you got older, you could
understand that they weren't brought up here, they were brought
up in the West Indies.[8]

When David was eight the family returned to Barbados for a visit,
where he met his grandparents and other family members for the first
time. He was, however, shocked by the houses which he described as
'huts' and the limited facilities. David attended school there.

I remember the kids taunting me and saying, 'English potato'
and 'English this ...' and I remember I run home from school.
I ran across the fields all the way back home. My mum sent
me all the way back to school. I didn't want to stay. I cried my
heart out! It seemed too tough for me. Seemed too tough.[9]

The visit evoked a mixed response, of familial acceptance and
public displacement. Nevertheless, it enabled flesh to be put on his
parents memories, as Barbados also entered into his own. He left 'loving
Barbados' and with a curiosity about his parents' relationship to the
island. Whereas before they rarely talked about Barbados, except by
comparison, now David and his siblings could and did ask questions.
Why had they left?

I suppose there was gold on the road ... that was part of the
reasons, that was the answer they gave me ... I said, 'Why
didn't you go to America? We could have been Americans!'
'Because they had American accents.' They said there were
some going to America, and there were some going to England, and they decided to come to England. And I think a lot
of their friends and relations came over here as well.[10]

The visit, and his maturing years, resulted in a growing awareness
of his parents' background and his own immediate environment. Prior
to the visit to Barbados, David and his siblings identified primarily with
the children in their London neighbourhood, among whom his parents'
attitudes, behaviour and ethnicity flagged a difference which they
neither liked nor understood. Ironically, it was that childhood visit to
Barbados which put this primary identity in profile. In their neighbourhood in London, there were a number of Bajan friends and relatives
who, for Beryl and her husband, had offered a continuity with 'home',
contacts and support. For David, it now became a source of culture and
heritage and, ultimately, a model. At the same time, and by contrast,

David was growing up in the world of the working-class inner city, where he became increasingly aware of his own ethnicity. As a keen football player and fan, he experienced discrimination and racial taunts. At secondary school he was subjected to a playground culture of white racial harassment.

> ... all these big white guys just roaming around the school with big DMs and ... the things you associate with this racist cult of skinheads ... some would have shaven heads, and they were never friendly ... they'd write in chalk NF[11] on your back ... teachers did nothing ... some of the teachers probably were like that, anyway.[12]

A harassment replicated, though 'more subtly' in the education system with its failure to 'push' and encourage black children, and, after school, in the apprenticeship system. Unlike his parents whose commitment to Britain remained temporary and who learn 'to put it (racism) behind you and look ahead, ' David, and many of his generation, refuse to do so. Racism, he says, he has now learnt to handle.

> I'm not aggressive, but I (look at them) as if to say, 'Well, I'm not scared of you. Anything you can give me, I can give back, and I will.' That's the only way I handle it now. I won't run from it. It doesn't scare me. It would have to be a group of them to scare me. But one to one, it doesn't scare me. And I can't laugh it off .... I just say what I've got to say back.[13]

In terms of identity, David is assertive of his own ethnicity, which is now given another dimension as he identifies his cultural values with his parents and the Barbadian community. David is now buying his own home, and lives most of the time with his girlfriend and daughter. He is not married. But then, neither were his maternal grandparents in Barbados, nor were his own parents until after the birth of their children. His family arrangements conform to many of the traditional patterns of marriage and family prevalent in Barbados, with deferred marriage, emphasis on consanguineal rather than conjugal ties, and within that a recognition of the role of grandmothers in the care and upbringing of children. Young children in Barbados have privileged access to their grandparent's generation, a feature which David missed out on in Beryl's decision not to return her children to their grandmother's care in Barbados. David's own daughter is, however, cared for most of the week by his mother. Ironically, David's household and family arrangements, as with others in this sample and elsewhere, are conforming increasingly to the Caribbean rather than the British 'norm' of family structure. Longevity in Britain has not weakened traditional family forms. On the contrary, as the generations extend, it has enabled them to be reconstructed and, with this reconstruction, a strengthening of the cultural ties with Barbados and a positive espousal of Barbadian culture.

Two years ago Beryl's husband was made redundant and has been out of work ever since. However, Beryl's mother, Eugenie, died recently leaving Beryl her house. With the children grown up, with poor prospects in England, and now with a house in Barbados, she and her husband plan finally to go 'home'. 'We've come a long way,' Beryl says, 'It was hard. These shores are really rough shores, I can tell you.' Her return will create a 'void' for David, whose relationship with his parents is 'close.' But it will also establish direct links for him with Barbados which, at the moment, are at one remove. More particularly, they will create links for his young daughter. It is this prospect which is forcing him to rethink his own sense of self. He is black British; he is also British West Indian. The impending social and emotional disruption to David's family life, at the point where it was beginning to replicate Barbadian custom, has forced him to reappraise his own position:

> I can really see a resemblance in the parenting ... I'm very much like my dad ... I feel she (daughter) is going to be brought up very similar ... I don't want her to have her education here ... in fact, I would like her to have some education in Barbados ... she's already been to Barbados ... she'll always have that link ... I would love to, like every year, try and get down there ... I'd definitely like her to have that link still. I hope to think that she could do down there and stay for months when she's older.[14]

As a young child growing up in London, David considered himself British. As an adolescent, that identity was qualified by his awareness of ethnicity. But as an adult, his Barbadian heritage has now entered the equation. This shift is partly the function of maturity and awareness; but it is also related to the shifting life cycle of his family of origin and creation. His parent's absence will strengthen David's links with Barbados and become a part of his daughter's cultural inheritance. 'You never know, ' David added, 'I might be down there ...'

As ties with the Caribbean are replicated across generations, and as the family structures continue to provide links and continuities, other aspects of migrant Caribbean culture in Britain are evolving. For instance, David's aim is to own his own business. All the Barbadians in this sample wished their children to take full advantage of the opportunities afforded in Britain, a not unusual goal given the genesis of Barbadian migration. David's ambitions clearly conform to this ethos of self-improvement. At the same time, he argues,

> if you're white ... there's always someone ... a dad, who always (or) he's got a mate, he's getting a job in his law office, or his engineering firm, 'Get your boy over, we'll teach him a bit about heating, we'll find room for him.' That's the advantage they've got at the moment, and what black kids haven't got.[15]

For his parents and their generation, the Barbadian migrant networks established in Britain were essential for survival. Migrants entered into the 'grapevine' before they left Barbados, and became fully-fledged members of it on arrival. It was through the grapevine that accommodation and employment were found. The grapevine replicated village structures left behind (indeed, were often comprised of kin and former neighbours) and sustained the values of support and sharing which had been part of the social fabric of Barbados. David's ambition to own his business is located not so much in the profit ethos but in the desire to reproduce on a more permanent basis the migrant networks of his parents' generation and provide support for his and others' children. Black people, he argues, need their own structures and infrastructures in order to succeed. At the same time, he is determined to move out of the inner city, and what he considers the 'wrong attitudes' of many of the young blacks within it. Although his identity is clear, 'I'm black, that's for sure', nevertheless there is a very clear distancing from a young, black inner-city culture, which he and other informants clearly identify with Jamaica (and anarchy) and a more positive avowal of his Barbadian heritage.

David's views are also echoed by Peter, who was born in Reading in 1967 and is the father of two young children. He is now separated from their mother, but shares the child care with her and his own mother. Like David, his own sense of allegiance is mobile:

> I belong to whoever wants me ... if British people don't want me, what's the point of making yourself part of something that doesn't want you? And if the Bajans don't want me, then why make yourself ... feeling you're Bajan, when they don't want you either? If the Chinese want me ... I'll be Chinese. I'm who wants me ... I don't see myself as anything. I mean, if the West Indies are playing cricket, I want the West Indies to win. Any football team with the most blacks in it, I want them to win.[16]

Peter's parents migrated to England as children, to join their re-
spective parents who had already settled there. Peter's maternal grandmother, Estelle, was born in 1930 but raised by her maternal grandmother, a plantation labourer. In 1950 Estelle gave birth to Peter's
mother, Beulah. When Estelle migrated to Britain in 1956, she left
Beulah in the care of this grandmother. 'My first image,' Beulah recalls,
'is of my great-grandmother,'

> I went everywhere with (her) ... to the fields, when she was
> hoeing .... She put me under a guava tree ... 'Bo-bo, sit there
> till I come back.' ... And bedtime ... I would be washed,
> nightdress on, and then I would sit on her lap ... and we would
> talk ... and as she talked, she would be rocking me and singing
> ... she told me Nancy stories, which frightened me to death.[17]

Like Jasper, Beulah 'can feel her presence even now.' Beulah's
great-great uncle had migrated to Cuba in 1920. Beulah recalls how her
great-grandmother

> used to tell me ... all these stories ... about her brother who
> went to Cuba. She never saw him again and I always remem-
> ber as a little girl thinking how sad this was. It was a memory
> that stayed with me, how sad it was that he went away and
> they never saw him again.[18]

Her uncle's absence became an emblem for her own sense of loss,
of her father to England (Beulah was her father's 'outside' child, but he
retained a close relationship with her) and then her mother. England was
a distant, extrinsic location.

> My mother sent me a blonde dolly, which I hated ... bit by bit
> ... over a period ... I completely destroyed this dolly, because
> I hated the blonde hair. Interestingly, now I see it in intellec-
> tual terms. The blonde dolly was alien to me, as a black child
> who had never seen a blonde person ... I hated it. I resented
> my mother.[19]

In time, however,

> there was a letter, my grandmother ... looked funny. And she
> wasn't happy. She was doing an awful lot of hymn singing.
> We do hymn singing, when we're upset. I think she said,
> 'Child, your mother wants you' ... I actually did tell her I
> didn't want to go ... I remember having this tremendous
> resentment against my mother, for wanting me, because I
> didn't want to leave my grandmother.[20]

This resentment was compounded in England, when Beulah had to share her mother with a new stepfather and four half-siblings and experience an adolescence in a strange and often hostile environment. Her family loyalties remained firmly attached to her great-grandmother in Barbados, and were reinforced by her relationship with her own father whose own sense of self, family and black identity was a source of guidance, comfort and inspiration.

> (He) is what you would consider a true black man, black in complexion, and black of mind ... He would always preach to us that you are as good, if not better, than anybody else you meet .... He would tell us that people were racist, but we were not to allow that to get in our way ... we had to try and overcome whatever in our lives was an obstacle ... So consequently I grew up always with this ... feeling of confidence in myself which the others (siblings) haven't got, they don't have that at all, so they're not together.[21]

Nevertheless, the extent of her anglicisation was brought home to her when, after twenty years, she returned to Barbados for a visit. She was thirty years old.

> I'll never forget this feeling ... do you know what really got me? The men ... I'm seeing these men. They're tall. Black men in England aren't tall, they're not erect, they're always working as if they've got a burden ... these men look(ed) so proud ... I'm looking at these people and I'm thinking 'These people are so beautiful' ... from the day I stepped off the plane, I've been native. Because I was pretty English before that ... I had a complete turnabout ... those are the things, as a black woman, born in the Caribbean ... (that) took on a new meaning for me ... black men, black professionals, just a sense of pride that I think the black man in Britain has lost as a result of living in a culture that is ... alien and hostile and I didn't realise until I went back, that we had changed, and we've adapted to accommodate living here ... if you're proud in England, and you're black, you're seen as uppity, or having a chip on your shoulder.[22]

She made up her mind them to return to Barbados and, as Peter recalls, to impart to her children

> the knowledge that she had of the island, and the love of the island, she'd told me all about that ... things that happened ... I don't know if it's the black culture ... but speaking from my

experience as being a *half-Barbadian* is the ability to comprehend things ... with my (great) gran, as an old lady, she was
very, very good at recalling things ... the same with my mum,
the same with my dad.[23]

As a result

> I always knew where I came from ... because it was obvious
> that these people here didn't want you being here ... you didn't
> want to be associated with something that doesn't want you.
> Nobody does. You go back home to Barbados and you see
> warmth, you see acceptance, and then you're here and you see
> all the reverse things, which world are you going to be part of?
> From an early age ... a child meets racism here ... I can't
> associate myself with something like that, I can't do it, be-
> cause you're not made to feel welcome here ... why should
> you fight to be accepted? You shouldn't have to do that ... if
> a white kid gets born tomorrow ... he's accepted. So why
> shouldn't my children be accepted?[24]

As a child, Peter returned to Barbados. Unlike David, 'My mum
and dad gave me such a good insight into what the place would be like.
It was like, for me, going home ... (so) I wasn't shocked at the conditions
... I went out there knowing both sides, knowing that it is a beautiful
country and knowing that some parts of it are a poor place.'[25]

Peter's grandparents were the generation who had migrated in the
1950s and as a result he was surrounded by uncles, aunts and cousins
from both sides who gathered together once or twice a week. He stayed
regularly with his maternal grandmother who helped look after him
while his mother worked. Family life in Britain retained many of the
traditional features of Barbados and Barbados, at first hand and at one
remove, was a prominent feature of his childhood reinforced by his
parents' – and in particular his mother's – determination to return, to
which end they both worked, saved and invested. Barbados, and its
absence, for Beulah and her husband assumed a metaphorical importance, and entered centrally into Peter's cultural heritage and imagination. 'Home' had a physical presence beyond Britain. In the meantime,
Barbadian culture was retained in the shape and fabric of his family life,
and replicated and reinforced by the Barbadian community in Reading.

In many other ways, his experience of schooling, of his apprenticeship (as a professional footballer) and his own experience in business
(he is a car trader) were comparable to David. Like David, he feels he
needs to recreate a black network for the next generation to inherit.

I was at school with a lot of white guys .... When they left school ... they went and worked with their dad ... half of them couldn't read or write, but they didn't need to ... I want the opportunity that if my kids say to me '... I can't get on with school' ... I just want to say, 'alright, this is my business, car trading, you come and learn this with me ... then when I think you're ready to run the business, then you run the business.'[26]

A move which would have profound cultural and political implications:

We've strayed from back home, with Barbados ... we are a close people ... and that's the only way we could have got through, living back home, by being close, by sharing the food, by sisters raising brothers, so that their mum could go out to work, by going out and milking the cows, by going out and bringing home the water ... they're not bothered about the family values any more ... white people get on with blacks alright, but we're not a threat to them, because we haven't got anything. We'll never be a threat until we come together and have our own businesses and own things and make money, and handle money, we'll never be a threat, so we can always be people's friends ... coming here we've been westernised. Those family values that made us strong people, we've come here and those values have gone out of the window, and that's why we can't get forward as a people any more.[27]

Peter's father, a fork-lift driver, took early retirement. Beulah, a health visitor, who studied part-time for a university degree and is now completing a Master's degree, has secured work in Barbados. They leave England this year, giving their house to Peter. Peter's maternal grandparents (who were not married, and have separate households and families) have also returned to the island. Yet despite his love for Barbados, and the positive role which Bajan culture played in his life, Peter does not wish to return there. He is uncertain how he could make a living and, more particularly, feels displaced there. By the same token, he is not committed to England and would consider re-migrating to Canada, as did his grandmother before her return to Barbados. England, for the time being, is where he will stay, and carve out an autonomous existence. Yet he has returned, with his children, for visits in recent years and it is their Barbadian heritage which he wishes to instill in them:

... if I don't tell my kids about Granny A and Grandad B and about my Mum and about how bad things were when they were alive, and cook them rice and peas and chicken and West Indian dishes, then they're not going to know anything else. If all they know is chips and swearing at their Mum and swearing at me, and going out to play, that's all they're ever going to know ... that's why people like the Jews are so strong because that's been in every generation, they remember the Holocaust, they remember the Bible, and that's been put through them, and that goes on and goes on ... and we forget. If you ask kids now about slavery, they couldn't even tell you about slavery, or when it was abolished or whatever ... you know, problems we had to go through, because they're not interested. All they're interested about is money. There's no values, they ain't got no values.[28]

Consequently, he is conscious of bringing up his children 'exactly the same way' as his parents reared him. Above all, however, he wishes to provide them with a firm identity.

People, by the way I speak, might say I'm racist. I'm very passionate about my people and I don't think why I shouldn't be ... when a black person is speaking passionately about his colour, and something he loves, then you start being called a racist. But what am I supposed to do? ... For too many years we've lived bad, and lived like dogs, and been the servants and been the workers .... It's no good one of us living good and ten living bad, we've all got to come together and make it better. And until we realise that, and know where we're going, then we're not going to end up with anything ... my kids are not going to have nothing. Their kids are not going to have nothing, and we're not going to end up with anything.[29]

This identity is one which, like David, he clearly distinguishes from the 'Jamaican' inner city.

A white person looks on a black man, they think we're all the same ... I went to Jamaica and I'm telling you that they haven't got nothing in common with Bajans ... they're just different people ... they've got a proudness in themselves that the Bajans haven't got ... but I think they carry that to the extreme, and too far, and they're giving black people a bad name ... they're an ignorant people ...[30]

However clear his identity, his allegiances remain migratory. His 'consolation of freedom' he finds in a continuing diaspora, the seeds of future wanderings. He feels displaced in Britain and in Barbados, although he passionately espouses its cultural values, which his parents refused to compromise, and locates his own ethnicity within them. He will, moreover, bring up his children to hold those values and retain their links with his parents in Barbados, thus continuing the contacts between Barbados and Britain, and the structures of the 'transnational' family which have been a consistent historic feature of Caribbean migration, supporting both the migrant and his/her family and accounting for the maintenance and resilience of an autonomous Caribbean culture in the host societies, a feature already noted for North America, with its long-standing traditions of Caribbean migration, but until recently, a new and under-researched phenomenon in Britain.[31]

Jeffrey's daughter Shola, born in Leeds in 1969, plans to return to the Caribbean.

I don't want to spend my last years over here. One thing England is good for is to make money, which you can't do in the Caribbean ... just the same way that, a long time ago, Britain had all these places colonised and ... took the gold away, or took whatever resources away and used it and abused it. It's almost like a reversal now. I'm not saying I'm over here to abuse the system, and to abuse money out of my employers, but it's a reversal now, where, yeh, we do want to go home eventually, but not until we've got a lot behind us, which we can't do just yet ... it's a case of making the best use of the years that coming up now, from experiences that I've had, and my parents have had, and not to make the same mistakes they've made.[32]

Shola is the eldest of Jeffrey's six children. Her mother was born in Jamaica. In terms of identity, Shola sees herself as 'everything' – British, Barbadian, Jamaican and, by adoption, Kittician.

When I go back to the West Indies, even my accent changes, or something about my voice ... people ask me there if I'm from certain parts. Like, in Jamaica, they'll ask me if I'm from East Kingston. In Barbados, they'll ask me if I'm from a certain part of Barbados. Either it's because I pick up the local dialect or something, and you can be just at home in all of these things. I'm not confused about my identity ... I'm equally at home anywhere.[33]

Mobile allegiances appear to be a common thread which runs through all the young people's narratives, running parallel with a positive black identity. But with Shola, and like other young women in the sample, her black identity was articulated as emerging alongside an awareness of gender. At first,

> when I sort of realised about what it's like to fancy a guy, I never used to see anything in black men at all. I could never sort of look at him and say, 'Oh, he's nice' or whatever. It was always, usually, a white guy with ginger hair and blue eyes![34]

Shola's sexuality became integrated with her black identity first 'when I met someone on holiday who was very persistent ... and realised that we were on the same wavelength' and, more particularly, as she began not only to experience, but to interpret and categorise the racism and sexism she experienced. She refused to be categorised:

> The only way for me to get on well with people is ... to become compliant, the phrase that I used was to become 'a happy, laughing, smiling nigger' ... but I can't be like that ... I'm not that sort of person ... now ... I switch off when I get to the door, do what I have to do, speak to who I have to speak to, keep myself to myself. Come out, and switch on again ... they don't want you to kick out ... against the system, or to break out of the mould that they've got you in.[35]

She became a black woman in Britain, her gender and ethnicity merged into a monolithic identity which imbued her with a confidence she is not prepared to compromise. As a result,

> white guys are intimidated by who I, when I come across them, initially, because I don't come across as very flirtatious or anything, it's a very sort of like, guarded ... approach to them ... when people first approach me ... they're not quite sure how to approach me, because I don't usually smile a lot and I've got this face that is just sort of unapproachable, so it's like, 'Don't mess with her.'[36]

It is a position which, by her own admission, makes for few friends. She 'switches off' at work and in public spaces, but at home ensures

> I've got people that I want around me ... anything that I don't want around me, usually has to go ... I feel safe ... I'm safe because I'm actually aware of what's going on ... safe ... with

the surroundings, with what I've made them ... who I choose to be with and who I choose to exclude.[37]

Racism, and her response to it, autonomy, has been placed by her in its historical context, the most appropriate rationale to contextualise her experiences. At one stage, she was interested in the teachings of the Black Muslims but found their attitudes to women, and their American bias, inappropriate. Racism in Britain she argues is 'ingrained' and

> will become subtler. I mean, it's very subtle now ... and we're being told that we've got a chip on our shoulder. But the fact is that we're carrying the anger and the experience of our parents and our grandparents and our great-grandparents, and our great-great-grandmothers who have been abused by slave masters and anger is then passed down through generations ... it's the repression of black anger that has led to a lot of explosions of violence among black people ... being torn away from family, and being torn away from homeland, forcefully, being abused ... there's no explanation for it ... and to see it happening today, but in different forms, it's very difficult to live with that, and then to be told you've got a chip on your shoulder when, in fact, this chip is a mile high and it's a great big sack of potatoes ... it's all happening again, it's a case of the slave and the slave master. If you don't fit into a particular mould, you're seen as a troublemaker. Now ... I've chosen areas of my life to pursue and things to pull away from.[38]

Shola trained as a radiographer, although she hopes to fulfil her earlier ambition to go to university and study medicine. She is active in the Elim Pentecostal Church and divides her leisure time between church activities, theatre ('black theatre, mainly') a modelling course and her friends. She is also a Special Constable. Children and marriage are on the back burner. Her primary focus is to travel, to earn money and, at the end of the day, to go to the Caribbean to live. England is an expedience towards her future elsewhere, rather than being a future in itself. Of the three young people cited here, Shola's ambitions are the most migratory, and her identity as well as allegiances the most clearly worked out, for which

> I thank God for parents who have, at least, shown me ... a path, or a way to take, rather than just being left to go any old how, and with no identity ... no family support.[39]

But what of parents' lives? Her mother, from Jamaica, is planning to remigrate to the United States. Although close to her mother, she finds her family in Jamaica greet you 'with their hands outstretched, and they want something.' It is the Barbadian heritage with which she finds most affinity. Jeffrey, you recall from Chapter 3, came to Britain in 1962 planning to stay for five years before travelling on. His plans mirrored those of his father, Garfield, who travelled with much the same ambitions, like his mother before him. Neither Garfield nor Jeffrey fulfilled their ambitions. Garfield lives in Barbados with his remaining daughter, on the remittances returned from his other children who migrated to North America. According to Garfield, Jeffrey never sends money. According to Jeffrey, he sent money home to Barbados every two weeks when he first arrived, but now

> He don't think ... I've got to pay for a mortgage ... I'm not in a room, *I'm not on my own* ... I have to keep the kids in school, have to buy the kids clothes, have to pay the gas bill, phone bill ... he don't think like that. (emphasis added)[40]

Although Jeffrey was a skilled worker, he did not always find regular employment. As a result, he travelled round England and Europe in search of work. He would return to Barbados 'tomorrow' he says, 'and build a ... nice house ... but I'm not in a position.'

It is not only the lack of funds which prevents his return. It is also loss of face. Jeffrey could return to live with his father in the family house but 'I wouldn't live with him.'

> When I'm in Barbados on holiday ... he says to me, 'Right, which house you buying?' or 'which land you wanting to buy? You also have a load of money.' I say, 'Well, Dad, I know what you think, but England's not all that good, you know, when we have a family.' I says, 'It's okay if you're on your own' ... if a man is on his own ... living in a room.[41]

Jeffrey argues that his father 'done well' and accounts for his success by the fact that his father 'was on his own.' Jeffrey's father also believes that Jeffrey 'done well', but his failure to return to Barbados or help out is the result either of parsimony or profligacy. The mythology of migration – of journey and reward – has become the means by which they interpreted and made sense of each other's lives. It was these implicit statements of unrealised dreams which Shola inherited. Shola cannot understand why her father does not return to Barbados because

> up till now, there's been nothing here for him. He's just been in jobs that ... don't last very long. And then promises of jobs in Germany, and then he has to come back again .... Life for him would be much better in Barbados.[42]

Like David, Barbados was held up as a point of moral comparison. She would be told how 'we are ungrateful, we don't realise how much we've got, compared to what they had, and we take everything for granted.' Nevertheless, as a child she travelled frequently to the Caribbean, to both Jamaica and Barbados. As a result, 'having seen what it's like over there now I appreciate myself things that I've got here. I don't take anything for granted ... like ... electricity ... (and) basic things like fridges ... (or) privacy.'[43]

As with many Barbadian families, a high priority was placed on education, a priority which, in Shola's case, was heightened by her father's experience of leaving school early, largely as a result of his father's absence. Shola left school with four 'A' levels and thirteen 'O' levels. Although she had applied for Cambridge University, she failed to get a place. She trained instead as a radiographer, moving to London two years ago. For her father, as for her grandfather, the reward of migration was located firmly back in Barbados, to return as rich men and build a 'nice house'. It is an ethos which Shola, though born in Britain, inherited (in much the same way that Sharon inherited from Orville). Shola has succeeded where her father and grandfather failed. Within the family, she is considered a success and is held up as a model,

> 'Oh, why can't you be like Shola?' or 'Look at Shola,' 'Shola this' and 'Shola that.' And I'm saying, 'But they're not Shola, they are ... different individuals in their own rights.' ... I've not particularly got anybody as my role model, I'm just sort of ... plodding on, and just making the best of what's available to me ... taking advantage of whatever situation ...[44]

Shola's comment, that 'one thing England is good for, is to make money' is not innocent; it contains within it the ambitions and rationale of at least two migrant generations. She intends to succeed where her father and grandfather failed. No missed opportunities, or distant dreams. She has learnt from her parents' mistakes. Small wonder she is held up as the family role model.

For Shola is 'on her own.' She has no children to support, and no remittances to return. Her earnings are her own. She took full advantage of the educational and economic opportunities offered. With a professional training, she can be relatively assured of a regular income. As a confident and assured young black woman she is, as she says, 'at home anywhere', free to make her own professional and domestic choices. Unlike her father she is not entrapped by, nor peripheral to, a hostile economy. Jeffrey's complaint, that he is 'not on his own' is also not culturally innocent. Caribbean living arrangements permit a wide range of individual choice for men and women, reflecting and reproducing not only a strong sense of individualism, but highly adaptive family structures which have, among other things, enabled and supported migration. Jeffrey considers himself weighed down by his domestic responsibilities. Such responsibilities, for his father, were shared by the wider family in the Caribbean, by his wife, her mother, by Jeffrey. This enabled Garfield to pursue his migrant career alone, but such support was denied to Jeffrey in England. Shola is not a pioneer migrant. At present, she has a family in England. But as she says, she 'has chosen' and the path she has chosen reflects the independence and responsibility characteristic of many Caribbean women. Already, she has established firm links with the Caribbean: she and a friend have been given land in St. Kitts. She has a stake in that culture which is certain to be passed on to her children.

> I will show them. I will tell them. I've been shown and told things, but I will tell them more, so they can avoid the mistakes that my parents have made, and mistakes that I have made. And hopefully be more aware ... of this racism that will eat away at them. But just to actually ride the storm ... which is what we have to do everyday.[45]

These three young people have had to come to terms with growing up black in Britain. Although all three have had different experiences, they have forged out a black identity which their parents, with their hearts, allegiances and ambitions still located in the Caribbean did not have to do to the same extent. The centrality of the family to Barbadian migration, and the centrality of Barbados to the family, ensured continuities between Barbados and Britain which provided the young people here with a framework on which to build their identities.

In the early literature of Caribbean migration to Britain emphasis was placed on the need to integrate and assimilate. This literature disregarded the culture of migration which had always precluded such assimilationist trends in favour of eventual return. To this end, parents imparted to their children a sense of Barbados and maintained the family structures across the ocean. As already indicated, some British-born children were sent back to Barbados or, like Beulah, left in Barbados until of an age when they could join their parents in Britain. Clearly, for those children, the links with Barbados are particularly strong, but for all children the prospect and reality of their parents' return has strengthened the cultural and emotional links with the island. The children and increasingly the grandchildren now play a critical role in fostering and maintaining those links. Paradoxically, the Barbadian community is becoming more, not less, creolised over time. Moreover, as the generations mature, the continuities in traditional family structure among the generation of Barbadians born or raised in Britain, suggest that the family itself may have become a statement of cultural and ethnic identity, as well as a vital mechanism in the strategy of survival. It will also offer a network of support for migrant families which will reinforce the cultural values of the family, and for the individuals within it, as well as providing – as they have done historically in the Caribbean – a trusted strategy for survival. At the same time, although the different Caribbean communities have joined together in pursuit of common political, economic, social and cultural goals, nevertheless the island communities still retain an awareness of cultural distinctiveness and, with the young Barbadians cited here, a determination to construct autonomous Barbadian identities in Britain which, if the current trends towards return continues, is likely to be enhanced rather than diminished by time.[46]

References

1   George Lamming, *In the Castle of my Skin*, London, Longman, 1953, p. 4 (abridged by M. Chamberlain).
2   This resistance to, and differentiation from, Jamaica was exploited by the Barbados Liaison Officer in his negotiations with prospective British employers, emphasising the long-standing reputation of Barbadians as hard-working, law-abiding and loyal colonials, unlike the Jamaicans who by implication were depicted as aggressive troublemakers.
3   Derek Walcott, 'The Schooner Flight' in *The Star-Apple Kingdom*, New York, Farrar, Strauss and Giroux, 1977.
4   BB77/1/1/B/35–36.
5   See Christine Barrow, 'Finding the Support: Strategies for Survival', *Social and Economic Studies*, June 1986, Vol 35 (2); Isa Maria Soto, 'West Indian Child Fostering: its role in Migrant Exchanges' in Constance Sutton and Elsa Chaney (eds), *Caribbean Life in New York City: Sociocultural Dimensions*, New York, Center for Migration Studies of New York, 1994.
6   BB65/1/1/A/29.
7   BB65/1/2/B/79.
8   BB77/1/1/A/6.
9   BB77/1/1/A/7.
10 BB77/1/1/A/11.
11 National Front, an extreme right wing racist party, whose younger members often wear the hall mark of shaven heads ('skinheads') and DMs (Doc Martin boots).
12 BB77/1/1/A/18.
13 BB77/1/1/A/23.
14 BB77/1/1/B/34.
15 BB771/1/B/41.
16 BB78/1/1/B/45.
17 BB50/1/1/2/33.
18 BB50/1/1/2/38.
19 BB45/1/2/1/56.

20   BB45/1/2/1/53.
21   BB45/1/1/1/2/27.
22   BB451/2/1/46.
23   BB78/1/1/1/8.
24   BB78.1/1/2/46.
25   BB78.1/1/1/9.
26   BB78/1/1/2/41.
27   BB78.1/1/2/29.
28   BB78.1/1/2/30–31.
29   BB78.1/1/2/49.
30   BB78.1/1/2/51.
31   See for instance Constance Sutton and Elsa Chaney (eds), *Caribbean Life in New York City: Sociocultural Dimensions*, New York, Center for Migration Studies of New York, 1994.
32   BB80/1/1/B/48.
33   BB80/1/1/2/51.
34   BB80/1/1/1/24.
35   BB80/1/1/2/34–5.
36   BB80/1/1/1/25.
37   BB80/1/2/1/55.
38   BB801/2/1/56–57.
39   *Ibid.*
40   BB2/1/2/1/66.
41   *Ibid.*
42   BB80/1/1/2/48.
43   BB80/1/1/A/4–5.
44   BB80/1/1/1/14.
45   BB80/1/2/1/57.
46   This is in contrast to the Caribbean communities in New York where a greater degree of cultural fusion has been remarked upon. Constance Sutton, 'The Caribbeanisation of New York City and the Emergence of a Transnational Socio-cultural system' in Constance Sutton and Elsa Chaney (eds), *Caribbean Life in New York City: Sociocultural Dimensions*, New York, Center for Migration Studies of New York, 1987.

PART TWO

Introduction

The emphasis in Part II is on family narratives. I am using the word family here to mean, simply, individuals related by kin, and/or individuals directly descended from each other. What constitutes a family is complicated and complex. The term itself is heavily laden with moral and cultural values. The Caribbean family, in particular, has in turn outraged, confused and defied definition by priests, reformers, sociologists and social anthropologists, from the eighteenth century to the present. Detailed data on the family has also succeeded in slipping through the empirical nets of successive Registrar Generals, of both Barbados and Britain. But it is not the intention here to contribute to the debate on the Caribbean family, nor to survey the copious literature, both historical and contemporary, which has been written about it. It is, simply, to present a selection of families which I hope reveal the diversity, and similarity, of migrant families and experience.

The five families here are represented in all but one case by directly descended generations. Some were 'inside' children, some 'outside', some parented children outside as well as within, the conjugal unit. The first three 'families' are *presented* as free-standing units, although it is clear from the narratives that wider family members – siblings, uncles, aunts, etc. – contributed to the social and material well-being of those family members. It is also clear that other adults – godparents, family friends, neighbours – often played a central role in the family and in the socialisation and care of young children.

The last two families are, however, presented within a wider kinship network. Here family relationships not only descend, but cross, the generations. I chose to present these families in this way for two reasons. First, because following a family through its network reveals how far the domestic unit has become globalised. This family moves in and out of Barbados, London and Reading. If it had been possible to pursue the network, we would find equally close family members in the United States and Canada, and descendants in Cuba and Panama. These family networks, were and are a vital component of the family structure and ethos, and were central in the migration and settlement process of this family in Britain, and internationally. Indeed, most of the families here refer to members across the world, and it is this international dimension which is one of the defining features of the Caribbean family. Second, and relatedly, the role of the family in socialisation is not a one-way traffic from an older to a younger generation. Siblings, cousins, as well as peers outside the family, play a keen role in the process. If we take migration as a value, as well as an adventure, then how those values are transmitted, and how those logistics are arranged, can be seen very clearly across generations as well as between them.

Not every member of a family was interviewed. Equally, not every member of a family interviewed has been presented here. The selection of families was, as I indicated in the Introduction, based on a quota sample, but who I interviewed within families was often random, the choice and preference of the individual concerned, or a choice imposed by another family member. An individual's relationship to, as well as with, family members will decide position and role within the family, as well as a perspective on the family. Selection is always an element.

It would be easy to argue that these narratives 'speak for themselves', to agree with Oscar Lewis in his early work, *The Children of Sanchez* that

> the tape recorder ... has made possible the beginning of a new kind of literature of social realism. With the aid of the tape recorder, unskilled, uneducated and even illiterate persons can talk about themselves and relate their observations and experiences in an uninhibited, spontaneous and natural manner.[1]

Social realism – or what Lewis termed in *Five Families*[2] 'ethnographic realism' – is merely one literary and artistic genre. It is an artefact. It seems, however, to be the one which is considered most appropriate to practitioners of oral history, and most appropriate to representations of the 'unskilled, uneducated and even illiterate.' Compelling reading though it may be, it assumes that the lives of, and stories told by, the unskilled and uneducated are unsuited to other modes of literary expression, that 'higher' art forms are not capable of rendering adequately the complexities and subtleties of their lives. There is a danger, also, that the illusion of authenticity created by social or ethnographic realism, blinds the reader to mistake verisimilitude for evidence, an illusion compounded by a stance of authorial invisibility.[3] Indeed, Lewis subtitled *Children of Sanchez*, an *Autobiography of a Mexican Family*. More seriously perhaps, the illusion of authenticity puts in place a historical closure, by framing the picture, binding the narrative and asserting a confidence that that was 'how it was'. Historians are perhaps guiltier than most of asserting 'how it was,' of present-ing history as both a linear progression and confined to periods. It is a view in popular currency, also, as we view the world through a tem-poral, rather than spatial, lens, and talk comfortably of eras which always end. Social change is far more dialectical, contrapuntal, if not contradictory, and 'eras', even if they exist beyond the historical imagi-nation, in fact cannot end, they merely transmute and transmit.

The narratives below are not, therefore, intended as social realism. But they are an artefact. They have been put through what Oscar Lewis described – though not meaning, perhaps, his insights to be turned against him – as the 'sieve of a middle-class' mind, in this case not a North American one, but an English, female one. The fiction of autho-rial invisibility has now been recognised. Debate on oral history has moved on since Oscar Lewis began his work, and the concept of autho-rial agency is now recognised as part of the historical debate. An interview involves two people, questions and responses, each asking and each replying within the context of their lives and interests, their priorities and prejudices. In addition, within the confines of our literary culture, tapes require to be transcribed. They are sounds which are not 'readable' until squeezed into a literary strait-jacket, for the spoken word, which is given sense and meaning through its paralanguage, through its hesitancies and repetitions, its unstructured and broken sen-tences, its rhythms, timbres, emphases, is a very different medium of communication to the written.[4] Furthermore, the interviews lasted several hours which when transcribed, ran to many pages of transcript. They needed editing, and choices had to be made.

The process of editing also necessarily disrupted the narrative structure of the interview, as much as the initial questions which I posed to the family members. In Part Two, I have analysed the interviews, identifying ways in which values were transmitted or transformed, memories contradicted or reinforced. In this section, my priority (and my editorial criterion) is more conventional, to highlight the material and social culture of a cross-section of Barbadians, for the empirical data it can reveal not only on the social history of Barbados in the early and mid-part of the twentieth century, and the social history of Barbadi-ans in Britain in the latter half of the twentieth century, but above all on the social context and history of migration.

References

1   Oscar Lewis, *The Children of Sanchez*, Harmondsworth, Penguin 1964. (First published, USA, 1961.)

2   Oscar Lewis, *Five Families: Mexican Case Studies in the Culture of Poverty*, London, Souvenir Press, 1976.
3   The first edition of my book *Fenwomen* assumed Lewis' stance of invisibility, a position from which I distanced myself in the new introduction to the second edition, published by Routledge in 1983.
4   Alessandro Portelli, 'The Peculiarities of Oral History', *History Workshop Journal*, 12, Autumn, 1981.

7 | Family One

Charles was born in 1913, the first of his mother's children. His father migrated to Panama before he was born and although his mother subsequently married, he was brought up by his maternal grandparents. His grandfather was a 'boss mason, carpenter, both' and his grandmother who 'was of the descendance half European', a schoolteacher and secretary. Charles migrated at the start of the Second World War and worked abroad as a clerk for most of his life.

When I were at the age of twelve years old my uncle, which is my mother brother, they lived in Panama, he used to send and help my grandmother. He said he want me to go to secondary school because the people in Panama who is educated get the best job. My grandmother had a brother and he worked on an estate as the bookkeeper. The white half could work there. So I was to go to Combermere. I had my money, my bag, my books, my khaki suit, everything ready. The money to be paid that my uncle send to pay for the school fees, it was eight dollars and eight cents. I will never forget this as long as I live. I was home on evening and my grandmother sister came very dressed. Two sisters came, two aunts and my grandmother get dress. I saw her boots, her umbrella and they leave. I do not know where they were going. But the next thing I heard, my uncle that was the bookkeeper at an estate in the country, had left for Canada. They ship him to Canada.

Three was, from the school that I was educated, to go to Combermere. One wrote his brothers in America to pay for him to go. My uncle send for me. They went on, but I couldn't go. My grandmother took the money and ship my uncle to Canada. And stead of she send me to school, she kept me at home. My grandfather died when I was thirteen years old and she went then and asked a man to learn me a trade, a tailor's trade.

My grandmother give me pocket change when I was a child. From the time I was going to school, she gave me one shilling and sixpence. When I start to learn trade, she give me two shilling every Saturday. She tell me she don't want me to smoke, she don't want me to drink, she don't want me to gamble. She told me the factory chimney send smoke, and gambling is what cause you not to go to Combermere. Your uncle go with all these white fellas and gamble and get heself in trouble, and I had to ship he out. So I don't gamble, I don't smoke, I don't drink.

One day I saw this girl about twenty yards away from me, and I had to wed so. I ask, who is this? I find she live up there, all the white people houses up there, theirs is the only coloured people house up there. I went home. My grandmother ask me, 'I notice something wrong with you. You sick something?' So I say, 'No, I ent sick.' I didn't tell her anything. Next day I went by and I wait. I ent see nobody pass. Three days, and nobody pass. So that week pass. The next week. One evening, I look and see. A young woman coming towards me, with a little child in her hand. So I ask her, 'Is this child yours?' She say, 'No, my sister child.' I tell her, 'The first child you ever have will be mine. I love you. I like you. I would like to be friendly with you.' She tell me, 'Mister, move from in front of me. My mother tell me don't stay in the road and talk to nobody. If you want to see me, you got to come up by my mother house.'

Next evening, I ent see nobody. The third evening, I see her coming down the road. I can't walk. I can't sleep. So many girls I had, so many girls I see, but however I turn, I always seeing this girl in the present to me. So I went to her. She tell me if I want to talk to her, tell her mother. I met the mother and I tell the mother that I like she and the mother started to laugh, the mother tell me, if you like her, you got to write to she father. I had a friend and he tell me he got the same problem and he show me a letter that he write then for a girl, so we make a copy and I fix it and post it.

I waiting up to this day for the answer. Up to this day. I ain't getting a letter and I can't see this girl. My friend tell me, man, I in the same position. I going to tell you that she does go to church. I go by church and wait for she there. I went home and I sit down on my grandmother bed. I say, 'Gran, I have something to tell you. You know the girl I tell you I see that I told you I like? Her mother tell me I can come home and see her. Gran, she the only woman I would marry to. I made you a promise that I not going to marry no woman till you dead.' She tell me, 'You sure? Do you know you got to look for money when the week come if you is a married man, and give your wife?' She tell me, 'Well, if you really going get married, I am behind you, I don't want to see you knock about, nor no woman put you in court for children.'

After that, in six months time, how old I was? Twenty-three. I marry 21st April, my birthday would be 5 May, to make me twenty-four. This was something that was God plan because God knew I would want somebody to take care of me. And he knew my grandmother wouldn't be alive. And the rest of the family had rob me. Well, we left for St. Lucia, get a home rent and they had the American bases in 1941. Well, my ambition, I rent a place and get two machines and I open a tailoring department, myself and four other people, in Vieux Fort. I land in 11th September and in September month I get a place and open up a tailors.

I went on the base to get a job working with the American. There everybody went for work. I stood aside. There were captain and a major sitting in their jeep and they hire everybody and when everybody pass, they close the gate. They call me. 'You looking for a job?' I said yes. 'And when you not come by here?' I says, 'It don't seem to make sense. You got so many people.' He tell me, 'Get in here.' He drive me right into headquarters. Honest as I am talking, carry me right into head-quarters, give me three forms, three leads, and an eraser. 'Can you fill out these three forms?' I fill out the three forms. One of the form, where you were born, age, parentage, any of your family this, anything, and I just answer to suit. So I fill out. Ever work anywhere in employment before? Well, this got me now. No. Any ability of trade? Complete tailor. Master tailor. Artist in the full sense of garments.

So that is how I turn to work. I did a job as clerk in the painting department, despatch work. I didn't went to Combermere, but I was really bright, man. But tailoring gave me sufficient because you have to know mathematics, you got to know the anatomy of the human body, you got to draft work, you got to know different angles. And Muriel, she's bright ahead of me. When I get the work in clerk, she help me, and I thank she. First thing she made me do, bought a dictionary, book algebras, different arithmetic, how to make up accounts, reports, all different things that I had. That started at seven o'clock in the morning. When six o'clock, I on the job. Till four and I work in the tailor shop from four and I go home ten, eleven. I go on the base and get work from the Americans. They gave me a travelling ticket, that I could travel on the American transport to take me in and out and I could go to the Commissary to buy food. Everybody suffering from food. I could get milk, ham, cheese, everything. Some people say I was lucky, but it wasn't that. I get work. And working tailoring the place. I do the cutting, and she sewing, and I sewing. That's how I made my money. And I work.

Well, it came that the base is going to close down. The Americans were going to Long Island so they decide to carry me so I go and went with them, doing clerk work. No where I go to live and there's no way my family can't come, I not staying and I don't want that job. I have seen too many homes broken up. I have seen too many men suffer. Don't matter what good job you got, if you are a married man and have a family and your family is not with you for a period of time, that going to mash up. I was alright in Long Island. I adjust myself. Only thing I ent want to do is to stay too long. The white people who contract, they finish the job and they came back to St. Lucia. Then the American close down completely and hand over the electric company, water company, telephone company and the Fire Department to the British Government. When the British establish everything, I still work with them, till I retire. I still contain my tailoring, never stop the tailoring.

And Irene. When everybody ask me, now, what about the daughter, man? This girl's bright, man, I say, she's in England, studying. I glad, man. I'll tell you something. I is a man does cry very quick. I miss her. I cry, yes. Definitely, I cry. I get in touch with people in England and I heard how rough things was in England. But then I realise something. She know how her mother, father love her, so she would never send and tell us anything that went wrong with her in England. Some other people might write and tell their family, but she wouldn't tell you. She won't waste time and paper tell you.

It's a pleasure talking to you. When I need to tell you the truth, that is something that come from my life that cause me to be talking to you, is my boy days. But I have no regret now. Never mind that I didn't get that opportunity to go to High School. But I made a oath, if I walk the road, pick paper bag, bottles and sell, my children got to get a secondary education. No disgrace to manual labour. I will not steal. But I will do every kind of work to see my children, my grandchildren as long as I alive, see they get a secondary education. I've made that vow, for what my family did me.

Muriel was born in 1916, in St. Michael. She married when she was nineteen and left shortly after with her husband to live in St. Lucia. She has two children, a daughter, Irene, in England, and a son who still lives in Barbados.

I came fourth, out of five children. My mother never work. She used to just a housekeeper, but she used to keep plenty animals, and kitchen garden. But she never work. My father was the one who do all the working. He was like a supervisor, one of those big stores in town. He worked there all his life. My mother father, he had a big home up Haggart Hall. Big, big upstairs house. Thirty, forty acres of land. He was a rich man. And all the land is still here. He had a lot of children in the States. They used to send him money, time after time, and then he bought this vast amount of land. He was a great man. He had a carriage horse, and carriage and a coachman to drive him. Come into town with this carpet over his legs. They used to call him the Chief. All the people in the neighbourhood could go to him and get something. He used to help. He had a quarry, too, you see, this is why he come so rich. Had people working for him, cutting stones, and then we had this amount of land. He had this amount of people working this acres and acres of land. Acres and acres of corn. He used to plant sugar cane, too. He used to plant everything.

My mother house was a very large house. It was a big wooden house. Big large front, three large bedrooms, dining room, kitchen. My mother had any amount of land because my grandfather had given her that land when she got married. We had a orchard. So much fruit trees. Any type of fruit we had, down in this orchard – soursop, pawpaw, guavas, cherries, mangoes, ackees, golden apples. I used to be like a boy, from tree to tree, picking fruits and eating. And then sometime my mother used to have over a hundred rabbit. Sometime a man would come kill three or four, and she will give the neighbours some and then the rest we going to have to eat. Fowls. Plenty fowls and turkeys, pigs, cows. We used to sell milk.

We used to help cook, help wash, although we used to have servants. We never work on the land. My mother had people help her. That was one thing my father never did. He never send us to the land, nor he never send us at the shop. We never went at the pipe for water. When it came to the neighbours and so round, my mother was very particular. We never used to play with the children in the neighbourhood. She felt we was a different breed. We were more elaborate in that neighbourhood. We would have our friends outside that would come at us, or we would go at them, but we never as children run about. Children in those days to me were very obedient. Very seldom did we misbehave. If we do anything that she didn't like, she would tell you, 'Wait, wait till your father come home!' He never spank, you will get the whole hod! She used to warn us, if you see a man that you like, or he like you, bring him home. I don't want nobody tell me that they saw you standing there round the corner.

My mother was Anglican, and she brought us up so. Every one of us had to go to Sunday School. She used to sing in the choir. I was a Sunday School teacher. My mother was a very particular person and a very religious person so I brought up my children the same way. Teach them to praise the Lord, bring them up in the church, send them to Sunday School, teach them to be good and honest. I didn't have no problem with my children. I have a son. I had no problem with him. He is married and every night, bless him, he don't want to sleep unless he call here. Every night he calls home to find out if me and the daddy is alright.

We went to the Elementary School. In those days, they didn't had a lot of high school. The Elementary School was just as good as the secondary schools now. You used to have to pay school fees, but it was just a small thing, four cents. I went right till I pass out, standard seven. I was very bright, too. I wanted to be a nurse, but in those days it used to be so hard to get onto the hospital. I believe my parents were a bit backward. They had a long saying that women ent born to have education because soon after you leave school, maybe you will get married. But they always look out for the boys. My eldest brother, they had the money on him. They say the boys is want to work to maintain the home. They would always look out for the boys more than the girls, because a woman role in the house. If I had my life to live over, I would be a brilliant woman some part in the world!

I went at a lady that used to take in girls to sew. I learned dressmaking. You would pay. I didn't working because I wasn't in need of anything. Soon after, I got married. He talk to my mother, tell my mother how he like me and so, he would like to get married to me and so. He had to write to my father for me. I was nineteen. But I could keep house. I used to help keep my mother house, never mind we had servants, so I had no problem when I got married. I had married in the home at my mothers, because the house was so big, she could rent then. The others had married and gone. I was the only girl then, so I married and live there and then we bought our own home, and move out. We stood in it till we went away and then we leave it for rent.

I had a big wedding in church. In those days, if you have twenty-four cars per marriage, that was a big wedding. I got so many gifts. The party carry right at my mother's home. They put up this large tarpaulin outside. We had butlers to serve. But virtually then the war broke out and we decided to go overseas to look for a better living. He went first to Trinidad, then St. Lucia and then when he get settle down, he send for me. When I first went with him, I used to feel strange, cor I ent accustom to living overseas. But I pick up myself and I led myself happy. We had some nice friends. We always keep ourselves up there, all of our friends, up there. I never bring down. My friends is always up there. I can speak to anybody, but I choose my friends. My friends are few and chosen. Doctors, lawyers, this body and that coming home. I had a few ordinary people too, but they were decent people. I keep myself up to date, and I keep up-to-date friends.

We bought a big home in St. Lucia. Man, we got a big house, man, high up, pillars and big verandah. We bought a lovely fishing boat. We had cows in St. Lucia giving milk. I never work. He never wanted me to work. He was working for enough money to keep us. There was only me and Irene. I used to do voluntary work, for the Ladies of Charity. That time now I had join the Catholic Church because I had no Anglican

Church where I was living. We would go every Friday and wrap parcels for the poor. We had a big register and we give each person a parcel, maybe rice, flour, sugar, soap, and then we have three or four people that too old to come and I would go house to house delivering those parcels. Different evening, we had to go to meetings, we used to go and visit the sick. A lot of people living in sin, we had to get them married. That was a happy time!

Then Irene won a scholarship to go to Puerto Rico to be a nurse. Eventually they rob her of it. So we send her up here to Barbados. She decided then to go to England. I say, well, if she want to go I wouldn't stay in her way. But then after she went away, I used to cry so much. I had miss her. But then I made myself accustom to that. There was nothing I could do about it, and I had the little boy then. All I could do is pray for her and put her in God's hand and ask God to send somebody to stay she about and protect her.

You can't do anything without God. That's my philosophy. So, I have no regrets. I'm quite happy and comfortable, just as you see me here, all the year, myself and him alone, happy and comfortable. Cook, eat, drink, sleep, lie down and go to church. No problem, no worries. I don't let what going outside worry me. That have nothing to do with me what going on outside. I'm a happy woman. Fit and healthy. After God. When you see me dress going out, my dear, stand one side and give me room!

> Irene was born in Barbados 1939, shortly before her parents migrated. She was brought up in St. Lucia and came to England to study nursing in 1960. She married, divorced and has now remarried. She is a health visitor, but in the course of her career got a First Class Honours degree in sociology, history and psychology at Leeds Polytechnic (as it then was).

My father emigrated to Trinidad in 1940. He married my mother and, it sounds silly, but for some reason he wasn't accepted by the family. He thought he was going to emigrate and make a life for himself and come back to Barbados and prove his worth. The war had just started and the Americans were building bases in the Caribbean, one in Trinidad and one in St. Lucia. I grew up in St. Lucia and went to school there. It was awful, from the point of view that my parents were Barbadian. For some reason, Barbadians, Trinidadians, Jamaicans, St. Lucians, they seem to have differences that sometimes white people don't always appreciate. You say, well, somebody's black, and that's it. But in terms of religion, speech, everything's different. And the St. Lucians tended not to like the

Barbadians very much. They felt that these people had come to rob them of their livelihood. It was said that Bajans always had the best jobs, the best houses. There was a lot of resentment. And the Bajans didn't really put any roots down. They would rent houses. My father bought a home and we sort of integrated into the society, but it was always, 'You're from Barbados, why don't you go back where you came from?' I was teased, and called 'Bajan', and all that kind of thing. I wanted to belong, to be accepted. So I learnt to speak patois. I joined the Catholic religion. Most of my friends were St. Lucians. I spoke like a St. Lucian. We would go to Barbados occasionally, but not that often. During the war people were scared to travel, and besides my mother gets travel-sick. So I missed out on all this grandma, grandad, aunts, uncles, cousins. Years later, when I met them, I always felt somehow an outsider, and thought perhaps I wouldn't emigrate. But then, here I am, telling you this!

I grew up in St. Lucia till I was about sixteen, seventeen. I wouldn't say that we were wealthy, but we had servants and the best of everything. During the war, when you couldn't get toys, I always had toys. And if you couldn't get shoes, there was always a cobbler. I used to have beautiful hand-made leather shoes. My parents were rather fastidious. It wasn't only material things. I had lots of books and all sorts of things like that, too. I was the one who had the ribbons and the French berets and all the accessory things. And, yes, I went to music lessons and all that sort of things. That created a lot of envy. My parents were strict and I think this was something they were criticised for in St. Lucia as well. You had very much a Barbadian community in St. Lucia, a very close community. They do all the things that they did in Barbados, and it was the same as how they brought their children up. The St. Lucians had a more sort of lazy way. We couldn't just go play out and anything. But I think because they lived in St. Lucia and it was very much like you live here in England – I think they felt strange and so that was in some way them trying to be secure.

But the whole thing came to a head for me when I realised I am a stranger, I am not a St. Lucian, was back in 1956. I won a scholarship to go to Puerto Rico to train as a nurse. I had wanted to be a nurse since I was thirteen. Because – it's difficult talking about wealth when you live in a country like England. Manor houses, and things like that. But I suppose everything is comparative, isn't it? At a very early age I was aware that I had more than most people. I can still remember lunch-time. My parents were very traditional people, so we always sat at the table and had lunch at twelve o'clock. And many a time I'd come home from school and be sitting having lunch and somebody would knock at the back door. And it would be some poor child who had gone to school in the morning – the same school as I went to – and maybe had breakfast, but no lunch. And they'd send them to my parents to ask for something to eat. I've seen where my mother has got up from the table and she'd give them what she had for herself and then she'd go into the kitchen and be giving things from the larder to these people. I would often come home and find her with bundles of my clothes that I had grown out of, and she'd give them to other people. It must have made me very guilty in some way. I would go and raid the larder and give to children. By the age of thirteen I decided that whatever I was going to do in life it was going to be something in caring. I was going to be a nurse.

My father didn't think it was a good idea, thought it wasn't good enough. Now, not many people could afford good schools. It was a privileged few who got to grammar school. If you were privileged enough to go grammar school, or a convent school, well, they thought even teaching, or working in a bank, anything like that would be better than nursing. Nursing just didn't have that kind of status. So at the age of sixteen or seventeen, I won a scholarship to go to Puerto Rico to train as a nurse. My passport was ready, my suitcase was packed. And then they said I couldn't go because I wasn't eighteen. That caused a lot of discontent. People were saying, 'Well, she's not a St. Lucian.' That was the first time that that was really coming home to me. That was, in many ways, a watershed in my life. My mother and father said to go back to school, but I didn't want to go. I left school, but went to relatives in Barbados and tried to further my education at the Modern High School.

For a while I thought this was wonderful, all my cousins and people. I used to wonder why my parents took me away from all that. Although my mother said that when my father sent for her, everybody says, 'You're not going to St. Lucia. That's no place to take a child.' But my father said, 'But now we're a family.' I think of things like that now, because my father is not an educated man, he didn't go to grammar school. But he certainly had a lot of good and strong qualities. That's how he saw it, that we were a family and you don't split a family up, you stay together. And he's always kept and maintained that. He always put his family first. You get people now saying that black men – I know people blame all sorts of things, they blame slavery, they blame the whole economic set up in the West Indies. They say black men don't have that kind of responsibility, that women are usually left to do everything. Well, it certainly wasn't the case in my family.

But I still wanted to be a nurse, to go to Canada, but the head-teacher told me that if I got my training in Canada I couldn't work anywhere else with that qualification. Remember, we were still under colonisation. Unless you had an English certificate, it was no use. So that's how I came here. For three years, I said, and if I liked it, I would do my midwifery which would have taken another year, and then I was going to go back to Barbados or Canada or America. I never came to England to stay. My mother didn't want me to come. She thought it was too far, but my father thought it was a good thing. If I was going to be a nurse I might as well go to England and do it properly, he said!

I came to England just as the whole influx of people from the Caribbean were coming. What we didn't realise was that you had this two-tier type of nursing, the enrolled nurses and the SRN and you had people working as auxilliaries. I applied to various hospitals and they would all write me back and say, 'My quota for colonial students is full. Reapply again.' In the end, I found someone who directed me to this assisted thing. There was a recruitment office, you had an interview and then you had to sit like an entrance test. Hundreds of people. Only five of us came through that batch, but then they found the hospital for you. I didn't know where I was going. I didn't know that England was such a vast place. I didn't know it was as cold. We were given a sort of manual that told us about the climate and the food. I had a cousin in England who was a nurse, and she used to send nursing journals home. But it still does not prepare you for what I found.

We came over on the boat, four of us came together, and all went to the same hospital. You had people who were coming to work in the hospitals, in the hotels, on the railway, women coming to join their husbands, children, all packed in like sardines. We were met by the British Council who pinned some things on us and put us on the train. We came initially to a hospital in Yorkshire. We thought we were never going to get there. We got to the hospital about eleven, twelve o'clock at night. We were starving, and they gave us this plate of cold salad. I mean, at home, that was a starter, or a side thing!

The size, the vastness of the place, was all so strange and different. The houses, the buildings, everything. I don't think anything in my imagination had prepared me for that. The greyness as well. England was very black and dull and grey, even though it was summer. We came over in June, and school was not till September. So they stuck a white overall on you and put you to work as an auxilliary. Basically, you were a skivvy. You gave tea, you did bedpans. If we were meant to be students, we really shouldn't have been doing that. But then they could justify that by saying it was one way of getting us socialised. But when one is young, and I mean all this, you are eager to please, you want to learn. I think racism is something that isn't always obvious. And then, in St. Lucia, at the convent, all the nuns were Irish or French, and fifty per cent of the children were white anyway, so I was quite used to mixing with white people, I didn't have any inhibitions or anything.

But then a number of us got disillusioned. I think we were homesick. I met this guy, and he came from St. Peter, in Barbados. He was very handsome, and you're young. So we got married. The career and everything went. According to sociologists, it doesn't matter what your education is, if you're black, you're all working class. I don't know how true that is. But we had a completely different upbringing. In many ways, I changed my way of living, my class, my status, the whole lot. We wanted different things. I wouldn't have minded, because in those days all black people lived the same way, we all lived wherever we could find to live. And life was rough. But my life certainly changed. At first, I didn't realise that and when I did, I thought it didn't matter because people get married for better or for worse. But life was hard, and I had five children, and he wasn't earning a lot of money and I couldn't work. We went to live in Leeds, not far from Chapel Town. In those days it wasn't inner city as bad as it is now. So we read, my children. Even when we were poor, if I couldn't afford it I would get books from the library. We'd be trailing round going to watch *Jane Eyre* and whatever was on at the local cinema. We'd be the only black people. The children now tell me that their friends used to laugh at the way we spoke. It was only after I met my present husband that he explained to me what had happened. That I was living in an environment, that we were poor, I was being a working-class mum with working-class children and had middle-class values and expectations, which wasn't good for my children at all. Like Elizabeth. She went to learn ballet. And the kids 'Why are you learning ballet? Why do you listen to classical music? Why aren't you into reggae?' But we weren't conscious of all these things.

That marriage ended. That was quite an awful time in my life. When I met my husband I knew that we came from different backgrounds. But this was England, and we were both young, and we had such bright ideas. I thought that all this would happen. In the West Indies, he didn't have the opportunity. But it didn't work out like that. Things were very bad with me. I went through a really bad period of depression. Although we were married, I didn't have a lot of support. My original idea was to get back home, but I didn't see how I could go home to Barbados with five kids and say to my parents, who were retired then, 'Here I am with five children, look after me.' So I thought nursing wouldn't keep me in luxury, but I could say I could earn my keep. So I went back to nursing, and got my SRN.

It was difficult, childminders and that sort of thing. Dashing about, buses and trains. What used to keep me going was that I could take my children and go home and get out of this awful marriage and England. I didn't blame the country, but I know that things didn't work out for me. I had many years when I was very unhappy and many years where

I didn't even correspond with my parents. I felt such a failure. But I qualified, and I got divorced but by then my eldest was fifteen and coming up to 'O' levels and it wasn't the right time to move her because I wanted to go back to Barbados. So I stayed. Within a year of qualifying I was a junior sister, then a senior sister. I kept that job for eight years, moved away from the area, bought my own home. Got a completely different life style for myself. I went to Leeds Polytechnic and did a part-time combined degree in sociology, history and psychology and I went to Leeds University and did a Health Visiting Course. Now I'm a Health Visitor.

To be truthful, I'd like to retire, to wind down. Life hasn't been easy, and I've done a lot. To come back and to get here, it's not been easy. I'm pretty tough, but I've had help from my second husband. That made the difference in my life. Now we are planning to go back to Barbados within the next two or three years. A lot go back to Barbados and when they get there, they find they can't fit in the society. We've been going home every two years and sometimes every year, so we know pretty much what Barbados is like. And we've kept contact with relatives and friends there. We've bought some land in St. George and we're thinking of building a house. I don't think my children will come to live there, but will come there on holiday. We'll make our base there. Yes.

> Elizabeth is the second of Irene's five children. She was born in 1962, and gave birth to her daughter, her only child, when she was eighteen. At one stage she was active on the Women's Committee of Leeds City Council. She is now divorced and a student at Leeds University.

I was watching an Oprah Winfrey show a couple of weeks ago and it went through people's homes, who hoarded things. They had a psychologist on and she was making assessment of people, why they do these things. She looked at their childhood, maybe they didn't have enough love. And I was laughing, because I have this fetish for shoes. I think I've got about three hundred pairs of shoes and I think, because when I was little, I could never ask for anything. It was always just enough for essentials. We never walked round dirty, we never went to school holey. But there was never any money for extras, like holidays, dolls. I always wanted a Cindy doll, and never had one. I used to sit and look at it for hours in the catalogue, but I knew that we couldn't. And I think that's where my obsession started with clothes then, because I used to make doll's clothes when I was about four or five, hand-sew them. I used to fold them all up in a pile, wash them, pretend to iron them.

We grew up very isolated, just the five of us. We never had uncles and aunts over here. My dad talked about Barbados a lot, how he grew up. My mum did in her way. She'd tell you about different parts of Barbados, land that her family owned. But she was always busy, she was always studying. Then I went to Barbados when I was twenty-one. Everywhere we went, 'This is your cousin, this is your uncle.' It felt like a real sense of belonging. It also made me understand Mum. I could see why she was the way she is, she's very much like her father. I loved it. I said, 'I'll give myself five years, and I'll come back.' That was ten years ago.

I went to a local school, from eight to when I was nearly thirteen. I really loved it, you know. Most of my friends were Polish, Jewish, Yugoslavian, Irish, and yet the school was predominantly black. We liked the same things. We liked the same books. I used to do ballet as well. We had more in common. Whereas my black friends, I never told them I did ballet. I kept it quiet for nine years. I didn't tell them because I thought they would laugh. And then my mum moved me to another school and I absolutely hated it. I stuck out like a sore thumb. There were four blacks in my year. By the end of the first week one of them had it in her head that I was a snob and spent the next three years persecuting me. Mum used to make us have extra lessons, just to make sure we were keeping up our head. So when I was in high school, I did well. I'd come top in English and Maths. I liked that, being the only black person in my class. I didn't mind schoolwork, but I hated the school. I couldn't wait to leave.

When I was sixteen I started at Art College. I had nowhere to work. You know, sharing a small three-bedroomed house with five children and two adults was just horrible at times. I had no space in the bedroom and there were always fights and arguments. Mum was very, very strict. I wanted to leave home. My mum went crazy about it at first then all of a sudden she softened. She was going with her second husband then and had found this house and there was no where for my sister and I to sleep, she had to get us somewhere! We ended up in a little back-to-back, but Mum used to come every day and check on us. Sometimes she'd turn up at eleven o'clock at night and we'd always know when she was coming, because they had this old banger that used to squeak when it came round the corner. I asked her a few years ago and she said she was always frightened that something was going to happen to us. She had no family or friends here.

Unfortunately for her, her worst fear came true – that one of us would get pregnant. I did, when I was very young, eighteen. She went absolutely crazy. I broke up with my husband within six months. My daughter was only three months old when I left him, and I had to come back to my Mum, you know, 'I told you, I warned you about him.' He was a Rasta. 'He's going to drag me down, he's not good enough.' When she gets annoyed she starts going on for hours and I had this young baby to look after and I used to just have to suffer it and take it. It was an absolute nightmare. I was doing a three-year HND course and my daughter was six weeks old when I went back to college. But I mean, they helped physically, they take her to the nursery, and pick her up, so I got a lot of support.

I left Art College, I had my qualifications. I wanted to work as a designer and here I was stuck with this baby. I was really broke so I took a job in a factory, as a machinist. I ended up being there for two years. It was horrible. I was so despondent, depressed but I couldn't break down, because I had this child to look after. I thought, well, I'll do something else. I'm not stupid. So I applied for a job with Leeds City Council. I ended up being there two years as well and absolutely hated it because I don't like office work. Then I decided I wanted to go to Art College which is what I should have done in the first place. Done my 'A' levels and gone straight to do my degree. So I started studying part time for my 'A' levels and working and passed History of Art and Sociology and I decided then I was going to try and get onto a fashion degree course. But Leeds University didn't offer one, or the Poly. I really had my heart set on going to St. Martin's. I applied to Manchester, had an interview with the Head of Department, but didn't get in. I thought maybe my portfolio wasn't up to scratch, but I couldn't get onto a foundation year because I had already had a grant to do my HND. So I licked my wounds, and left it for a year and got a job for a newspaper, working in the advertising department. I'd be sat there talking to customers, drawing, sketching all the time and I thought, 'This is ridiculous'. The years are rolling by. By this time, I'm twenty-seven, twenty-eight. I applied again, got an interview – same chap – I went to shake his hand and he pulled away. That's the first time something like that had ever happened to me. He says to me, 'I remember you. Why do you keep coming back here?' I was so angry. I said, 'Why shouldn't I? I've got every right to apply to go on a course if I want to.' I left there, for the first time in my life, having experienced something so blatant, in tears. I cried all the way home because I knew I had the talent.

At Art College, I won a competition for designers. They had this really big exhibition and fashion show at Grosvenor House. A few weeks later I was flicking through a magazine and I saw my clothes. And he didn't even look at my portfolio. I did complain, later, but it was hard to prove, but after what he'd done to me I was even more determined. I was now working with homeless women and battered wives and I sat at work one day and thought, 'I'm fed up with this.' I could do the job because I'd been there myself but I never felt fulfilled. Now I'm nearly thirty. So I looked through the prospectus for Leeds Poly. They had a new degree, statistics, sociology, psychology, like twelve different subjects. I rang them up and explained my situation. Three people interviewed me and I was offered a place straight away. I was really happy then, I thought, 'Somebody wanted me.'

I packed my job in and went. I was doing really well. Getting 'A's in things like law, statistics, that I'd never done before. I finished the year and went on holiday to Italy and was reading a *Vogue* magazine and I thought, 'I can't stand this because the only time I ever feel happy is when I'm working with fashion.' Then a friend of mine told me about this degree, at Leeds University, in fashion design. It was there all the time, and I was going all around. Actually, it was only about three years old. I got on the phone straightaway, got an interview, took my portfolio and she said to me, 'I don't see any reason why we can't offer you a place.' I could have died with joy, because that's what I wanted, all these years. I went straight into the second year and I've got one more year to do.

There's been one or two incidents there, but my dad always used to say, 'Always walk with your head high. Never be ashamed to be black.' I don't have to feel different because my skin is black. My mum always seemed to get on well with white people. I don't know if it's because of the way she grew up, her background, she just fitted in and she brought us up like that. My dad kind of encouraged you to think positive and I think I've taught that to my daughter. At the end of the day I tell her, 'If you cut my wrist and you cut Joe Bloggs wrists down the road, what will come out, but blood.' But it's always there. When I went to Barbados, it was a shock. I remember walking into a bank, and all the staff were black, and the bank manager. I've had my share of going for jobs and not being given them and it always crosses your mind, you know, if I was somewhere that was predominantly black I'd think, 'Oh well, I didn't perform on the day' or 'my qualifications weren't good enough' but here I always think, 'Was it because I'm black? What are they seeing when they look at me? This black face?' And then I get upset. I can't bear it. I think that's why I want to go and live in Barbados. They have black people in good jobs, positive role models. But here, I always have to be just that bit better. Like on this course, I showed some of the students how to draw. I thought, 'It's alright when you're white. It's their country and they let them in the door, but they've given me a hard time.'

8 | Family Two

Lorissa Clarke was born in St. Joseph in 1912, the eldest of eight children. Her mother was a maid, her father a driver. She looked after her siblings as a child and as a result did not go to school. She brought up eight children, five of her own and three stepchildren, six of whom have migrated, five to the United States, and one to Britain. She also raised some of her grandchildren. With the exception of a short period as a maid, she worked all her life as an agricultural worker.

There was this gentleman. He was a watchman. The first wife did dead and left three boys. One day he said to my mother, 'Miss Peg, I beg you for that little girl.' Cor, he had a mind upon me. He ask me if I will care the children for him, and whoever care the children for he, he will make them a wife. The eldest of his boys was eight when I took up with him, one was two and one did four. I only had my daughter Eva and she did going to school. The three boys I care for, so he married to me. We get up a Sunday morning and dress and went down that drive down at the church, and married and come back home.

That last June is twenty-five years that my husband die. When he go he tell me, 'Lorri, I going dead and left you and I don't want you to knock about, cause you raise my children and that is them home, so I going to look for a home to left for you and your children.' He build this home here for me and my children, so I rallying in the name of the Lord by myself.

Seven kids I carry. I had all of my baby working, heading cane, and everything, carrying basket and dung and everything. You band your back (with) a flour bag or something, keep yourself in subjection that if you should get a jerk, a fall, or anything, that will help keep your body tight. Cor I know I carry some big two hundred bundles of bush with one like this week, and next week, borning. If you got strength and you ent feeling no pains, you could work up till the day before you got it. I borne all my children at home. I beg the Lord, never did let me had to deliver neither one of my kids by a doctor. Well, he answer my prayer. I could stand home and holler for the Granny. She deliver thousands of babies.

155

She come here so, she ent looking at the baby, even if that born before she get there, she tending to you first, and then she will tend to the baby. You had to pay the Granny for attendance on the baby and the nine days. In them days you stay in bed nine days, drinking all bush tea, purging you out. All kind of bush. You pick nine of every bush and you boil up good bush tea and you drink it. Whenever you want water, they give you a cup full of that. Wash you out. The morning the baby bathing, you had to put the money there for them.

Three months after, I back at work. My same daughter, Eva that in England, mind my babies. She stand home and do the housework. Cause, I beg the Lord, not to let me send them in the field. And I keep them nigh and I went in the field and work, and she would stand home and she did get she education.

Me and my sister didn't get no education. My mother was a maid at the white people. Ain't no money then. Five dollars a month working, if so much. In them days my mother has to live in. My father raise me till he die. I did five years old with him (then) my aunty did raise me. My aunty used to do hawker work, selling starch. Had to walk from down in St. Joseph all up in St. Philips to get what you selling sell to get back home with the four cents to feed your family.

You had to pay a penny to go to school, every Monday morning, otherwise the schoolmaster ent going allow you to come in. When you can't got the penny to send, we had to stand at home. We had enough thing to do to help our mother. We had to bring water from miles. We time, you had to head water. You had to pick up wood. We used to had a rock fire outside out in the yard, next to the kitchen door and you put on that the iron pot, to cook in. No saucepan nor nothing so ent stirring yet. It used to be sweet enough, with wood, not with no gas nor nothing. Not even to iron your clothes, we use to had to iron we clothes with mahogany seeds, in a coal pot. A lot of work. The house had ground flooring, you had to sweep it, and you marl,[1] and keep it clean. White wood chairs that you had to scrub every weekend. We had to sleep just where they put we. Upon the floor. We get flour bags and make bed, and stuff them with khus khus grass, or sour grass.

We didn't have shoes then. We didn't had a lot of money, but we live, and we make it good. You didn't use to punish for no food. We ent use to hungry. Coconut, guava. You use to had breadsellers coming out, bread and fishcake, or mauby, but you can't trust[2] no more than a penny worth. Or you could plant potato and yam and thing in the same arrowroot,[3] dried peas and everything and you could reap them to help feed your family. We used to keep yardfowl, that you could get egg. And turkey. You keep pig, eight cent trusting and six cent if you buying it cash. The pork we used to keep in corn jars. Rub the salt and the sugar down there and pack it in that corn jar. It used to be sweet enough. Cow. Sheep. You raise them and you will kill and sell, or you send half at that person, half at the next, and half there and you keep half. When them one ready to kill it work back the same way.

But we couldn't run about. Nor get in no trouble. You couldn't do nothing so. You had to speak to everybody in the neighbourhood whether you parents and them agreeing or not, if not the same person will lash you and then you mother come home, you going to get more. Yes, we had to do all the work, and then when night coming, everybody done eating, we play there, with we parents, 'Hiddy Biddy,' 'Find your Massa gold ring', 'Puss in the corner.' Time is then ready to shut up. Every man makes to where they living, you come in and you go to your bed.

I start to work at twelve years. At twelve. Do work in the field. That time they used to got a little pond grass gang. When the big people pick the pond grass, you will carry it out that it won't grow back in the land. So I start at twelve. Some did only eight years old. I went at twelve. From the day I went work I get twelve cents. Six day, seventy-two cents. Boys and girls with me work for four cents per day, a shilling at the end of the week. But I ever had a working spirit so from the time I went out in the field to work I used to get twelve cents. There was a driver.[4] She tell you what to do, show you how you do it and then she watch you do it. She used to carry a whip, and if you do anything, she give you a lash or two. But I ain't got none of them, ain't got no lick. At eleven o'clock you take lunch and you come back at twelve and you work then till five upon a evening, then you make home to your parents.

I keep up with that, field work, from then till I retire at sixty-five. You had to make do with field cor at that time was more field work than any other work. They didn't have no black man in we days as overseer. It would be a manager and a bookkeeper, all white. 'Yes Sir,' or 'No Sir,' when you tell them anything. We worked hard enough. I know I work hard. Hard. Hard. You work. You work. You work. Very hard. I had no choice. I used to work in the gang, the women gang. Then, the bookman ask me if I could drive the old women, them who is loading cane. You get one pay. Stouch pay. Twenty dollars a day. Whatever the first-class men get, they will pay me. That for a day's work. The women in the gang, them get their pay. I get whatever the men get, the first-class men.

My daughter, Eva's, boyfriend went down to England when England gone down, and he send back for her. I couldn't do nothing but let she go down. She had she man, she had a child for one. She tell me so, 'Mum, now don't let me see you crying.' I say, 'I ent going to cry cor you ent dead! Still living.' Yes. I did miss her, but I had to let her go. She did leave one child here with me, them send for her before she did done school. When she first went to England, she write every week if she could. She used to write very good. My daughter down the road, she do all the reading and writing. But then, she say, 'Since the telephone and thing getting good,' she say, 'Mum, is better for to hear your voice than to write,' so she did call me every the ending of every month or the first of every month.

She the only one in England. The boys in America. All them children good. My boy, everything he send down from America for me, dresses and hat and anything that I want. I don't have to buy unless I feel like wearing something in Barbados. This apron here that I got on, he bring. He sends twenty-five dollars for me every month. And I look every day and whenever they write, I be thankful. Praise God.

All them children good. I be thankful for them. Praise the Lord for them. Thank God for them this morning. In Jesus' precious name.

Eva was born in 1934, the first of Lorissa's children. She left Barbados in 1956 to join her boyfriend, Tony, in England, leaving their eldest daughter with Lorissa. She married Tony in England and they brought this daughter over from Barbados. Eva had two more daughters and also brought up her grandson. Tony died a few years ago but she still lives in her house in West London with her two youngest daughters.

I was very small, about five, when my mum and dad separated. Mummy find out that he was messing about with this woman and she just pick me up and leave. She didn't stay. She went and rent this house, and my grandmother came to live with us. She was even stricter than my mum – and she was left-handed. It used to seem harder than if Mummy smacked you, like it used to have an extra sting in it!

I used to go down by my dad on Sundays. The lady he was married to, I didn't like her very much. One Sunday I went down there and she got very nasty. She went outside, and I shut her in the toilet, and went home. How my mum laughed. She say to me, 'You shouldn't have done that!' She was there till my dad came home!

Then we move into my step-dad's house. He was very good. He work in the plantation, the watchman.

I was about nine when my grandmother died. I start cooking for everybody, for the whole family. I stopped school then, after my grandmother died. My stepbrothers used to give me things to do when they come in from school and a lady living nearby us, she used to give me a lot of sums, and make me reading. My charge was just looking after the house – cooking, helping washing, doing ironing, keeping the place tidy. I was the eldest, and all the others was my stepfather children. They was all boys, so I was the only girl, so I had to do all the housework. My stepdad, he had two spots of land. One he used to plant canes on and the one by the house, he used to plant foodstuff. And then he rent two other bits and he used to plant canes and when time for the crop, we all had to muck in and help cut the canes. He would sell it to the factory. When I was big, about ten, I used to get up sometimes three o'clock in the morning and go out with my mum, to help her load cane, when the crop is in. Some mornings, I'm in a good sleep and Mummy will wake me up, 'Come, come, Eva, the truck is going to come early for the cane.' I used to get myself tidy and go with her, stay there till half seven, eight o'clock and then come home. I used to take her lunch to the cane field, and then I'll come home and I'll cook dinner for her and the family, until she get in.

When I was small they used to have a children's gang, to pick the grass. I used to be glad to do that, because there's extra money. You used to get about five dollars and something cents for the whole week. It was nice to get away from the house. If you're doing that, you can't be doing housework! I do all the cooking and all that for Mum, while she go to work, till I come up here. My stepdad used to keep pigs and he had cows, take the cows to the pasture in the morning. It was a nice childhood, really.

I had Myra when I was seventeen and Tony, my boyfriend, wanted to marry me then, but I said, 'No, I'm too young. I don't want to get married, so you forget that.' When you're seventeen, you're free. You could go where you want, you don't have a husband to look after. And plus, there was a lot of other girls used to come up to me and say, 'Tony is my boyfriend.' If you're married and he is going to run around, it wouldn't be very nice at seventeen to go through that kind of problem. So I said, 'No.'

He decided he was coming up here. He was an electrician. He had a couple of friends that came up here and they used to write and tell him how they're doing and so he decided he'd give it a try. Quite a few people was coming up at that time. People said jobs wasn't that hard to find, and so was accommodation, people rent you a room, and it was alright. The day he leave, I said, 'Why you go to England? You find a girlfriend up there, you won't remember me!' He keep writing. Then he say he missed me and ask me if I would like to join him. I was all excited. I ask my Mum if she wouldn't mind, and she said, 'He's missing you, and I'm going to miss you as well. But if that's what you want, then you're welcome to go.' My stepdad was very upset, 'Why he got to go away and send for you, to take you from us, from me and your mum.' This was the first time I ever saw him cry, was when I was leaving home. Tony send the money for me. Myra I left with Tony's mum and my mum. I was heartbroken. I couldn't see her. I saw her in the morning, before I was leaving home in the evening. And when come time for me to leave to go to the docks, I couldn't go to see her because she was crying, grabbing hold of me and things. I frightened to go to see her before I leave, or carry her to see me off. I don't think I would have come, because she would be crying. She was four. It was terrible. I say to Mum, 'I see you in five years.' I was hoping I can save some money, enough to go back home and build a home of my own, just to have somewhere for ourselves.

I got seasick about a couple of days after we was out at sea and all I do is lay there and cry and pray. 'Lord, I want my mum. I don't want to go to England now. If I'm sick now, I'll be sicker when I get to England.' The ship was packed with people. We slept in bunks. And there was one lady, she looked after everybody that was ill. She had ginger tea, and all different things she made and give you to settle your stomach. She was like a mother to the whole ship. Even the men, when they get ill, she used to look after them. A lot of them was young. It was horrible to begin, you know, everybody crying because they missed who they leave behind. And then after, everybody then get to know each other. It was alright then, till when you reach here, and saying goodbye to everybody. You start crying. You're saying goodbye to people that you don't know if you're going to see them again.

It took us eighteen days to get here and then when we got off, we went to Genoa, and cross over from there then, to London, on the train. Everything was strange to you. All this is different to home. I was all excited, what with coming along on the bus, watching everything that was around. Tony was living in Swiss Cottage, at a Irish lady named Mary. When she sober, she was very nice. But when she had the beer, she used to, 'What you bastards doing in my house? Get out of my house!'

Tony was on the top, at the front. The big rooms was the double rooms. There was a bloke at the back, then another couple down the front, and at the back of them someone else. And then there was two sisters, and a white lady. Mary, she had the basement. The big rooms, you had a cooker in. The sink was on the top of the stairs and then we all had to go down to the first floor, to the bathroom. Apart from this white lady, they were all Barbadians. We lived good. We used to give each other, used to share everything we had.

But I leave all that space at home, to come and live in one room, to do everything in this room. I said, 'Couldn't you get two rooms?' He was working in a factory, and the wages wasn't that much. By the time you pay the rent, and you buy food, the money used to be finished. After two weeks I was fed up in the house, just looking out of the window, watching the people go by. I was bored. I was just going out of my mind. You're accustomed to moving about and doing things, and staying in the house waiting for him to come in from work, it was terrible. So I say to him, 'If I've got to stay this much longer, I want to go back to my mum.' He took me to the Labour Exchange and I got a job working in the catering department in a hospital. It was all strange. Before, you do what you want to do, when you feel like. But you got to work, you've got to get to work for a certain time.

I was the only West Indian for a long time. Some was a bit funny, a few of them was a bit prejudice. One manager kept picking on me. One Christmas when I got my money, I see it was short. The manager paid the others theirs. I knock on her door, I said, 'I don't know for you, but I have a daughter at home that I have to look after, and my money is important for me,' I said, 'I want my money on my wages next week, otherwise I'm going to sling you some place.' She put the money in. One day she had me so mad, she start picking on me again. There was no one there, and I took the dishcloth and rub her face with it. I say to her, 'Next time, I'm going to stick your face in the water, I won't just rub your face.' That's the only time I find any malice or anything against me, because I get on well with everybody that was there. Irish. German. Spanish. Italian. One, I used to look on like a mum. She had a daughter in America and she used to say how she missing her, so I say, 'My mum must be missing me the same way how she's missing her daughter.' I'd give her cuddles, I used to tell her, 'Come, let me give you a hug. You can imagine it's your daughter hugging you.'

After I came up here, Tony asked me a couple of times to marry and I said no. Then the next time he say, 'I'm going to ask you one more time, and if you say no, I won't ask you again.' I say, well, I was older, and we was living together I have Myra and if I have any more kids, I would like them to be born in wedlock. So then we did, got married at Primrose Hill Church. I had the girls from my work, Irish girls, and the people in the house. A friend took the pictures, only he put the old film back in the camera, so all the pictures was taken one on top of the other. There was about four, and those was the four pictures I got and I send one for my mum, one for my dad, one for Tony's mum, and we kept the other one. The party was in my room. We just take the things out. I make a screen to shut off the cooker.

We live at Swiss Cottage three years, then a friend of ours bought a house in Kentish Town, and we shared. We lived there for about five years and we moved then to Regent's Park, to another friend, in 1961.

I used to put something down every week. We used to save the money somehow. Saving and sending money back for Myra and Mum. When the five years come and it passed, and I was still here, and every year from then, I was saying, 'I'm going to go home in the next two years, the next three years.'

I was eight years before I send for Myra. A lot of people send for their kids, whether they want to come or not. And they come, and then they're not happy. And I said, 'I've got a kid at home. If she send and say to me, "Mum, I want to be with you," at the word, and I will send.' And that's what happened. She just wrote one day, 'Mum, I'd like to be in England with you.' And we just got the money and we sent for her. I was all excited. I didn't know what to do first. I don't know if to hug her, kiss her. I just grab hold of her and just stay there holding her all the time. Then I hold her off, and look at her, and hug her again. That was a lovely day. But when I brought Myra up, she (the landlady) started getting funny, I say, 'I don't mind what you do to me, but not with my children. I think I'll kill anybody that did hurt my kids.' They send the welfare to see us. We had the kitchen, the bedroom and the sitting-room. Myra used to sleep in the sitting-room. The welfare lady came and said, 'It's too small, and the walls was damp.' She put me on an emergency housing and they offered us a flat. We took that. My first lot of furniture was when we moved to the flat. All the places (before) was furnished rooms. You had to buy the lot. I felt good. I sat down, 'These are all mine!' And I felt great about that. Furniture which is second-hand, you don't know where they've been or who they've come from. I used to make covers and cover them up, spray them, get this Dettol water and wash it first, before I sit on it. Then I had Margaret, and Louisa, and we lived there for nineteen years, until they moved us here to this house in 1990.

When I had Margaret I stopped work. I wanted to look after her because my parents bring up Myra and I want to do that myself. I haven't worked since. Do the odd homework, making tassels and wools and buttons and things. But not going out to a job. Looking after kids for anyone. I just help out. They pay me sometimes, sometimes they don't pay me.

It was nearly eighteen years before I went back home. I been four times since. I might go home to live. Margaret like it at home, and so does Louisa. Myra say when she reach forty-five she want to be in Barbados living, she want to be in the sunshine. In the last part of my life, I'm getting too old for the cold weather. But if the kids say they would like to go down there to live, I would try and do my best to make us a home down there.

Margaret was born in 1967, the second of Eva's daughters, and the first to be born in England. She and her sisters and nephew were brought up in a flat in Paddington until rehoused a few years ago by the council. She is unmarried and lives at home with her mother and younger sister. Her father – Eva's husband – died two years ago. Margaret is a seamstress by trade.

My gran was much more strict with my mum than Mum would ever have been with us! Mum had to do her chores and everything before she was allowed to go outside the house. I didn't have any chores to do. Mum used to do everything for us, the washing, the ironing, the cleaning. She said that she was at home and Dad's at work, and we're at school, so she'd tidy up in the daytime so it would be nice for us when we came home. And like, with boys and parties. She'd trust me to go out. I know she wouldn't have been allowed to do that. She would have to sneak out. My dad wasn't strict with me at all. Anything I wanted to do, he would go out of his way to make sure I would be able to do it. I remember my sixteenth birthday party. We had the sitting-room to ourselves and had loud music, and my dad said, 'Turn it up!' My dad was in among everyone, having a great time. And the police came because someone had complained about the noise and my dad came to the door and he just says, 'My daughter's sixteenth birthday, so I'm not turning down the music.' One of the policeman, his dad was friends with my dad, so my dad invited half the police force over after they finished their shift. There were still people complaining about the noise and everytime someone complained, he just turned the music up a bit more. The police came over again and one of their own policeman answered the door, and they couldn't believe that half the police force was in the party. There's nothing they could really do, is there? My dad, that was one great glory for my dad. He won that one! He loved parties. He loved loud music.

A lot of my dad's friends, and Mum's friends, they were very close. I called them auntie and uncle. It's sort of like a mark of respect. They were people that you'd see a lot, at least every week. I had those kind of influences. And Dad would talk about Barbados any chance he got, and Mum, talked about what it was like when they were growing up, always telling us stories. Mum always talks about her family when she talks about Barbados. Fun to listen to how things were then. They've changed so much. And the way Mum described Gran. We were practically terrified of her. But she was nothing like what Mum had explained, how tough she was and everything. She wasn't like that. She was really kind, and hugging and kissing. Mum didn't have any pictures of her, and she always used to say she was just big. But when we first saw her, I remember thinking, 'She's *big*!' Really big! I was six then. When I went again, I was twenty. I like it when I go on holiday, get sort of like a bonding with Gran. We'd talk. She'd tell me about Mum and the other kids, and what it was like bringing them up. She will ask me, 'Does your mother make you clean your room and stuff like that?' And she'd ask if I have to do the washing up and everything and I say, 'No.' Then she'll say, 'I'll have to talk to that woman, make you do more.' But she'd do it jokingly. She was a good laugh. I didn't know that she was so funny. My gran was funny! But the way Mum described her, she was really strict and firm. I'd like to have her around all the time, but I have to make do with the holidays and phone calls. I feel closer every time that we talk. It's like you wished that you had her around all the time, from when you was little. I have to make up for it now.

When I left school, I went to the London College of Fashion, to do tailoring. The first year was brilliant. And then the second year, it was just repetitive. A lot of the stuff they were teaching me, I was learning already because I had a part-time job, just round the corner. He used to make jackets and coats and I worked for him later, after I finished college, part-time. He's the only person I actually ever worked for. Now I'm trained to do stuff by myself. I don't think I could work for anybody else. I don't respond to orders. I wouldn't want to do factory work, just being told, 'Sew that up there.' I want to be involved. At the moment, I'm just doing whatever comes along, mostly from word of mouth, like Mum's friends. People will want stuff made for them, if they're going on holiday, or if they've seen something that they want, but can't afford it. People bring me a picture and say, 'I want that, but it's like £500. You could make it for me a lot cheaper.' A lot of Bajan people do like their clothes made. A lot of West Indian people like their clothes made for them. I'm going to advertise, but I have to get a portfolio done up so that I've got something to show. It's not a brilliant living, but it gets me by.

I'd seriously consider going to live in Barbados if I thought that I could make a really good living over there. The only thing is, you're in a Catch 22. You're never going to be happy, whichever country you're in, you're going to be missing somebody. The majority of my friends will have to come with me and the rest of my family would have to come down, definitely! But if Mum went and left – I'd be alright about it, because I know she wants to go back. I'd most probably be down there a lot more than I do go now because I don't think, like, the amount of time I could spend away from Gran, I couldn't spend that long away from Mum. I suppose with Gran, I don't know why, but inside I feel she's going to be there forever and that I'll always have time to be with her. Realistically, I shouldn't think like that.

I don't think of myself as British. I was born British, I was born in Britain, but I think of myself as West Indian, as from Barbados. My bloodstream comes from there, that's where my ancestors are from, so that's what I believe myself to be. It's just like I was just born here. Most of my friend's parents are like Mummy. They cling to their roots a lot. They even, though they are here, they do certain things that they would do over there. Like on certain occasions, there's certain types of food. They will make a thing about specially preparing it, the traditional ways. It pulls the kids into it as well.

Sometimes you feel like you don't fit in, in this country. Sometimes you feel you just want to get hold of the government and strangle them. The way they are messing up the education of children. It's going to be the black children that are going to suffer the most. The way they treat mothers, the way they treat you when you haven't got a job. All I can say is, that once it gets really bad, I am gone. I am out of here. But if I had a child, I don't know if I'd want to have a child in Barbados. It's easier to bring up a young child over here than it would be over there. The child care system is much better over here. But bringing up a child over there would be good for the child. It's a lot safer than it is over here. The education is pretty good. But I don't think I'm ready to go there to live. I don't know why I say that I would like to go over there to live, I don't think I'd be ready to go yet. I'd only go if Mum was over there. She'd have to be there. It would have to be like a whole family move. Home, at the moment, is this house. But I have two homes. I've got a home with my gran as well. That is also where I'm always welcome. I've got two homes. The best of both worlds.

Notes

1   Marl is ground coral or limestone, used to cover floors.
2   To purchase on credit.
3   Her aunt used to grow arrowroot from which she extract the starch to sell.
4   The person in charge of a gang of labourers. The term and the position originated under slavery.

9 | Family Three

Olive was born in St. Philip, Barbados in 1926. She was her mother's only child. She emigrated to England in 1956 to join her husband, and brought her five children over four or five years later. She was widowed and in 1987, when she retired from the hospital in which she worked, she returned to Barbados with her eldest son and his family.

My mother leave me very small, as a baby, from Trinidad. My father died there, and she came back home, with the little baby and her parents look after me from then until I was twenty. I never knew my mum, not until I had my second baby three months, and then she came home. But she always write. She was working in Trinidad, with some white lady there, just like how young girls going to England. When you grow up, you go into a place, and you may get a job there. Then she leave Trinidad and went onto Panama and meet her husband there and he took her from Panama to Jamaica. She resides there. Our family love to travel. I love to travel. But she never had any more children but me. I'm the only one. But I was with her mother from the time I know myself. A very, very loving grandmother. She love the dirt I walk on.

She was a cook. She never work in a plantation. She uses to work at a plantation, by the time I know her. Our family belong to the kitchen, all of them. My grandmother, and then my mother, she picked up in Jamaica and had restaurants. Everything you could think of was food. My great-grandmother, that is my mother grandmother, she was a cook, too. Have a big, big oven, big wood oven. Made bread, cake, fishcake, muffin, salt bread, turnover, and selling on Saturdays. All the family's cook. Every one. A cousin of mine, my mother's sister, cook as well. Everyone is cook. We just belong to the kitchen.

My parents never come out in the plantation. None of us. None of us at all. My grandfather, he was a fisherman. We had three boats, *The Pearl*, *The Iris*, and *The Cornwallis* and you know everyday was fish, fish, fish! Flying fish, sea eggs and the pot. He fished off Skeete Bay and Consett Bay, the East Coast. They can read the clouds better than the man at the airport. They have the sailboat and can tell if you're going to get this cloud coming here, or if it's going that way. When he had a good catch, you go into town, by boat, into Bridgetown Harbour and sell.

He was what we call 'half a doctor'. If you had bad sick, he will cure you. Different things he would give you, different bush tea. He send at the beach and tell me, 'Go and get a pan of sea water, go to the shop and get some Epsom Salts, get some coal.' I don't know what he's making but whatever he done, he give us some. Then you know some people have like harelip, funny lips. You come to him, and that should get better. Anything at all. I never went to a doctor yet. At that time we used to pick all the different bush – Christmas bush, Cercy bush, all kind of bush and come and boil it. Very bitter. And you drink that. The cold get better, the 'flu get better, everything get better. Used to boil the shark oil. I had to drink it. He'd have a special pot for that, to make shark oil, if he catch a shark. Or if you had a lame foot, you come to him and he will put a bit of bread, and blue soap, some aloes, put it on your leg and in two days that foot get better. But he never tell us. Like now, I should do something, but I can't because he never told me what to do.

My grandfather went away after I was born. He was in Cuba and send for my two uncles. I don't know what they went down there to do. He never done talk to us like how we would talk to our children. Very different. He been there for many years. And then when the two boys went, they send back to Mum. They're always sending. My mother brother went to Curaçao. He used to send out a lot of clothes, pretty bath towels, powder, everything you could think of. He send my Confirmation dress. I never seen a dress and the shoes the like. Voile, with a lovely pattern. I can see it now. Then he came down here then for good. He had a lovely bungalow in Christchurch. But the other uncle in Cuba, he never came back. Then after my mother could get grown up, she went to Trinidad.

We never suffer. We had the garden. My mother, my grandmother was working. When the yams was selling over the plantation she would go and get a hundred pounds, sweet potatoes, bananas. We never hungry. But strict. They were so strict. Didn't like me to mix. But my dear Grandma, she was lovely. I never knew a mother, I just knew her. She never slapped me, she never shout at me. She would tell my grandfather off. 'You shout at me, but not this child.'

My grandmother used to get us up at four o'clock every morning and make my grandfather tea. And then she knead the bread and make some Johnny cakes, and cook sweet potatoes, I eat some. Then she comb my hair, tie it with a scarf, and I go back to bed, and she going on to work. I will get up then, take the sheep and goat, go to the yard[1] to her for another breakfast, I go the plantation, and she had breakfast there for me. Then I run to school. I finish school at seventh standard and went to

learn to sew and I make her dresses and her pinafore, and I could iron
good. The mistress used to say, 'Cook, who iron your apron?' Almost
now I could picture her there, sitting in her chair, combing her hair.
When I say my prayers, I could feel her presence within me.

We never a big, big family. Nearby was my grandfather sister.
They used to come. All the family comes at you, you never go to the
family. They come to you. Well, really, my family was away. My two
uncle was in Cuba, my mother was away. Great-grandma lived near us.
I never had to work. I never work yet, until I went to live in England
after my husband had gone down in 1956.

> Jasper was born in 1945 and joined his parents in England in
> 1961, when he was fifteen. He married when he was nineteen
> and has two children. In 1987 he returned to Barbados with
> his mother and his wife. His daughter has now joined them in
> Barbados. Jasper is a lecturer at the Community College.

We all were a big sort of happy family until emigration started to
Britain. We were living in St. Philip and my great-grandmother was a
cook with the plantation. I often went to the plantation with her, playing
with all the young white kids. Colour meant nothing. But I think it was
very unusual. Growing up among whites, I felt no different. Probably
that's one of the reasons that I got on so well in England, because I've
never had any discrimination inflicted against me.

My great-grandfather died about 1950. He was a fisherman, and
had one leg and I remember him being very tall and these crutches
seemed to be very, very long. The thing I remember most of all was his
coffin when he died, this long black coffin being took away and the
undertakers had these tall hats and monkey suits and they were very
frightening. The wake went on for about a day and a night. When they
heard he was dead all his old fishermen friends gathered, plus all the
neighbours from around. One of the things about that period is that most
West Indian men believe that they should have more than one woman in
their lives, so my great-grandfather had about three women, and all
three had a number of children from him. Your wife accepted that you
have to have an outside woman, your wife accepted your outside children, and this all became part of the family. So his children, and his
grandchildren from his outside relationships came so the house was
filled with a whole lot of family and me, being a little boy, they all fell
in love with me. I thought that was a wonderful period when he died.

Family back then meant something. The family relationship was
very strong. Relatives used to travel for miles to bring food, provisions,

breadfruit, sweet potatoes, yams. And when you were reaping, you would take to them. We all, at that time, lived off the land. So when one of the old cousins were growing things like sweet potatoes, we'd be growing cassavas and eddoes. We'd do a swap, and this wonderful family relationship was because we all belonged to one person, my great-grandfather. He was the common denominator, he was the person that kept us together as a family, so the outside family and the inside family, all were family.

His other women called my great-grandmother, 'Sis.' She was married to him, so the respect was paid to her. I upset my mum, 'Why do they call Ma, "Sis?"' She says, 'Well, "Sis" came from his outside women, so they're like they're all sisters, and all have the same man.' Of course, back then, times were hard and for a woman to bring up a family completely on her own would have been very difficult. My grandfather was a fisherman, and he owned his own boats, he was able to support his family at home, plus his outside relationships as well, so he was considered fairly wealthy. He was obviously there for all of them. My great-grandmother I loved dearly. I grew up with her. Everywhere she went, I was with her. I was with her when she died. She was so much a part of me. I have got some rather old-fashioned beliefs. I believe still that the spirits of the dead live on. So I sometimes believe that my great-grandmother is still looking after me. This is why I feel I've been so fortunate in all the things I've achieved in life, because of the love of my great-grandmother.

The house that we lived at was quite a lovely house, a typical West Indian house, two gables, shed roof and a kitchen and attached to the kitchen was a lovely large oven that was my great-great-grandmother's oven. Our whole family's always been in cooking. The oven was made of brick and was a focal point of my life as a little boy. I grew up in front of the oven. There's nothing there now, just the piece of land which is still our land which has been handed down from the family, from Lola to her daughter, which was my great-grandmother, to my grandmother, to my mother, and I suppose my mother pass it on to me.

I never knew my great-great grandmother, I only ever heard of her. Her name was Lola. In fact, there's a corner in St. Philip known as Lola's Corner because that's where she baked and that's where everyone came. She baked cakes, bread. Everyone converged there every Friday and Saturday because they used to be paid then. Men would trust bread and credit the stuff they require all week and then come Saturday, they'll pay her, then she can go to town and pay her suppliers. After a lot of hard work, a lot of flour kneaded for bread, she was able to buy the land from the plantation. She bought just over an acre and that cost her just over ten dollars. But ten dollars back in the 1880s was a fortune. She had to work long and hard because at that time they used to sell bread for a hà'penny. But she got the land off the plantation and I would like it to continue in my name, and my son's name. It's not the best place for building, it's on a corner, but it's where we lived. And it was a good place for a bakers because everyone knew where it was and converged on that place.

My father went off to Britain late in 1953. It was a very exciting time because everyone on the island was talking about emigration to Britain. I loved talking to the old fellas sitting under this huge machineal tree, passing these stories on about how they went off to Curaçao and they went off to Panama and they was building the canal and they went off to Cuba and Aruba and found the oil. These men were talking about emigration to Britain. It was the new thing. I remember my dad saying to my mother, 'Look, things in Barbados right now are a little bit tight, so I would like to emigrate to Britain, but we haven't got the money.' So my grandmother from Jamaica sent the money to my father. I remember him promising my mother that he will go off to England, work hard, and send for her and the children. He also promised he's going to pay back 'that woman'. He always referred to my grandmother as 'that woman'. I don't think he got on terribly well with her. But she was instrumental in helping him to get to Britain so that, in turn, he could help us to get to Britain.

The feeling of Daddy going away was dreadful. I felt very sad because Britain seemed so far. I might not see my Daddy again – this was the dread, this was the fear that came over us, more than anything else. And it was the time the Mau Mau in Africa were throwing the British out and here in the Caribbean the Federation was being brought together by men like Bustamante and Grantley Adams and Eric Williams and Forbes Burnham. These were names, you know. Bustamante stuck in my mind. And one of the ships which was owned by the Italian line was hijacked by Africans on the high seas and we were all very worried, 'Have they hijacked our ships with our people?' Of course this was Africa but I didn't know the difference. As far as I was concerned these – of course, the British being in control of Barbados make it clear that these were terrorists, the word sounded very terrifying you know – these terrorists were killing everything in sight!

It was a Friday morning when one of these huge black American cars came by and took him off to town with his little valise. And that was the last I saw of him before I saw him in England some five or six years later. We felt alone. It was a very, very sad time, my sister crying an awful lot, my mother crying an awful lot. It was a very difficult period for us but my grandmother in Jamaica was very supportive and very helpful. She used to send money for us, so we be always looking for the postman. But my father put in place, before he left, a system where we were able to take credit from our two local shops. When he first went to Britain it was very difficult so he wasn't able to send back much right away. But we didn't have the overheads we have today, we didn't have to worry about electricity bill, or water bill and things like that because the local standpipe was just round the corner and we had the old kerosene lamps. We always wait for letters from my father. One of the first letters had a picture of my father and a postal order for two pounds. It was almost a fortune. You looked forward to the letters from my dad. He knew to say how well he was doing in England. He done that just to keep up my mother's confidence, to give her moral support, because if he told her things that were bad, or the Teddy Boys kicked the hell out of him, she would probably lose all hope. So he told her he was doing quite well. He had been a chauffeur here in Barbados, so he got a job first as a driver with London Transport.

Two years later he send for my mother. My brothers and sisters went to my grandmother in Jamaica, and I stayed with another relative who had nine children. I became the tenth. She loved and treated me exactly the same as her own. I remember as a youngster in England, my first job, the old lady wrote and said, 'Things are very difficult in Barbados and I would like some glasses, but they cost fifty dollars.' I had a saving of eleven pounds and ten shillings, the equivalent of fifty dollars, and I send it all to this lady, to be able to do something for her because she'd done so much for me.

I was there until about 1961, when I got the letter from my mother to join her, and the postal order. I had a passport and a lovely valise suitcase. That was a marvellous, wonderful feeling. I was going to join my mother, my father and my sister. The whole family packed the suitcase. Now, everyone in Barbados thought all the West Indians in Britain were suffering terribly for lack of food. So in the suitcase was a couple of short trousers, a couple of shirts and there was yams and sweet potatoes, and breadfruit. There was eggs, pumpkins. I'm walking through the airport with a suitcase of food. There's sugar cane syrup, molasses – good for the blood pressure in Britain – and bush, for making bush tea. And flying fish – fry them, cook them, pack them tightly and wrap them in brown paper!

I fell in love with BOAC. The stewardesses were very kind to me, they gave my flying wings, a book to log the hours, the Captain signed it. I didn't want to get off the aeroplane. Anyway, I had to make my way to the terminal. I walked through customs and the first time I saw so many white people doing ordinary work, sweeping, hammering. I said, 'Whites don't do that!' My mum was waiting for me and she was crying and I was crying and we all hugging. And then the next exciting part was the travel on the train. I'd never travelled on a train in all my life. From Heathrow to Victoria, from Victoria to Birmingham. Run, run, run across London, and the traffic and the double-deck buses. My mother was so tired she slept all the way from London to Birmingham. She said, 'When we get to Snow Hill in Birmingham, wake me.' Well, I was so excited, all of this, the smells of Britain, the smoke from the train, the diesel, the smell of gasworks, the smoke belching out of these huge chimneys. My mum was still sleeping when we arrive in Wolverhampton. 'Oh my God,' she says, 'I've gone past Birmingham!' So I dragged this suitcase of food out of the train and we ran to the other side and got the train back to Birmingham, made our way to the bus and she took me home to where she live.

But it was at the top of this three-storey building, the attic floor. Just one large room with a stove and a little table and a sink. It wasn't what I was accustomed to, and I started crying and crying. My bed was the table, as it folded the headboard acted as the table. That was the part I hated most. I felt so constricted, so restricted. My mum wouldn't let me out because of the Teddy Boys. My mum wanted me to go back to school and I thought I really would like to work. I wanted to be a motor mechanic. I wanted to work for Rolls Royce. A cousin of ours took me to the Youth Employment Exchange and this fella behind the desk said, 'What would you like to do?' I said, 'I would like to work for Rolls Royce. I would like to be a motor mechanic.' He looks at me in amazement. 'I'm sorry, you'll have to try something else. The manufacturing company up the road are taking apprentices, would you like to try them?' I never knew what that was, but I said, 'Yes, if that will get me into Rolls Royce.'

So off I went. The foreman took me down on the factory floor. This place must have been about a mile long. Hundreds of machines, old-fashioned machines with the old large belts that run from overhead, huge spindles, belts running from one machine to another. This room filled with moving belts and machinery and noise and smell. The smell of swarf, of suds, coolant. I vomit. The foreman gives me half a crown. 'Right,' he says, 'go and buy yourself a little bottle of brandy.' I brought it back to him. 'Drink it,' he says, 'that'll settle your stomach, boy.' The brandy worked and the smells of the swarf and the suds went away. I was the only black in the shop, but this foreman really looked after me.

I stuck it for three years. It was supposed to be a five-year apprenticeship. By then I was courting my wife and it wasn't enough money. So the bus company wanted conductors. I applied and they took me right away and my wages went up from five pounds five shillings a week to nine pounds eighteen shillings. Then my wife and I got married when I was nineteen and we left home to live a married life together. It was a period of my life then that I had to be mature, to save money to buy a house, and soon after, our son came and then I became a man. In fact, I remember quite clearly the day I became a man. I was working on the buses and went to work one morning at four o'clock. There was an English fellow booking you in and I said, 'Good morning, Mr. Snow.' His name was Johnnie Snow. 'Morning, Mr. Snow.' He says, 'Well, Sambo.' I said, 'Mr Snow, I said "Good morning" to you. I said "Good morning, Mr. Snow." I didn't say, "Good morning, honky, whitey, John Bull" or anything else. I just said, "Good morning, Mr. Snow." If you can't call me by my proper name, just don't call me anything.' That morning, I became a man. I wouldn't tolerate anything like that. There were other times, after, when I had to exert myself.

After I got used to Britain I took full advantage of all the opportunities that were offered. I joined the Air Cadets, got my pilots licence. In 1970, I came back to Barbados. The government then seemed hell-bent on developing tourism and I said to myself, if they are going to need tourists, they are going to need chefs and I think there'll be opportunity there in case I ever return to Barbados. Cooking I've always loved. It's been in my blood. I've always cooked at home. So I went to a technical college in Birmingham and was accepted on a catering course. But I was a bus driver. I went to the superintendent of the bus company and asked for day release. He was good to me and made up the day's pay with overtime. The other students, all were in catering, in the trade. Then this man was travelling on my bus once, and he was in chef's trousers. I said to him, 'I'm at college, learning to be a chef.' 'Really?' he says, 'How do you get on being on the buses and learning to be a chef?' 'Well, it's difficult, because I'd like some experience, but I can't get any anywhere because I can't leave the buses.' 'Well,' he says, 'I'm the Chef in charge of the hospital. When you've got some time off, in the evenings, or in the mornings, come around. I'll help you out.'

He was very, very helpful to me. And while I was working with him one day the Superintendent of five of the National Health Service Hospital kitchens came round – and offered me a job in one of the hospitals, as third cook. It was a lot less money, and the lads in the kitchen used to make derogatory remarks. I used to look out of the window of the hospital and saw the buses driving past, and I used to cry. I missed my mates, the independence. But I gave it a chance and within four weeks was made pastry chef, then I was offered a position as Assistant Head Chef at another hospital but turned it down. The travelling would have been too much. Within about a month, the City of Birmingham Social Services advertise for a Chef in Charge of three senior citizen homes. So I applied for the job and got it and from there I started climbing. By then, my wife and I realised that the only way that you can make money in England is to buy and sell houses, and we did that. Sold our first house, made a profit, used that as a deposit on the second house, made a profit, bought a brand new house in Redditch – and I apply for a job in Redditch as a Head Chef with a dairy company, one of the largest dairies in Britain. I got it and the company sent me to college again to do catering management. And I became one of their catering managers, and the first black catering manager they had. I worked so well for them that they had me then as a troubleshooter, if there was a problem in any other unit, they would send me off to the unit. They also use me as a training officer as well.

Now, within four years of working for them I wanted my own business. I was hell bent on my own restaurant, a Caribbean restaurant in Birmingham. I looked around and searched and I found a building. But during that period a lot of things happened in my life. I became a freemason and I got a lot of help in that area. I was also a member of the Police Liaison Committee. But I got this building in the city of Birmingham and invest six thousand pounds of my hard earned money in turning that place into a restaurant. The firm I worked for were very helpful and more or less gave me, from their warehouse, stainless steel tables, stoves, a Hobart machine. In fact, when I left them, they said to me, 'If you're not successful, your job is always here.'

So I started the business and after three years my wife and staff were able to handle it. The turnover was good and things were going relatively well. I was making a living from it, but I wasn't actually paying myself a salary. I couldn't save any. So I called my old company and they took me back and I let my wife continue with the business. In the evenings I would make my way to the restaurant and any production they needed for the night or the next morning, all that would be done. Most nights, I used to be leaving the business eleven, twelve at night. I never refused anyone. It might be two in the morning, a car will pull up outside the restaurant, and knock on the door. I say, 'Hi, how are you doing? What can I do for you?' I remember this English lady said to me, 'You're always the same, from nine o'clock in the morning to two o'clock in the morning. Where do you get all this energy from?' I thought, God knows! I'm so tired!

But then, 1986, there was a bit of a recession, things were getting pretty tight, people weren't spending as much as they were, the turnover wasn't as great. I had to lay off some staff. My mother retired from the hospital where she worked and said she would like to go back to Barbados. My wife and I always wanted to come back, so we thought that was an opportune time. Our kids were grown up. So we sold our home, sold the business. I went over to England with a little suitcase filled with food and I came back to Barbados twenty-seven and a half years later with a huge forty-foot container, with my car and everything else. From a little suitcase. I believe in achieving. Life is so short, and time is so very important. I've got clocks all around me, you know. I love clocks, because time is important. If you waste time, you waste your life. This is why I buy all these clocks.

> Michael is Jasper's eldest child, and only son. He was born in 1965, and has a daughter although he is now divorced from his wife. He left school at sixteen and entered retailing. He has been a car sales executive for the past four years, and sales-man of the year for the past three. He lives in Birmingham.

My father wanted me to join the police force, or the RAF. I still think there is prejudice in the police force, just because of the colour of your skin. My cousin's been pulled because of that. That's probably the only reason why I didn't join the police, although my father said the idea behind me joining the police was to have more black police officers around, and make it easy on black people. I could see his point of view but I thought, no, it wasn't me, at the time. I like my features too much to be attacked!

There's still a lot of prejudice around but, to be fair, I just see it as the person's ignorance. But I'm fortunate. I think it's happened once or twice, but I haven't thought about it. I don't think, because you'd crack up. I am conscious for my daughter because she's mixed race. I do try to offer her the best of both cultures because she's brought up in a predominantly white background, with her mother and obviously the only contact my daughter has with black is myself. I try to make her aware, try to give her the best of both cultures though I know she's not really getting my culture, because my parents aren't here to advise her. My parents would say to me, ideally, if they had the choice, they would like her to be in Barbados. They feel for her. They wish she could be brought up there and probably better than perhaps I can do, or my ex-wife will probably do. I've asked my ex-wife and she said yes, then she decided against it. I think it would give my ex-wife a break, so she can sort her life out and start afresh. I wish my parents could be here, take some of the burden off.

My father was looked after by his grandmother for a fair length of time. I think the idea has come from there. I think it's a great idea. My mother's not working in Barbados so she'll spend more time with her, teach her the wrongs and rights and spend a lot more time with her. I think if she could be brought up in a black environment she'll see the black side of her culture. I think she'd appreciate that and benefit from that. I give her Barbadian food, rice and peas, chicken, fish, fruit. Basically tell her where my parents have come from. The roots, as it were. Just give her an idea of where I've come from and where she's partly from. She's been to Barbados. She's got the basics. She remembers the food, she remembers my grandmother.

I think, deep down, my parents wanted me to marry a black girl. But when we moved to Redditch, we wasn't in the right environment, there was no black people around. How can they expect me to mix with black girls? They put me in that position! Then when my parents went back, I felt strange. My grandmother went, my parents went, my sister went and I'm thinking, 'My family's gone!' But I thought, 'I've got my own family', with my daughter and my wife at the time. I miss them, though, to be perfectly frank with you. I appreciate time with them. And I've got uncles and aunts and cousins in Birmingham. I see my aunt every week, if I want anything, they're there for me, and they ring me.

I wouldn't be tempted to live in Barbados. It's very slow. The people are very, very slow and the way of life is, period, very slow. I couldn't relate to that. I think being a black British going out there I wouldn't feel too comfortable either. They look at you and think, 'You're black, yes,' then they think, 'You're British, and you've got money.' Perhaps somewhere else in the world, America, Canada. My father's got some relatives in that part of the world. If I had the opportunity, I'd like to go. Even Europe, perhaps. I don't know what I want to do. I want to stay with my daughter until she's sorted out but I've got no real ties here and with my parents back in Barbados, I can do practically anything. I can't say I'm British, but I'm black. Obviously, I feel proud that my father's from that part of the world. When people don't know me, they ask me if I was born here, or in Barbados or Jamaica. I feel bad about that because I don't really like being related to the Jamaicans, their attitudes and their ignorance. As a rule, they seem to have a chip on their shoulder as regards to life. They call us Small Islanders. They think Jamaica is a bigger island, they think they're bigger and better. But being they're black, we relate to each other, especially in a town you don't know, just because a person's black, you acknowledge them. But the people I mix with, like my cousin, my best mate, they're Bajan/ Kittician, so we just hang around each other, so the Jamaicans don't bother us. I only relate to Barbados.

Notes

1   The plantation yard, where she worked.

10 | Family Four

Herman was born in 1917. Like his parents, and great grandparents he was an agricultural labourer all his life. He has
always lived in Barbados, with the exception of a brief time
working in the United States. His younger brother, Roy, went
regularly to the United States, and he had a number of uncles
and aunts who had migrated there. He and his wife have one
child, their son Vernon, who was the first of this family to
come to England. Herman also had a daughter from another
partner, who was brought up by his wife.

My mother was a very hard-working peasant of Barbados. Very poor,
but very honest. She worked at various estate plantation, heading cane,
working, cutting bush. She worked in gangs. She gave birth for eight
children. Three die. My father lose one of his legs at the age of nineteen.
He had a strong body and he rear all of us with that one leg. He work on
an estate. He watch, he drove mule cart, and then he had a freight cart.
He also was supervisor in the road. He had what they call a wooden foot,
a peg. On one occasion he and another fella been in a race, and my father
won. And even at times, if he want to hit either one of us, he could leap
and catch either one of us even if we was running.

My father married to my mother in 1929. Well, of course, we was
born already. I know (all) my grandparents, but I didn't know my father
father because he die when I was quite small. Agriculture. All in agriculture. You see, under the colonialism in those years, certain rules, we find
it tough, very tough. Things were not so bright. Work hard, small wages.
That was a very oppressive time. When I know my mother, she was
renting house. She rent house till 1934, then my father bought this place.
But I come along a very poor boy.

My father rent land but in those days there was such restriction on
the estate and watchman would soon turn. You couldn't raise your
stocks. You get a bit of grass they will haul you and carry you in the yard
and the manager would send you to the station, convict you. You didn't
raise too many animals in those days. He plant yams, potatoes, grains
and so on. Six type of corn we had. Cane corn, Indian corn. We took it

to the mill and we get some flour to help boil coo coo and dumplings and bakes. That's the most he does get. No money. You couldn't get all that you would eat. Mother was so poor she couldn't feed us as she like. Some nights, you go to sleep hungry because small wages and many of us. She couldn't feed us as we like, so we did hungry, and that's that. Many times she has somethings, she give it to us, she do without. I know on many occasions that been asleep with no food whatsoever. She didn't have to give us it, tears in her eyes. Yes, I been through all of that. So that's the reason why I give God the glory, thank Him for the change and this present day.

We ate off calabash. Wasn't no stove. Pot. Nothing over it whatsoever. When it rain, it was terrible. No food. You used to have to cook something with trash, or go in the hill, get bit of backgrowing, wood or so on. The facilities is far better now but before, before Mr. Errol Walton Barrow took up the government, it was not so. In those days, you could get regular employment but no money for it. Half the time. You work every day from morning till night, regular employment, but no money. Pay you just small wages. The only sense we had, the Barbados Workers Union, that fight to increase. It would start up in the early 1940s and then, in time, things raise. And that is how we see the people in Barbados. Everybody is very, very, very flat. No clothes. If you got pants, you got more patches than crease. You couldn't tell the colour of the pants, you have so many different patterns. You eat meal from the bag, your parent tie the bag and wash them, and get a seamstress to make a suit for that. You had to wear to school that and when you come home on Friday, take off and wash it, cor didn't had the second suit. Never wear shoes, not until I was the age of seventeen. She didn't able to give us not even a pair of pump, for sixty cents, she didn't able. So the first pair of shoes that I put on my feet, at the age of seventeen, I import from England. We blend together, a group of us, and send away for this. Twelve of us boys. I want a pair of shoes, another want a pair and so on. If the shoe ten shillings at that time, we gave one man this shilling, the other fella, he give him, then he had a certain amount to send.

We all slept on the floor. The mother didn't had beds. We had bags, that bring rice in, that would be our mattresses. On Christmas, you will go to beg the managers for bit of grass to put in the mattress. They only allow you a certain amount, because grass at that time was very valuable to the estate, so they used to don't give it away so easy. Mother was strict, and very proud for it too. Fetch water. Long journey, because sometime you have to go in the spring, sometimes go in the pond. We was under all obligation to help in the land. Nor we couldn't abuse people. My father was so strict that he wouldn't allow us to visit other people home. We couldn't run about so. Always under control. If any person see a child going astray at that time, (they) would go up to the parent and complain. Some people would whip you and then tell the parent what happen. I was always told that all men is of God, regardless of your colour. So I was taught to respect all. I had the concept that is the will of God that the white man should have the riches in his hand rather than have the black. This is not a belief. This is what I know. I was brought up mostly Pilgrim Holiness.

I went to elementary school. Was one penny per week, but that penny per week was as hard as going up the hill Golgotha where Jesus travel. Mother tried to send us all to school, but it was very hard. A penny. The teachers was very strict. One day, in the second standard, I was reading from a book called *The Graphic Reader*. I couldn't get the word 'breathe'. The teacher beat me very badly, so I promise that if I grew up to a man, I would beat him and so, years after, one day, I met he. I says, 'Stop. You were my teacher.' He say, 'Yes.' I say, 'You beat me very badly at school and I going to beat you now.' So he said, 'Before you hit me, wait. I would like to ask you a few questions.' I said, 'Alright.' He said, 'Can you write?' I say, 'Yes.' 'Can you read?' I say, 'Yes.' 'Can any person fool you easily?' I say, 'No.' He said, 'That what I done for you.' And my heart melt, and I have to beg him a million pardon for using such words to him.

Eight years of age, went to work. This was in the vacation time now. A very small boy, at the age of eight, for five cents a day, picking grass, or beetle. You pick beetle by the pint. A shilling for this pint. But it's a time before you will get a pint. It was very rough, very hard. I did pick these beetle in the day time, early upon a morning. In the day time, beetle lay about. A shilling. It meant a lot in those days, when I was a boy. I was under all obligation to give my mother the money. We couldn't do what we like with it. I could only do as I like with my money after I decide to court this lady here. At twelve, my father did take me from school and carry me to work with this yoke of oxen, to an estate. I lead the oxen that very crop season. One ox did name Rowen, and one ox did name Bourne. You would say, 'High, Rowen, back, Bourne.' At the end I went to another estate. Weeding, forking, digging cane hole and so on. Wherever things look a little better, I would go. I been as far as estate in St. Andrew. Six, seven miles, walk that evening, or sleep over. And it was all of my work until the last six years of my working days. I worked the school meal programme, but my whole life was agriculture.

I met my wife one night, going to practice for a Service of Song. I had the opportunity to let her know how much I love her, it was a burning love in my heart for her. She was just seventeen, I was nineteen.

We was going to the church, it was a biblical teaching from the bible. If you really want to serve God and if you love different people, you should marry. And therefore we marry, at that early age. We had our problems, we ask God to help us. I was only earning three dollars a week. In those days, it didn't take so much money for a wedding. You will take enough ground provisions. People was more loving and liberal. They would give you. So two poor people, we marry, we didn't had no money. We had no chairs, we didn't had this and that, but we still marry. We rent a house. Twelve cents a week. One room. Then we rent thirty cents a week. Then we rent two shillings a week until God help us to get a little place and we didn't had to pay no rent.

1946 I went on the emigration to Florida, weeding grass, cutting cane plants. I didn't stay long there, about five months. The money was good, but not sufficient. They want to do excessive work, but they ent increasing the money. I didn't agree with that, so that means that I had to come home. We live in a camp. It wasn't so good because over a thousand of us were there, Barbadians, Jamaicans. You had some things, chinks,[1] and mosquito like giants. On nights, you may put on a light and you see the chinks crawling round like soldiers and their eyes staring at you. I didn't make so much money, I didn't so fortunate to bring back no money. I came back as I went.

Before I went I was superintendent (on the estate) I came back and go up to another estate and work there for fifteen years, as a superintendent. Vernon was born in 1937. The riot break out the month after he born, and my mother tell me I was born in a riot year, too. 1917 was a riot year. The riot, mentally, it affect me. People who I knew, they lose their life. Millions regret to see that they live to see such happen, when they look on the bodies of some that get shot. The police coming through with guns and firing off at people. People were suffering. Small wages and at that time they didn't getting very little work. But it brought out some good, because then they had a Commission and then from this is the results of the Union. 'Cause the working class was working and ent getting enough wages and that was what brought this on. Somebody lose a life so that others might live.

But I never think that I would wish agriculture for my son. Although, in agriculture, it is something good in a sense, but the wages was small, so my wife and I decide that, despite our condition, we had no money, I would decide to send our son to a secondary school under all condition. And so we did. We had no money. We send him to school because God keep our health up. We simply send him to school, offer our health, not money. He was fortunate to win a scholarship but was rob out of it. This was what you call a Vestry scholarship. But it was favouritism, and he won it but the scholarship given to another boy. We pay every cent. It was nine dollars and sixty cents a quarter. I will have to ask God now to tell you how we pay. He help us along that line. So poor, no money, but we had the will and He help us. That's the only way that I could answer, cor we had to pay every cent. Had to buy books, everything. Lunch. Clothes. But God help us. The glorious God. The honour is to Him. Nothing to us.

Vernon did well. He never fail an exam all through school. So then he leave school, his years was up in 1955. He say he want to go to England. I didn't have the money, but I borrow and he leave us at the age of eighteen. I can't describe my feelings to know that, so young, and going somewhere he don't know people, wondering what would befall of him also. But there's one gentleman who was down there. I send and ask him to receive him and so he did. He didn't have to wander about nor nothing. But it was terrible with both of us to know the only son we have leave at that age.

> Born in 1937, Vernon lives with his wife, a Barbadian, in South London. He came to Britain in 1955 and he and his wife bought their house in 1968, when they married. They have no children. Vernon was the first of the family to 'go down', preceding his uncle Roy by a few months, his cousin Beryl and his cousin Beulah by a few years. Vernon was brought up Pilgrim Holiness. At the age of eleven, he won a scholarship to a secondary school but this place was reallocated to another child, who was an Anglican. He eventually secured his place at secondary school through the help of a member of the Parish Vestry, who was also the local Barbados Labour Party MP, for whom Herman worked on a voluntary basis. This man 'had all this influence ... and the system was that lots of people, like my father, were kind of unpaid workers for these people politically ... and if you supported a party, these people would tend to look after you. Apart from this religious side to it, if the local MP was really interested they would push you in that regard.'

We had a very poor house, what you would call a shack, really. I was brought up Pilgrim Holiness, in that sort of religious atmosphere. I wasn't allowed to swear. I had to be polite to people in the streets. If you meet a neighbour, and everybody in Barbados is a neighbour, you had to greet them. You had to be particular about the way you conduct yourself in public. You had to be careful of your clothes, our books, our pens. They were all expensive. I had to help. My parents would leave home early in the morning and from an early age I would have to do things, come home evening and go and get shopping. I may even cook for them before they come home maybe eight, or half-past eight. We had no toys. Things like cricket balls, we had to knit them ourselves, get a stone, wrap it in rags and then twine and knit this ball until it was a solid thing. That's how people like Garfield Sobers started. Make kites, play warri, dig the holes in the ground. We never had sophisticated toys, only the white people, the more wealthy people, had those. I had to do my homework by a little paraffin lamp. We had no electricity. The school regime was pretty tough and we were poor people who had nothing. We had no books. We would borrow from the library, and swap them around.

I came to England on the 14th November 1955 at the age of eighteen. When I was in the fourth form at school there was all this going on about the immigration of Jamaicans to England so when I left school I decided I'm not going to hang about in Barbados because, at that time, one had to wait quite a little while before you could pick up a job. So I decided I would just come to England. You regarded it as some kind of opportunity. The concept of coming to England took over from the old opportunity system where Barbadians used to go to the United States. My father went to the States, cut canes in Florida, working for a three-year contract or a five-year contract and come back home. My uncle Roy, he spent a lot of time in America, and my mother's brother. Barbadians are great migrators, you know. You will find a Barbadian anywhere in the world. Barbadians just have this one thing of moving out, all the time. Then the opportunity to come to England blossomed. Lots of people, girls and boys, coming to England as nurses and bus conductors, working on the railway, working at Lyons. Do you remember Lyons? The tea shops? It didn't matter what you were doing, it was a break to get away. Of course, this sort of thing was very helpful to the island. These people coming out were making room for new people. It also worked the reverse way. A lot of money was going back into the economy in Barbados. Some people, like me, had the idea that I'd be back in five years. Some fellas came up here, were able to do a degree part-time in five or six years, and went home.

I had no idea what I was going to do. But you know, in Barbados, people regard the outside world as wealthy. They always go to places like the States which are developed countries. We never heard anything bad said about any of these countries. In the case of Britain, nothing was said. There weren't any adverse things being said.

As I said, at that time, there was this euphoria, people willing to take a chance. I was only eighteen. I had only just left school. I had never worked. It just came into my head, like that. Everybody was going to England. My friends, all the people I grew up with, they were leaving, so it just came into my head. I wasn't sponsored by London Transport. I just told my father I wanted to come to England and he agreed. He didn't have the money and went to see this MP who helped him, financially, and with references, that sort of thing. We booked the journey to England, got the passports and so ready. My parents prepared everything and the night before I left there was a little party. As a party, as you would have it, it was a very poor affair. We couldn't afford any drinks, any rum. We didn't have any records. We just made local eats, and sang hymns, to a sort of marine theme. All my friends came around, wish me goodbye, and it was very, very sad.

I left Barbados in the evening and boarded ship. The first time I had ever been on a ship in my life. They were mainly Barbadians, but one or two Jamaicans or Trinidadians got on elsewhere. We felt pretty terrible. There were new diets to us. But we involve ourselves, making our own entertainment to make sure that our spirits didn't sink. We didn't dwell on the experience of leaving home because, don't forget, in a way it was a kind of hope as well. We were like pioneers, really. I landed in Plymouth on the 14th November and the first thing that struck me was the awful cold, and the smog, and these little terraced houses. Coming up on the train, we were wondering what they were. We knew a lot about sixteenth, and seventeenth and eighteenth century England, because we were taught it, and we had seen films on the mobile cinema about Britain. A lot of films about the war.

I had some one here to meet me, from my village. He received me here. He was also receiving his cousin, that was sort of like my friend. He took me to Streatham. They were living in a double room with a Jamaican family and got a single room for me and my friend. He and his wife had to look after me quite considerably because when I came I had about ten pounds in cash to tide me over. If I hadn't been sent to somebody like him, who actually knew my parents, who had an interest in making sure my welfare was okay, I could have suffered immensely. Because you had nothing. I knew no one. I stayed with him for about two months. In those days, the Jamaicans held sway as far as accommodation was concerned. The whites wouldn't let you accommodation so most of it was controlled by Jamaicans who had been out here ten years before, had bought houses and let them out in rooms, three or four in a room, you living like flies in these places in those days. I mean, they were pretty horrible. Lots of Jamaicans, they were very unscrupulous. They exploited, and we had to put up with it. There were frequent rows in these little rooms. If you wanted to have a bath, there was only one. You had to put your sixpence in and then somebody would come and use it! Looking back, you had to sympathise with them. We were all struggling, you see.

Arriving November brought me right into Christmas, first Christmas ever spent away from home. What happen, one evening me and my friend were walking and we met a West Indian gentleman. He saw us just walking in the cold. We had nothing on. We had no coats. We just had like little pullovers on, windcheater, the old style West Indian felt hats that we used to import from England, and our trousers, in the old Zoot fashion. This man, he came from Barbados, he noticed us and he realised that we were West Indians and he stopped and talked to us, invited us over to his home in Balham and we spent that Christmas with him and his family. He sort of took us in, like he adopted us. He had been here from the days of the RAF, during the war. I subsequently went to live with him and we stayed with them for about three years and other West Indians came and stayed. We had like a big family there. I enjoyed my time with him immensely. He introduced us to the League of Coloured People, which is defunct now. Every Saturday night, we used to go to this place. We met other West Indians, we used to dance, calypsos, the old, real old-fashioned calypsos, Lord Kitchener and so on. Many of the people there were students, from the West Indian Student Union. Or sometimes, they had all these West Indian girls at all the hospitals, and they wanted to meet boys. We used to live for this sort of thing. You might get somebody go to a hospital and say some young ladies at this hospital want to meet some boys, and you would go down there at the weekend. That sort of thing would go on for years and then gradually the girls, and the boys, got married off and the social pattern changed. But you had to do special things to meet people in those days because you were new. The indigenous people didn't accept you readily, they regard you as an intruder.

It took me ages before I got a job because I was not skilled in anything. I just had a formal education. I remember having to sign on to the Labour Exchange. That was very traumatic. I found a lot of problems with jobs. There was some kind of discrimination because people didn't want to accept my Oxford and Cambridge Certificates, even though they were corrected in this country and the system was the same. I had to find manual work, as a kitchen porter at a biscuit factory. When I eventually left I applied to the Civil Service, for a clerical officer – and I was called up in the army! See, we were British subjects, under the old colonial system, and we were eligible for anything. That surprised me in that a lot of things that we applied for here, they were denied us at the time. I had to go in the army. So, rather than going there as a conscript, I signed up for six years. This was about 1960. I was posted to Hong Kong, and then a local posting in London. Imagine me, even when I was in the army, I had just as good 'O' levels as some of my English comrades and the intake with me were selected for Officer grades and I wasn't. That was one of the things that make me decide to come out because I saw it wasn't fair at all. I bought myself out. It cost twelve pounds. And then when I came out, I still couldn't get a clerical job, so had to do different manual jobs again, factories, that sort of thing. I applied then to the Post Office. At the time, it was still in the Civil Service and it was then that I did get in to the Civil Service, and have been there since.

But things were very hard at first. You know you had to send money home to your parents. They were expecting this. People were working two, three, four years before they could save anything, because they had to pay back what they came with. This is the kind of background we had, not only home, but here as well. Then you had to keep yourself in clothes. There was a firm in Brixton that used to do a kind of credit thing, salesmen who used to visit all these West Indians. They would take maybe two shillings a week, and that way you were able to buy clothes, shoes, and eventually you could buy furniture from them. I remember that's the way I had to live, for about seven years, till eventually I found myself a bit more independent financially and could go and buy things out of a store. If I were able at the time to get a better job, in keeping with the sort of education I had, it would have made a significant difference.

When I first came here my plans were that I would try and take a degree in economics, and go back home. But I never do a degree. I found out that you would have been over-educated for the jobs you were given to do. I stuck it out but I feel that if I had been treated a bit more fairly here I could have done a lot better. There's all sorts of things we found out here that, had we known, we wouldn't have come. It was pretty rough in the fifties. First, you give yourself a five-year plan, and then it went to ten-year plan and then fifteen-year plan and when you get to about twenty years, you give up altogether. In the background of your mind you're always hoping that this miraculous opportunity for you to go back home will turn up. Everybody hopes to go back to their place of birth. I'm saying I'm going back home whenever I retire. But circumstances change. I understand there's a lot of crime there. I have to take all that into account. I'll be getting old. You don't want to go back somewhere where you don't have the strength to fend for yourself. Your parents will probably be dead. Lots of your relatives will be dead. I have to look at things in that light. They don't have the social welfare structure at home like they have here. I've contributed into the system, I can stay here till I die, and probably be well looked after. I have to look at it in that light, whether I can afford to go home and gamble on that.

You don't know what kind of health you will gain in that time. Although I'm hopeful that I will go back to Barbados and I'm yearning, I haven't lived there. I'm virtually an Englishman. I've lived thirty-seven years here. I cannot count the eighteen years I live in Barbados. I would be more terrified to walk around in Barbados now than I would to walk around here. Nobody would care anything about me now, they regard me as a foreigner. I have to look at things in that light.

> Louise is Herman's sister-in-law. She was born in 1923 and worked as an agricultural labourer until ill-health forced her to leave the land and open a small shop. Her father died when she was ten years old, and her mother when she was a young woman. As a result, as well as bringing up her two children by herself, she also raised her youngest brother, and provided a home to a younger sister. Both her children and her nephew migrated to England. Louise married after the children left.

My father die in 1934 leaving six of us. The last little boy was four months old. Well, then, my mother she had to go out to work. And I, being the second eldest, my sister, Herman's wife, she was the eldest and she was already working, I was ten years old and I used to have to stay home from school then to keep house and the little boy. My mother, she would had a cow and she would milk it and we would take the milk and scald it, and you would pick some garden balsam and wash it and put it in the milk. It had a very sweet taste. People say it did cooling but it used to be good and during the day we would go at that milk. Or she would cook potatoes and salt fish, or yam and salt fish and we, all during the day, would always got that to eat. We used to eat out of something called conaree, a bowl, made out of clay. It used to come down from St. Andrew selling them. When I see the baby crying or anything so, I give it milk. So I would feed it and time to sleep would carry it to sleep in my mother bed. I look after the little boy save when I was working in a little gang, picking grass. My grandmother used to keep the little boy for that time. Then about twelve years old, I had to went to work, in the third-class gang.

We live on my father land. His father had this amount of land so he share it up between his children and give them all a little some. He did Panama, and buy the land and my father house put on that land. Things wasn't so expensive as it is now. People would give. Any family was in to plant yams and corn and other people were not, and if I got corn and you ent got none, I would give you some. If you got yam and I got none, you would give me some. That is how we used to live down inside there.

It didn't so much of borrowing, they would give you, if they know you want.

We didn't a lot of clothes. We would go to school and thing barefoot but we always had a pair of pumps to go to Sunday School. My mother was an Anglican, then the last three years of her life she was a Pilgrim Holiness. My grandmother was an Adventist.

That time we did go to school at five. I had to leave at ten, but I reach fourth standard. And went to work at twelve. The first day I went, I had a basket and you would have to pack the plants. The person who was bringing the third-class,[2] she wait till I done pack the plant and she lash me. I stand up and cry. A watchman there, he and my father was first cousins, my father used to do the watching, after my father die, he got the job. He come in, he tell me you stand up and watch me, so I watch him as he does pack it. He say when you come back now you be able to do it, so when I come back now, I could manage it, because I didn't want no more lashes. I get twelve cents a day. I been in the third-class gang till I must be big, about fifteen, and went working with the big people, heading cane, for eighteen cent a day. Then I leave the third-class gang and went tending mason. A carpenter build a tray for me, my mother gave me a pair of pumps, that the cement mortar and lime would not cut your feet. You would carry the mason tools, carry the buckets, for twenty cents.

I left then and work back on the estate, weeding and so on, but that was when I catch up with trouble, my first child, by the manager, a white man. My mother didn't know anything about it not until she found out I was pregnant. Somebody tell her. She ask me if it were true. I tell her, 'Yes.' She ask me who it were. I tell her. And she started to cry. She say to me, 'I going to make sure you telling me the truth.' She carry me to him. He say, 'Well, I can't sure, but I believe.' At that time, I would had to say I love him. But she wouldn't let me go on, she say, no, you can't go on with that. I was seventeen. He was twenty-seven. But he help with the child. I had the baby home and then, you know, my mother did like it.

I stay home a certain time then I went back to work, agriculture. I work a little time and then my daughter there, myself and her father getting great, and then I was with her. She was born in 1943, Beryl's father left her eight months old and went down to Trinidad. He send money a certain time and then after he get tie up with marriage and so on, he stop supporting her. My mother look after my children and a sister that I had home, my mother last daughter. I work till 1955, when Janet,[3] I stop working agriculture at that time and I was up here keeping shop. I had a house with a shed roof and I start with the two children. The three of us used to run the shop, they used to make mauby, they used to ginger beer, they used to lemonade. I used to make fishcakes, go to Speightstown for coconuts, and a man would bring down bread three times a week to sell.

My son went to secondary school. He father used to give me money every month. Then the two of them went in England, my son in April and Beryl in November, the same year, 1961. I pay and help send them both. We all work as one with the shop and I promise that whatever, if there's anything, I would spend some on them. They wanted to go. I said, well, if they go and they make it, it will be alright, but if they don't make it, they must work for as much as would pay the fare to come back. It wasn't a lot of nothing to pack, just only the clothes. I pack a suitcase for them, and Vernon's mother give him a box, and the box did heavy, with something to take for Vernon. Vernon receive all two of them.

I used to cry every day, when I used to put the food, I used to cry, say I want them, I wonder if, how they is getting through and so on. My husband he used to tell me, 'I can't understand, you send them over to England and now crying, constant crying, crying, crying.'

> Beryl is Vernon's first cousin. She was born in 1942. Her father went to Trinidad shortly after her birth, and she did not meet him again until an adult. She came to England in 1961. She was met by Vernon on arrival and lived with him until she moved into her own accommodation with her boyfriend, whom she married in 1968. She has four children. In 1980, they moved into a council house. Her husband is now unemployed. Beryl worked first as a machinist, and then in administration. She now does a school crossing patrol.

Lots of children grew up without their fathers, I don't hold it against my father because, travelling now, I can understand why it probably went the way it was with him being abroad. But I still felt part of his family. They told me I looked like them, anyway! I think they felt duty-bound because I was so much like them. My grandmother would loan anything she had, and my uncle would help. He's a dentist in America now, he was fairly well educated and he would come round and make sure I did my homework, make sure I'm doing well.

My brother's father looked after him. He looked after his education, and he used to support him weekly. When I won a place at secondary school, because my mother was on her own, she couldn't afford it. I lost out there. My brother's father send him, because he was able to. I badly wanted to go to secondary school. I suffered in that way.

I really want to learn shorthand and typing and she said she couldn't afford that either. So I was stuck in her shop till I came to England.

By then I started to see a boyfriend. She didn't like that one bit. So protective, I suppose, something like that. Then he came up to England. People were emigrating to England. Vernon was here. My uncle was there, too. My mother had her new found husband and she asked my brother if he wanted to come to England, and she just asked me if I wanted to go. I felt I had the opportunity then, of the education that I wanted. Then I suppose, my boyfriend was there, I thought, 'Well, there's an ideal opportunity.' She probably thought, 'Well, England is very big, ' I think she didn't think probably, he was so far away that I probably wouldn't see him!

A number of people had come abroad anyway. The jobs in Barbados were very selective, and they had this thing about not employing too dark a person. Barbados was then run by your top white people and you had to be very fair to really get through. I felt I couldn't make it. But I had no idea what England was like. All I knew that this England was paved with gold, and it's the Mother Country, that's what we were ever taught, because we were still under British rule. I hadn't the faintest idea what it was like. My boyfriend never spoke of it. My brother never talked about it. I suppose it might sort of put off people. I just said, 'Yes,' and came over on the *Sorriento*, with my flannelette pyjamas and a tailored jacket. I still love that jacket, it was nice and warm and good, and I made the skirt.

The ship docked at Southampton and Vernon and my brother met me here. I didn't even know where I was. It was night, it was winter. I think they came to Queen's Road Station. They're walking, but I was just following them, I didn't know where I was going. I didn't know anything till the following day I got up. Seeing the family again was my first thought, and seeing my boyfriend. I felt that I'd come from somewhere and away from the mother, and all that restricted area. I was glad for the freedom. Seeing them again, I was ecstatic. I felt I was still home because I'd come to, and I'd found my family.

They brought me to Peckham. They had a flat, three rooms, a basement flat. But it was scary in the night. Once the lights went off, you used to hear these funny noises. It was very scary for me, for the first weeks. My brother used to work shift-work and if they're working nights, I was all by myself. The bed was by the window, and I didn't like that one bit. When they're working, that's when I creep into their bed.

Because I had Vernon and my brother, I settled a little bit better. I felt if I was on my own, I would never have settled easy. I managed to settle in the end. But I had to, because I didn't have the fare to get back. I thought it was horrible. The buildings were dirty, and the streets with all the dog mess. It's such a different way of life to get used to, that it didn't really seem to be the right place for me. And people kissing in the street. Oh, that was very, very nasty to me! They were very discreet with their kissing and thing in Barbados, but here is people kissing and cuddling up and things, under trees, and on the buses. It looked really, really rude. And they eat fish and chips out of paper, newspaper. I felt it was a bit primitive. At least those kinds of things we never did. It was things about that you would respect yourself for. And a basement flat, too. You couldn't really see anywhere. There was no daylight. I came in the heart of winter, it was just too dark to me. I have to stop and think a couple of times, 'Was this made for me?' You know, with this dark area, these dark places and this cold. It was truly cold. We were wrapped up all day and all night. I have to say, it was dreadful.

I didn't want to make mother feel bad, 'cos I know that she would worry and so we just wrote the usual, and, 'We okay,' and, 'We both fine,' and, 'It's cold' and things like that. But we never really told her that it was that bad. We never did, because she probably would pine and worry and think that it was her fault for sending us. No, we never let her know.

I didn't get my first job, as a machinist, until the New Year, but the pay was very, very small. Then after time went by, you get to know the place, and I can shop around. So I had numerous dress-making jobs in Aldgate, until I fell pregnant with my eldest son. I went into finishing work then. But I really was interested in doing nursing because I felt at least it's a career, a better career. But I was pregnant. I would have to find someone to keep the baby day and night, and Vernon said they don't train people in London, I would have to go to the country. And then to go up in the country, to be learning, away by yourself, the others here in Peckham, have to make friends, find people to be with, that didn't seem too right. So I abandoned the idea.

When we had my son we moved. Going round, looking for rooms, or whatever to rent, you know, 'Vacancy for room or flat to let'. Well, by the time you got there, they just slammed the door. Those were the first signs of prejudice that I've experienced. They opened and they slammed the door. And you go back to that same lot two days later, and the room is still there, or the flat is still vacant. That's where the prejudice really hit home. That was low, and that was from the heart. But I suppose you have to put it behind you and try to move on, you can't really let it pull you down. It's fortunate that, most times, you come across black people that were here before, had a home, and they would let you a room.

Because I was young and fit, I felt you had the will and strength to carry on. You see, a lot of us coming here when we're young helped us a lot. I used to find it in the shops as well. People didn't want to serve you, they never touch your hand. Even when I was working in Shell and I delivered the mail and the man in the sorting room, his hand brushed mine and he said, 'But your hands are soft!' So I said, 'What do you expect?' Because I was black, my skin was probably tough like nails.

My son was born in 1962. We lived first in the same house with Vernon. It was owned by a Greek, and we lived on the top. Then my boyfriend found another room, a bigger space. We shared kitchen. Throughout the whole time, wherever we moved, we shared a kitchen. You just get a room, and the kitchen, on the landing. Awful, Oh my God! A shilling a time for the gas, and you put in that shilling and by the time you've put that in, somebody else come in and start cooking. We had to share the bath, the toilets. We shared all the amenities except the room we live in, everything in that one room. But the sharing was awful, really. Some weeks it used to cause a lot of arguments with people. We used to even go to the public baths to bathe, you could get a big tub of water and be in there as long as you like. We'd go there every Saturday and have a decent bath. It was like Heaven!

1971 – eleven years later – we got our own place. I had all the children then, four of them. We had to go to the Council then. They had this house, a half-way house, for down and outs. My husband said, 'No,' he's not taking his children there, he's got more respect than that. We had a social worker and she got the children in a nursery school and the Council managed to give us a place down Rotherhithe. The girls shared a room, and the boys shared a room and we had our own room, we had a kitchen and living-room, and it was all to ourselves. When I got my own kitchen, I'm telling you, that was like Heaven. I could then cook when I want, cook how I like, it was like you were somebody now. You now became somebody. Before you were just a person, but you were nobody, you were just a bare frame of a person.

The children were happy and the school was just across the road. But they had a little factory not far away from there, and two of the children got lead in their blood. I kept going to the doctor, but he wasn't able to do anything. It was only after some other families had the problem and they checked. We, the whole group of them, tried to take the council to court. It was a dead loss. I think today, if it happened, it would be a much stronger fight. But at that time the money was not there to fight a council with the money they had.

The council had to get us out, but they were nasty. They move all the other people that had to move into nice accommodation. When come our turn, they move us in a old block. It was dreadful. My husband just went for them. My daughter had lost a lot of her teeth and her hair and she was just sleeping all the time. Eventually, they moved us on to North

Peckham, central heating, overflowing water. It was only luck that got us from down there because that lead got into the children's bloodstream. They were under specialist care at the hospital for a long time. But when we got here, that was a lot better. They all began to be a lot healthier and started to grow then.

But we had people upstairs who used to make so much noise, and the accommodation was small. I had to go up every day to the council, had to make a lot of noise, go up there every day at the office, every day with some complaints. I told them, 'I don't want any maisonette, I don't want any flat. I want a house.' We had to battle against the council. That's where some of the prejudice that we felt came in as well. We move down here, to this house, in 1980. But we battled to come this far. It's only by the strength and health that has got us this far, really, because if you had sat back and let it get to you, it would have drove you back downhill and you'd be down there forever. You would have cracked up.

And again, the schools didn't do well for the children. You always heard of England, the education and the universities that they have here. Our papers used to come up there to be marked, from back home. I couldn't change the system myself, but with us backing them up, and pushing them a little bit more, we got them where they are. My kids know the standard of education in Barbados is very high. When we went back in 1975, they went to school in Barbados for a while, and that's when they knew it was high. But they have to accept the system here, and do their best. When they were all here in the evening, we used to have our evening discussions on the Sunday, after we have our meal, we sit round the table and chat and chat, just sit and laugh. Today, they are loving children, and they're good, and they've done their best, and the education as it was here for they, they use it. They all did very well, really. One works for the Post Office, another is a service engineer, one works in a lab, and one works for an airline.

I went back to work when the youngest was eleven, part-time. My husband was on shift work so, between us, we were always home and around with them. They were never by themselves. I felt the children were well cared for. I knew that you can't really have children and don't care for them. I feel very, very strong about that. I feel very, very strong about children not having their parents with them, and not be there with them when they need them. I don't know if because that I did not have my father, but I felt that no way that my children would be the same. They should have a father to be there for them. I love children, come what may, and I love the two grandchildren I've got dearly, and I feel very close to them as well. One spends every weekend with us. Children is our tomorrow, and we should care for them.

I think I've had enough of England. I think it would be better to get back now and get the sun in our bones. If health stand by us, I'm definintely looking forward to going back to Barbados. I think it's time to retire. The hardest trouble to get over is the children, not seeing them as you used to. I suppose you know they're well. But, as I told you before, that when I write to my mother I never used to tell her that so and so is a problem, not to keep her all the time worrying. I feel they'll do just the same.

England would be a better place if there wasn't so much discrimination, that's the truth. I just hope that some of the things that happen to us don't happen to them, because I don't think they would take it as lightly. They can only inherit Barbados, but they were actually born here. Let's hope it gets better, not worse because if it gets any worse, it will be very sad for a lot of us people here, and my children might be caught up in it. These shores are really rough shores.

> David is Beryl's second son. He was born in 1966 in South London, and works as a service engineer. He is single, with one child and lives 'ninety-eight per cent' with his girlfriend and 'two per cent' with his sister, with whom he bought a flat.

My father was more strict than my mother. When you get older, you realise it was for the best, and there's nothing wrong with the way he brought you up, because you tend to carry it down in the way you're teaching your kids now. I can see the exact thing, how my mother and father brought me up. Roles sort of come up. They were strict about everything. We didn't play out every day. He would say, 'Come and read a book,' 'Go in our room and learn the times tables,' and then come back and recite it to him. Our parents seemed to be that more stricter than the other children on the estate. I used to sit at the window sometimes and watch the kids running out to play. Every Sunday, we used to go to Sunday School, used to dress up smart, a little tie, and all that.

They didn't talk much about Barbados. They would draw a reference sometimes, like if we misbehave, 'If I was back home now, you wouldn't get away with that.' As we got older, you could understand that they weren't brought up here, they were brought up in the West Indies, and we asked more questions, say, 'Oh, what was it like going to school?' Because then we understood more. When we was young, we couldn't say, we didn't really care, all we wanted to do was go out and play.

We actually went to school down in the West Indies for a little while, and we could see the difference in the schooling. I was eight. I didn't like the school, but I loved Barbados. I mean, we was allowed to go out and play. It was brilliant. I've always loved Barbados. But when we had to go to school I remember the kids taunting me and saying, 'English potato,' and 'English this ...' I remember, I run home from school. I ran across the fields all the way back home. The fact that I was English. I just took to my heels and I came along home. My mum sent me all the way back to school. I didn't want to stay! I cried my heart out! It seemed too tough for me.

I remember that first visit. When we got in, I kept thinking to myself, 'It's just huts.' That's what we were saying to ourselves, 'It's just huts, look at these huts.' We stayed at my grandmother's. She was a stern lady, but she took to me. She was a lovely woman. I met lots of family members. In Barbados, you have a lot of families and you seem to find that a lot of the people that are around you are your relations. It was good meeting them. I've been to Barbados a total of about five times now. You asked more then. It was only about two days ago I actually asked my dad how the war affected Barbados. I mean, I know this is going back some, and it's coming off track a bit, but that's getting to the point of me being inquisitive, as I'm getting older. I never even thought to ask that question until the other day. As you're getting older, you ask more questions. When I was younger, I used to ask my dad about his girlfriends, or his school, or where did you live. Or why they left Barbados. They said, workwise, it was better for them to come over here. I suppose there was gold on the road, as well. That was the answer they gave me. I asked them, 'Well, why didn't you go to America? We could have been American!' 'Because they had American accents.' They said there were some going to America, and there were some going to England, and they decided to come to England. A lot of their friends and relations came over here as well. We have got a few family here. Really close ones.

I enjoyed my junior school more than secondary school. It was more relaxing. The pressures started coming on in the secondary school. I was bullied for about three years, by one particular guy. I can always remember being so keen to learn, he took that excitement out. It wasn't a racially motivated thing, because he would pick on black and white. It took me to the third year for me to hit back, and then the bullying was over. The school I went to, in my first year, was about thirty per cent black but going up after that there was only, like one or two black at the school. As youngsters, all we knew was that the white guys above were NF. That was the general term for someone that didn't like black. But it wasn't deep-rooted bullying, constant picking on you. It was more like a white culture of racism. All these big white guys, roaming round the school with big DMs and the sort of things you associate with this racist cult of skinheads. Some would have shaven heads and they were never friendly. It didn't seem to be a big issue for the school. Some of the teachers were probably like that anyway. But I felt the system was biased, a bit racist. When I look back, a lot of friends of mine who are black have done very well, and could have done better with that extra push. But they weren't giving it to the black kids, they were giving that mainly to a lot of the white kids. There wasn't any black kids in the top classes (streams), and in the bottom classes they were virtually all black kids. And when you weigh that up, and the lessons they used to teach up in the A classes, like physics. I never ever got to learn physics. But the top two classes learned physics. I can't say there was something blatant about it, there was a sneaky way about it, but when I look back, I think, 'Why wasn't I allowed to do that?'

My parents decided to change me from that school, to a better school. They couldn't see me getting anywhere where I was. Going to this new school was a different culture. There was a load of white kids up there, but the black kids and the white kids seemed to be on the same level. It was weird. It really hit me. I thought, 'I'm doing this. I'm doing computer studies.' I was doing 'O' level chemistry, I was doing these subjects I wasn't getting the chance to do before. I stayed on then, for a year in the Sixth form. Looking back, at school, you never got the chance to excel.

Out of school, I was made conscious of racism. I've always loved football, and I went to play Sunday football for a team. I was the only black guy. The majority of them were alright, none of them ever really came out and said, 'You black this ..., you black that.' But common sense tells you that there was this feeling that one or two didn't like you. After a season, I didn't play for them any more. But on one occasion. I think this is probably the worst area of racism I have ever witnessed. Every other Saturday I used to go down to East London to watch West Ham play. I was about twelve. We was always, like, the only black kids. We went on the tubes, all packed with supporters, I can always remember someone saying, 'Black niggers on the tube,' and all that sort of stuff. I mean, we'd got our West Ham hats on, scarves on, they've got theirs on, but they say we're too black to support West Ham. We were the only black guys on the tube and they were making the sort of taunts, the remarks, the comments. I decided I wasn't going to support West Ham from there.

Now, it's different to then. Then I'd be scared by racism. Now, I've witnessed it at work. I handle it. I'm not aggressive, but I look as if to say, 'Well, I'm not scared of you. Anything you can give me, I can give back and I will.' That's the only way I handle it now. I won't run from it. It doesn't scare me. And I can't laugh it off.

My dad used to always drum into my head to get a trade. When I left school I went on a YTS scheme, telecommunications. But I couldn't see much of a future, so I went back to the Careers Office and got an apprenticeship in heating, ventilating. Four year apprenticeship, and I'm still with the same company. I took off from there, work-wise. There was a bit of racism on the firm, really. When I started there was only two black guys in the whole entire firm and this is a very big firm. As an apprentice, I always had to work with the poxy engineer. I would say poxy, because I can look back now at who was the better engineer. I think to myself, 'Why would they put me with him, if they wanted me to be any good in the future?' I don't know if this was racism, or favouritism. There's lots of black people there now. Now, being older and maturer, I see general workmen's resentment, not a colour thing.

My daughter is two now. I can really see a resemblance in the parenting. I'm very much like my dad and I can see the caring, loving nature in my girlfriend, from my mum. So I think there's a very similar upbringing. I feel she's going to be brought up very similar, education-wise. My parents made an effort to find a good school, even though I had to travel that bit more. That's what I totally intend to do with my little girl but I hope, by then, to move to an area where the education is better. My advice to my daughter is get a good education, learn as much as you can. In fact, I would even like her to have some sort of education in Barbados. I feel that the education is that bit stronger there. They have that push.

Yet I always see my future as being here, and for my kids, as here. I see myself as British West Indian. I don't know how you sort that out! At school, you was black, West Indian. The West Indies would play England at cricket, we all rooted for the West Indies. 'Go on West Indies! Give England a thrashing!' Now, when it comes to music, there's Reggae music, rap music, this is British, this is *our* English music and we're saying, 'Yeh, we're English.' It chops and changes. Realistically, I'm British, black British.

I don't really see myself going back to the West Indies. But if my parents go back to Barbados, I would really miss them, because they are my support. My mum is here for me. My dad is here for me. If I'm not sure about something, I phone them up. They're the ones I turn to, even at twenty-seven. So I would really miss them, miss them deeply. I see them, speak to them, virtually every day. I'm close to all of them, my sisters, brother. That close. If they were to move, they'd be a very big hole. They have my little girl at the weekends. But if they're in Barbados, my daughter will always have that link. I would love to try and get down there every year, so they can see how's she developing. I hope to think that she could go down there and stay.

What is my future here? I'd like to think that I can own my own house, have a happy family, my own car, and be living comfortable on a wage, not having to be continually doing overtime. I don't want to be an engineer all my life. Somewhere along the line I'd like to own my own business. I always feel that a white has always got someone, a dad, a mate, 'Get your boy over, we'll find room for him.' That's the advantages they've got at the moment, and what black kids haven't got. If I own my business, if my children can't get their own work, I can turn round and say, 'Well, come and work for me.' That's what I want in life, but not here, in this part of South London. I feel in the future that will happen. Everything's new now. It's changing. West Indians had kids, but their kids are having kids. It's a new era. I feel in fifteen years time, you'll see a big change, because it's got to change. Black guys are going to college and learning. They're getting decent jobs, managerial positions. I've seen it change with my own eyes.

I see some of the younger kids that have grown up here, they've been brought up with the wrong attitudes. I'm not going to use the word 'chip' because that's what's used way back, as soon as you argue a point, they say you've got a chip on your shoulder. I won't say that, but they've got a bad attitude. I can see their futures are bleak. Unless they really get theirself a nice strong education while they're young, I can see them struggling later on in life. I don't want my daughter growing up with that.

Notes

1   Chinks are bed-bugs.
2   Third-class gang, also known as the third gang, of children who worked on the plantation.
3   Hurricane Janet.

11 | Family Five

Violet was born in St. Andrew in 1914. Her mother's brother migrated to Panama and lost touch with the family. She had three children, but never married. Her two eldest children migrated to England, but her youngest daughter, a school teacher, lived close by and visited her mother daily. Before I interviewed her, Violet gave me a large bunch of ginger to 'grater' for ginger tea to ward off the cold in England. She worked as a hawker all her life, retiring only at the end of 1992. She died in 1994.

My mother had four children, but only two of us alive. The rest dead, when they was little babies. My mother used to work at the estate. The estate rent them spots and you put your house and thing on. In those days, they didn't no money, only eighteen cents a day, six pints for six cents, five pints for ten cent, according. My dad was a blacksmith. He met and married to somebody else and he and she went to Cuba or Trinidad, one of them places. But my mother stick to we and I went to sixth standard. In those days very few children could go that far with school cause as they get a certain age they had to left and go to work. But my mother didn't see it so. I did the only little girl child she had, and a boy, and she work and raise me up and send me to school.

My mother used to live with my grandmother, a old, old woman and after she dead, my mother then left home. She stand and care my grandfather. My grandfather used to work the land. Reap canes upon a year, plant enough food, cassava, yam, eddoes. When it come to Christmas time, you should see the people banging at my grandfather for cassava to make pone. Yams. Coolie eddoes, white eddoes, girl! My father father, he used to work land. And he had a mule. Used to gather meat[1] and sell it.

We grow ground provision but the other things, rice, flour, salt meat, you still have to buy from Miss Downey. If my mother got money she would buy, if she ain't got the money she would credit where she get money. When she worked, she pay Miss Downey. She could go back trusting again. Once you ent pay, you can't trust, or they may not put debt on top of debt. My mother raise pigs, sheep and goat. People used to thief, thief all. They will steal people's stocks, cow and all they used to steal. I raise pigs. They don't steal pigs cor they make enough noise. When they get big, I call the speculator. I will call and ask him how much pounds he thought it would give and I will then engage and work out the grade. The speculator pay little or nothing. You the down, and he take the up. I say, I raise it, buy feed to feed it and them get the up and I get the down? Uh, uh. Let me get the up too. So I used to kill a pig, regular. Used to kill pig, man.

I went to sixth standard, and I stop there. I must have been about twelve years. I start work. Five shillings a month, cooking and washing. I used to live at the mistress. She was a schoolmistress. Then when I was seventeen, I had Sweetgirl. When I had she, my grandmother did living and I used to left she with my grandmother. After I had them children and they did get big I say I going to have to go and do something else that will help the situation, so that these children upon a morning I had to give them money to get their lunch and then give them something to eat when they come home, clothes for their wear. I starts selling, start hawkering, man. I pick up some customers and I get enough work. Man, it does sell, everybody used to say, she get to buy better than the big women went down ever since! They defile you. If you never say nothing, nobody can't say so. No, had to keep your mouth and I put their kind of obeah back-part of my head.

I buy from different people, estates and everything. That time banana twelve and fourteen cents for a hundred. Sell three for a penny. Buy and sell tomatoes, everything that I could get. Anybody got two butter beans or anything so, you would sell them. In town, in the market in Bridgetown. I will get upon the same place on a morning, two o'clock, three o'clock in the morning and go out and catch a bus. It did take long to get to Bridgetown cor that time you had to stop and take the next body all the time. Start early and get in town before the day clean out. You couldn't make it everyday. I had to go out and buy goods and bring it home. I would make it sometimes twice a week. Got something to eat, then go back on a Saturday. They would trust and then they would pay you. That is how I get through. All my life. Gathering and selling. And grandmother look after Sweetgirl and them. She would go in the ground and work and come back and set on the pot and thing. When I come home I get they something to eat.

Their father had to give me. I go in court for them. He didn't living with me. He went and married to somebody else. And they had to help find him, help put the money in my hand. My son went first to England. I raise the money at a join meeting. Join meeting with people, six, eight, ten, twelve, all the people that you could get and you carry along two dollars a week, so when you get turn you muster it. I raise the money at the meeting. I bought a valise for him. I trust it. I say to he, 'You not only young and will be ignorant, you ent got no sense, so I tell you what sensible children will do. Always put down, if no more than fifty cent, put it down upon a week. When you get a dollar, you will get two and you will muster and muster so you will be able to send for your sister.' He used to send money for me, he used to send the money good for me.

Then Sweetgirl go to England and left she children. My mother still look after them when she did first (go) then my mother dead, so I had to see to them. I didn't feel too despondent when Sweetgirl go because I figured that she had two children and if she go along and work she would be able one day to send for them. And so said, so done. The little girl, I did love. I will miss she, but that's where she belong, if she with she mother, she the best side of the bush so and she would come along better than here in Barbados. The mother send for her, and I did very glad and then the boy began to get a little mannish and she do the same for he, too. Sweetgirl used to help me good, too. So my youngest girl, she pass her test to go to secondary school and she is now a school-teacher. She get a good salary.

I still used to sell when them going to school. All my life. I stop now three months ago but I didn't use to carry a big tray, I got a basket. Make a pad and put it on my head. After the bus get so congested, I couldn't worry a tray. Even now, when I got two banana here, I does sell a girl down the road. I pay a worker now to cut so. A day's sport. Thirty-five dollars. I have half a acre. Bananas, breadfruit, shaddock, pears. The breadfruit I did give away. Only time you will get money for them is that when breadfruit scarce. I plant ginger. Anybody that will carry it, I will give them. You think you come here and you have half a pound of ginger? No, man. The Lord don't stingey with me. He give we every-thing that He can. So, you can still give somebody piece and got some for yourself.

Estelle 'Sweetgirl' was born in 1930, the eldest of Violet's three children. Her father was the 'village transporter,' and, like her mother, bought and sold produce. Although she was brought up by her grandmother she remains very close to her father. She had two children in Barbados, one, her eldest daughter Beulah, by Roy. She migrated to England in 1956 and left Beulah and her son with her grandmother. She married in England in 1958 and had four more children. In 1987 she was widowed but married again, to a Barbadian, and

remigrated in 1991 to Canada. She and her second husband
have now returned to Barbados to live.

Everybody knew everybody. Everybody watch everybody, everybody
cared for everybody. Everybody shared everybody's food. You would
always know who ain't got much to live on. When you cook, you don't
say, 'That will do.' No, you cook a pot of food and anybody who doesn't
have food, you say, 'Come.' We always had plenty. Sometimes my
mother would buy a hundred and fifty flying fish. Frying, one o'clock,
two o'clock in the morning, cause they had no freezers. People pass, she
say, 'Come in, come and get a fish.' I think this is why she's so happy
now she's old, cause everybody just mucks in with her.

I left school at fifteen, when I was in seventh standard. I stayed on
a further year, they teach you gardening, then I learnt how to dressmake
with one of the village ladies. But before I went to learn to sew with her,
I went to the Singer Machine Company to learn to design patterns. Then
I bought a machine and began to sew. I made a good living. I used to got
myself look so smart. I used to work in the government, too, giving the
men who worked building roads their water and do their messages.

I was young when I got pregnant, and that's my Beulah. I was
nineteen. You didn't have any boyfriends until you were sixteen. I think
we were too protected. You protect your daughter so much, the next
thing you see her pregnant. Some chap comes along with a bit more
ideas than what you have. He falls in love. Then you're there pregnant
and each time now that the little stomach seem to be coming up you're
wearing something bigger and bigger till you can't wear nothing better.
By then, they all know you're pregnant. But Granny loved me and
Granny would do the babysitting for me while I go out. I was nineteen
years old and I went to dances, to weddings, to parties. Name it, and I
just went there. I never liked going to the big dancehalls, I never had that
kind of night-life. And then we used to have Service of Song, mostly
religious. I remember the rumbas but I didn't enjoy them kind of things,
singing them things cause I still kept my faith, so I would never sing
things that contradicts my faith.

Beulah was pride and joy. My grandmother loved that little girl.
Beulah's father wanted to marry me. They said I was too young. My
grandmother said, 'The child doesn't do her any harm. She'll have it,
she'll be alright,' she said, 'but you be sure that you really want to get
married to her. She's too young.' But Beulah's father would support her,
and he still do. They're still very close. He always supported her, so I
didn't have no problems, moneywise. Then I went back to work.

Well, emigration was on. They would call out the firms out in
England and the hospitals where the vacancies were on the Rediffusion.

You would always hear how many hundred jobs this one got, or the other one got and the hotels, you know, lapping the girls up, because they didn't have to give much money. But they didn't let you know that they didn't have much place to live, you know, finding somewhere to live was difficult. They didn't let you know any of that. Most of your friends had gone and they'd be writing you letters, said, 'Oh, why don't you come up?' You know, 'Things are good. Why don't you come up and see the place?' By then I was living fairly comfortable. I was working. I had my dressmaking. I was living at my grandmothers. So I think, 'Well, instead of me coming to England, why don't I give my brother the fare and let him go?' So that's what I do. I paid my brother's fare and let him come. We weren't used to a lot of money and what they could work for was double at what money we could get in Barbados. When he say what he could work for and what he used to send for my mother well, money gets to your head. I said, 'I've got to go and have a try.' So I decide then to leave my job, pack up my dressmaking and come to England. I had enough of my own money. I just went along to the ship's agent and paid my fare, on the *Napoli*, Italian ship, about sixty-five pounds, that was all.

I left Beulah and the boy, 'cause I'd had another child by then. I never bothered about it. I knew they was in good hands. Cause it was Granny who used to do all the work on Beulah. I didn't feel any way guilty. To me, at times, I wonder if she was mine or Granny's. She was only mine, sometimes, by name and I used to make her clothes and she was happy, a happy little girl. I used to make her so pretty. So when I had to leave her, I just kiss her goodbye down the waterfront. I kissed them all.

Knowing I came here, when I was leaving, I got a tailor to make me a nice jacket and I made a skirt, so I had a nice outfit. And when I came to Victoria my brother bought me a lovely red coat, fitted one. And I was this pretty young girl in this lovely red coat. I've never had a coat to fit me like that. I first look at the houses and I wonder what's these things on the roof for? I only knew factories had chimney, and I said, 'Well, they must be short of labour with all these factories!' But that's what I thought, the first minute I look out of Victoria Station. I said to my brother, 'Well, they must got a big shortage here for labour, with all these factories!'

My brother was living in Reading and he took me there. I was expecting to find a nice little room with every little thing there tucked away for me. I ended up sharing my brother's bed and in that room there was three more young chaps on beds. I didn't expect to sleep with strangers in the same room. But I was such a happy person I never let it bother me. We just take it for fun. We're young people, but you didn't let your parents know your problems. Whatever the problem was, you always sent home a happy face. You never bad talk. You didn't tell them the bad things. You put up with it. I think, by not telling things, more came!

I stayed there for about three weeks until my brother sorted me out and then I was sharing a room with two more girls. We shared everything. Kitchen, cooking. Whoever came in would put the dinner on, whoever was in first would cook. Soon after that, I got married. He came from the same district in Barbados and he was one of the chaps that used to sleep in the room with my brother. In those days, women were pretty scarce, and when one get you talking he would just keep you at it! You would get make a fuss of and you're not used to that kind of thing! By the time I got married, I had a nice room, well furnished.

Two days, I had my first job and I worked ever since. It was in a canning factory. It was hard to begin with, cause it's not what you're used to do. But once I got into it, you really work. I used to earn a lot of bonuses and I used to send money back, because I had Beulah and the boy and Granny. Everybody mucked in at the factory, everybody loved everybody. There were more Barbadians that anybody else. Then after a while I went to the hospital to work, scrubbing. I scrub that hospital so clean, on my hands and knees. I really work hard in that hospital. I worked there for thirteen years and had about three more children and then I went at another hospital. By this time, I went up a bit higher. I was doing auxiliary work there and I do that there for twenty years, until I retire.

I got the first job through a Barbadian friend. All the boys and girls were always working, nobody sat around. If anybody was sick, you would always be one of us to go and look after them, make sure they're all right. You would bring them in your room till they were better. We'd eat together, and drink together and laugh and talk together and you meet at this one this Sunday, pool the drinks, eat, had fun. But you always kept together. We couldn't get West Indian food. We used to get the Patna rice, and that was hard to cook cause we're used to brown rice. We couldn't get cornmeal or okras for coo coo, but we used to take the semolina and make it into coo coo and we found a Continental shop that used to sell them other things. I don't know who was the first ones that bring the cornmeal, but they soon begin to have the vision to say, 'If we've got these people here, let's give them a shop.' So they begin to bring over and import little things. There was one shop in Reading, Mr. Pollard. No white man could go in there and say anything about a nigger because he would ask them to leave. He said, 'Before the blacks came, my name was Pollard. But now I'm *Mr.* Pollard.' He was white, but he was all the blacks' friend and by then his trade was really hitting off. And then he would start delivering the groceries for us. We used to take our list there Thursday and when we come home with our wages Friday, the groceries were there and we paid them.

Gradually we kind of integrated with the English, once they have found out we didn't have tails, they said! But we certainly had prejudice. If you hear a room was for rent, by the time you get there, it was gone, when they saw it was a black person, 'What a shame, the room has gone this morning.' But I never used to feel discouraged because I thought they're not used to people like us, they're not used to strangers. You can't really get vexed with them.

Then we bought our first house. We paid £850 for it, three bed-rooms, on one of the little scruffy streets of Reading. This man had lots of houses. In the war, he just scooped them up when people died and word got out among the blacks that this man sells houses. So one black person got into him and they were introducing all the others, so that's how we got our house. By the time I got pregnant the second time, we moved in this dirty, bug-ridden, three-bedroom house and that place was hell. There was bugs everywhere. You pulled the wallpaper off and it make you sick. We couldn't sleep that first night. The next morning the neighbour tell us how to go to the Sanitary Inspector and he come and flit[2] this place and then it was alright. My husband, him and his friends, had every room stripped down and they painted it up, new wallpaper, new carpet, new everything. And this little furniture shop in the town used to supply all the blacks, one introduce the next, and he would come and furnish everywhere for you till you paid. Went along every Saturday and paid him. But it was good. You were independent. Own your own house, you know. We were very grateful to these kind of people, but I suppose that was good business for him.

I brought Beulah over and she went off to live with her natural father 'cause he loved her, and his wife loved her. She was nine, ten. Then when the boy was fourteen I brought him over. At home, I hadn't been used to bringing the children up on my own without Grandma, so I got a childminder. I went back to work every time I had one. It was a good thing. I still get my full pension, because I worked for it and it paid off beautiful in my old age. I had an Englishwoman mind the babies, thirty shillings a week to keep the baby. When the children start to go to school I would work evenings, when my husband come home and work all day Saturday. I used to go two in the morning, walk about two miles to scrub the hospital to be back in time for my husband to go off to work and get the children ready for school. But still, we managed to get a nice three-bedroom, new house. That's my working, you know and it all paid off because the children then, they all had a good life, not like the life I had in Barbados. They had enough room to sleep, good beds, good house.

I'm retired now and going home to live. I would love to be able to look after my mother, and my father, both of them when they can't look after themselves. I feel so committed to go back to my parents. I was glad I leave Barbados cause I've been able to help my mother. You're pleased about those things. Some people come and they never remember their parents. They can't go back cause they got nowhere to go. But I was glad we left home, my brother and I. We manage to help her to build her house. You feel good going home to your mother.

> Beulah was Muriel's first born, Roy's second child and Vernon's first cousin. She was raised by her great-grandmother. Beulah joined her mother in England when she was ten years old. She trained as a nurse, then as a midwife, finishing her career in England as a health visitor, having graduated in the meantime with a BA in combined studies, and a MA. She married when she was seventeen and has two sons. She and her husband returned to Barbados at the end of 1994, where she now works as a health visitor and social worker.

I was a grandmother child. First borns in Barbados usually are. My great-grandmother was everything to me. I can feel her presence even now. She used to sing me to sleep. I don't remember that money was hard or that I ever wanted for food or clothing, because my mother always worked and my great-grandmother worked in the fields too. I slept in a four-poster bed with her. She told me Nancy stories which frighten me to death, even now. She had these wierd brown eyes, a very deep, deep brown, unusual brown and she used to look at me and I used to feel a little bit afraid, as if there were things she knew that were kind of mystical! I went everywhere with my great-grandmother. I remember her taking me to the fields when she was hoeing, she'd put me under a shade, a guava tree and she'd say, 'Bobo, sit there till I come back.' And I would sit under the tree and watch her hoeing. Bedtime, I always sat on her lap and as she talked she would be rocking me and she would be singing. She'd tell me stories about when she was little, the house made of wattle, her sisters and a brother who went to Cuba and how she never saw him again. And I always remember as a little girl, thinking how sad this was. It was a memory that stayed with me, how sad it was that he went away and they never saw him again. I fell asleep on my grand-mother's lap. Whenever it rained my grandmother went to bed and took me with her. When we had Hurricane Janet in 1955, we spent it in bed. I always have this image of being safe in a big bed and to this day, if I am upset, I go in the bed and I cover my head up with the quilt.

I remember my great-grandmother being the focal point of my life and my mother was this woman who wafted in smelling of perfume, with nail polish, wide skirts, thin waist, laughing, and out she'd waft again. She was like the relief in my life, the pleasure bit. And, I'll have to say this, I've never recovered from the fact that she had other children. My brother who came after me was born in the West Indies and he is very much part of me, but I feel bereaved since she's had the other four children. I still can't come to terms with sharing her.

When she emigrated to Canada I was devastated. After she went through the barriers, I caved in. If I walked through this house and looked at something that was hers, I would burst out crying. She has an old dressing-gown that she left in the house the morning she left. When I'm upset I put it on and I sleep with it. Sometimes I go and I wrap it round my neck. I can smell her on this dressing-gown, which is ridiculous. I am forty-two years old!

My father was the village ram. And he would admit it. He was young, he was handsome, he loved women and he had a wonderful time. I always remember him. He used to strut around the village. He was a bus driver and in that time, if you were a bus driver in Barbados you had all the girls and all the prestige. He would be strutting around and he would come and see me, pick me up, throw me up in the air. My great-grandmother adored him. I remember him collecting me and taking me down to his family in St. Lucy and I used to feel like a little treasure, because my mother was a dressmaker and when she knew he was coming she would dress me up in the prettiest dress. She used to show off about me, and I think he also was the passion of her life. He was her first love. Both of them are always telling me, and I'm very conscious of it with both of them, that I was very much a love-child for both of them. He would collect me and carry me down to St. Lucy to my grandmother who would then parade me through the village and she'd just show me off. She'd take me to the village shop and she'd put me on the counter and my dress would fan out. I can remember this, as a three-year-old, being paraded round the village, and taking me to his wife's home, being with my sister who was only four months older than me.

I remember the day he went to England. I must have been five. I remember my stepmother, and my mother, and a couple of other girl-friends that my father had, past or present, at the quayside. They would be all saying to him, 'Roy! Roy! Roy!' and he was so blatant. He was kissing all of them, and they all adored him, although he's obviously done dirties on most of them. And they started to quarrel! I can remember this, and I can remember the dress my mother had on that day. I mean, in these times, one woman would have the decency to stay home, to save the embarrassment. But they all turned up. When my mother left, I can remember her going to have her passport done, seeing it, her trotting to places for injections, buying new clothes, making new clothes, buying a suitcase. Crying bitterly at the quayside. My mother had on a white organza blouse the day she left. I always remember thinking how pretty she looked, but I was devastated. After that, just as the evening was coming, I used to look out on my grandmother's back step and imagine where my mother was. I used to look as far as the horizons I could see, and I used to imagine what my mother was doing. I suppose that's the way a child misses her mother, by imagining what she's doing. But my mother was always constant, even though she was away, because religiously, every month, she sent our money. She also used to send parcels, lovely clothes. Looking back, it could not have been easy for her to amass them. And toys. She sent my brother a London Transport bus which was the envy of the whole village. She sent me a blonde dolly, which I hated. She sent her sister – who was younger than me – a brunette. It was smaller than mine. Bit by bit, I couldn't do it for my great-grandmother to see, but over a period of probably a month, I had completely destroyed this dolly, because I hated the blonde hair. Now I see it in intellectual terms, the blonde dolly was alien to me, as a black child who had never seen a blonde person. But my mother, thinking I was her little girl, she sent me the biggest, prettiest doll England had to offer. I hated it. I resented my mother. I was angry with her for sending my aunt the pretty little brunette, which was more to what I was used to. I resented this aunt for having this dolly, not parting with it, to let me borrow it. Bit by bit I used to have accidents with this dolly, the big one. I dropped it, so it got a bruise. I remember hitting it with a stone. Another time, I actually took a rock and bashed its face in. By the time it was finished with, you couldn't recognise it as a dolly.

Then one day I got home and there was a letter and my great-grandmother looked funny. She wasn't happy. She was doing an awful lot of hymn-singing. We do hymn-singing when we're upset. She said, 'Child, your mother wants you.' I didn't understand what she meant. She said, 'Your mother wants you up there.' I actually did tell her I didn't want to go. I was quite adamant for a long time. I had this tremendous resentment against my mother for wanting me, because I didn't want to leave my great-grandmother. I believe it was my father's idea that I should come to England and live with him. He paid the fare. I was very unhappy. I remember crying and as the day is getting nearer, crying even more. They spent all this time creaming my skin, I had to have my hair done better than usual. They stopped me going out to play in case I got cuts and scratches, because I wasn't to be scruffy when I got to my mother! I was forbidden to climb trees. They took me to get my passport done, my injections, queuing up down the MO, with great resentment. It was devastating when I parted from my grandmother. At times in my life when I've been vulnerable, I still dream about her.

I was excited about England because of all the things I had been taught in school. I was fussed over on the plane by the stewardesses, and when I got to my mother, I thought she was incredibly silly. She was giggling, the sheer pleasure of seeing me, fussing over me. And then there was this man, very imposing black man, which was my father. I hadn't seen him since I was five. He was at the airport, and we went to my father's. My father lived in Notting Hill which in the 1960s was one of the filthiest parts of London. I was shocked. The houses were all close stuck together, they looked so dirty and they were so tall. The flat inside was nice, but the house was the pits. Everything was dirty and noisy. We stayed there one evening and then came back to Reading. I was shocked by that as well, because my mother lived in one room with this husband. I spent the rest of that week in Reading, then I went to live in London with my father.

He was very strict on discipline and I was used to living with an indulgent great-grandmother! Every other weekend I would go to Reading and that was like a treat. I was spoilt, I got more food. My father's household was very poor. My mother had this network of friends that we visited. We danced. I'd have no housework to do. I got more food. I listened to gossip. Then my father got in terrible financial straits and we were evicted. My mother didn't know. We were homeless. We ended up in a transit van and my father would drive round looking for accommodation. They'd say, 'No blacks, no children.' Driving round London. To me, that is the real hard stark picture of immigration. They slammed the door in his face, 'Shove off! No blacks, or dogs!' And he drove. We lived in the transit van for more than two weeks, stopping off at toilets and baths. Food would be chips. My father used to look as if he'd failed us.

For us children, we found it a giggle because we didn't have any discipline, we didn't have any school. Eventually he made this decision and I know it was something that wrecked him. We all went to this council home but it didn't take men. It was one of the most horrendous places in England, Newington Lodge. Subsequently it was condemned. It was a place for people who were homeless. We were in a room, where once you'd slept and cleared up, you had to be out on the streets all day. We shared it with another woman. My stepmother spent most of her day crying. My father used to visit us daily. We got dysentery and ended up in hospital.

Meanwhile, all this time my mother apparently is sending messages all over West London, to all the black grapevines, where is her child? My father is very proud so he was hoping to get things right before he contacts my mother. Meanwhile, my mother's had a baby. I don't actually remember my mother being pregnant but when I saw my sister, she was three months old. You can imagine how my mother, a woman who's pregnant and can't find her first child is getting on. She must have been frantic. Every weekend she sent my uncle from Reading to London to try the grapevine. Where was I? Had anybody seen my father? And my father, because he's embarrassed, has gone underground.

Eventually the day came when he found a flat in Peckham. Two rooms and we moved in there. He still didn't tell my mother, but she found out. He was wanting to get on his feet and then tell her. She turned up at the door and what she didn't call him you couldn't repeat. My mother had, before she went to Jesus, the most abysmal tongue and temper. She cursed him like a trooper and she gave it to him. My father is the most sensitive of men. He cries at the drop of a hat. He begged her. She wouldn't have any of it. He cried. He was devastated. He packed my clothes and he sits me on my lap, 'Remember that I love you. I don't want you to go. I always want to keep you, just like the others.'

I went to school then in Reading. I loved school, have always loved school. I read before I went to school. I took the eleven-plus. Now we know they were racially biased. 'Choose a dish that you would like for tea.' What did that mean to me? 'What is your favourite seaside?' I didn't have that background and those kinds of tests discriminated against children like me. I ended up in the 'D' stream of a secondary modern. And after the first tests there, went up to the 'A' stream. The headmaster was a wonderful man and I will never forget him. He and I were friends till he died last year. He supported me right through school. I went to a school in Reading in 1961 where the headmaster would cane children for shouting racist jokes. This was the kind of philosophy he had. His teachers were the same. He was a man ahead of his time with regard to children of different cultures. He encouraged me and supported my career and helped me get into the Royal Berks Hospital to train as a nurse and at that time black girls never got a look in there.

And off I went at eighteen. But I was married by then. I conspired to get myself pregnant. I was seventeen. To me, I was so grown-up, I was so confident and I wanted a son. We went and got married, had a lovely wedding, lived in this bedsit and had this baby, a son, exactly what I visualised he would be. We were so over the moon with this child, over the moon. Those were extremely happy years and I started my training when I was eighteen. I lied to Matron that my mother was looking after the baby, but we kept him between us and my aunt, with whom we were sharing a house, looked after him. And we saved. God! How we saved. In fifteen months we had a deposit for a house on my student wages and his working in a factory. We lived on nothing. I had one dress. I used to patch and mend my husband's jeans, his underpants. I'd buy something for the baby each month when I was paid. But we had such fun, you know. I wasn't conscious that we had life hard, but looking back, we must have done. We moved into our house when I was nineteen. We had nothing. Bought everything on HP and every month I would walk round Reading with my wages to all the people I owed HP. We muddled along like that. And then I carried on. As soon as I finished one course, I would enroll for another. I finished my SRN, midwifery. Then we had another son. I was thirty now, and we went to the Caribbean.

From the age of thirty when I first stepped back in the island, and I shall never forget this feeling, when I was stepping down the steps I felt so good, the heat on my body. Do you know what really got me? The men. I had never seen so many black men in one place. Obviously, living in Reading, the circle of black men is pretty limited. So I'm looking through the airport and I'm seeing these men. They're tall. Black men in England aren't tall, they're not erect, they're always working as if they've got a burden – well, they have, living in England! And these men look so proud. I'm going dizzy. I'm looking at the people and thinking, 'These people are so beautiful.' To me, those are the things, as a black woman born in the Caribbean and being brought up in this country, sort of took on a new meaning for me. Black men, black professionals, a sense of pride that I think the black man in Britain has lost as a result of living in a culture that is alien and hostile and I didn't realise until I went back that we have changed, and we've adapted to accommodate living here. From the day I stepped off that plane, I've been native. I was pretty English before that. I had a complete turnabout. I came back to England four weeks later and I said to my husband, 'I'm saving. I'm going back.'

If you're proud in England, and you're black, you're seen as uppity, or having a chip on your shoulder. If you are articulate in England, and you're black, you're seen in many spheres as trying to get one up. It's so nice to see black people who are not proving anything, not proving that they have become this in their profession, they just *are* the people they are. That's how I want to operate. I don't ever want to feel that I've got to be apologising because I am black. I just want to be me. When I say this to some people they say, 'But suppose you don't get a job with the status you have here?' or they say you might have problems financially. I say, 'I don't care. We came to Britain and lived the most appalling lives and I feel that if we survived in England, I can survive anywhere else, and certainly the country I was born in.' England has been good for us, as immigrants, if we take out the good things and use them to our advantage. I never have trouble fitting in when I go home. I cast off the clothing of where I've come from, and I fit in. I keep up with the politics, the economy, I slip into dialect, I sweet talk, and I stand my ground. I'm prepared to be pretty humble, I wouldn't feel that I've got to live with a certain class of people. My family are villagers. To me, it would be ridiculous, just because I have got a certain profession, not to relate to those people. I would miss out an awful lot. I'm optimistic about going to live there. Considering what I started out with, twenty-five years ago, in one grotty bedsit, the two of us, and a child and before I was eighteen, and we survived. I don't see that anything in my life could be any harder.

> Roy is Herman's brother, and Beulah's father. He was born in St. Lucy in 1929, and was the youngest of the eight children. He migrated to England in 1956 and returned to Barbados to live in 1992, and practises now as a Minister of Religion, although his earlier working life has embraced a number of careers. By the time Roy was born their father had become a supervisor and a transporter, who owned two donkeys and a horse, and was the only black person for 'miles around' to do so. As a result, Roy did not experience the extreme poverty which Herman had lived through and the family was considered 'better off' than many of their neighbours. Roy has seven children, four by his wife whom he married in 1951, and three by other partners. Two of Herman and Roy's uncles and four of their aunts lived in the United States. Roy left school at fifteen. His mother wanted him to be apprenticed to a mason because, 'she wanted to avoid committing me to the agricultural work at all costs, ' but Roy was determined to go to the United States, although you had to be twenty-one to qualify.

Well, this is a bit of deception now. My brother, who was twenty-eight, registered and got a slip to go off (to the United States) but decided he wouldn't go, so he let me use his slip. Fortunately, I was big and I present myself as my brother, his name, his slip and I got through. My mother was crying her eyes out but I was very cocky and ready and raring to go. We were sent to the Union Bag and Paper Corporation in Savannah, Georgia. I was the youngest person on the trip. Not once did I let on. Fortunately there was no one at my factory who was from my district. I behave older and I was big enough to get away with it.

Racial discrimination hit us smack in the face. We couldn't understand it, but it was a hard pill to swallow. I was away about seven month, living on an ex-army camp. All the nights now, I was missing my mother and when the bigger men didn't seems to worry, I would burst into the odd tear and off a letter would go. What we earn was a big lift on what we were getting here. A certain amount was extracted from our board, yet I would get enough in my hand to go into town on pay day, buy a coke or a beer, have something to send for my mother, something to buy clothes, and there was a compulsory savings taken out automatically, so when I came home I had a few more clothes, more shoes, a little cash in my pocket, a few things for my mother and I was able to come home and pay thirty dollars to learn to drive.

Well, that was another deception now. They ask you if you was twenty-one. I was only just gone sixteen! I was lucky enough to get a job soon after as a driver. I was in the job for four months when the immigration to America started up again. This is 1946 now and I applied for a slip then in my own name. I put something down there, twenty-something, to make sure I got there. This time I went to work for the sugar corporation in Florida, hoeing. While I was there, there were men driving the tractors and every spare moment I get I would go over to the tractor, steal some ideas and talk some of them into letting me have a go. I remember my scripture, 'Ask and you shall be given, seek and you shall find.' I catch on quickly and knew how to drive a tractor and I took notice of how they use to use this contour ploughing, instead of cane holes. Then I was transferred to Montana to get the sugar beets out before the cold. I was still only sixteen years old but nobody knew that.

I volunteer for cook, so when the others out there in the cold now, fingers burning off doing these beets, I was inside cooking, feeding myself. It was a blessing from my mum. They even give me a gun to shoot ducks. Never handle a gun in my life. 'Can you use a rifle?' Believe me, I said, 'Yes!' I came home the same year, 1946 and in 1947 and I got a tip off for this job, one of the best jobs in the Parish, paying the most money. I went to the (plantation) manager, 'Can you drive a tractor?' I said, 'Yes.' All the experience I had in driving a tractor was what happen down in Florida! He had two tractors stand in the yard and one he put me on, to see what I could do. Happens to be one of the caterpillars which I had had experience on, even remember how to start it, everything. The following week now I got to get into this ploughing and this is something worthwhile preserving for history. I said to him, 'They dig cane holes here to plant canes in but in the United States they don't dig cane holes.' I said, 'They dig out a drain and when it come to hilly places, they contour it.' I explain it to him in detail. He thought it was a marvellous idea. No doubt he sell it as his idea. But if I went now and put it in print and say that I was the man who was responsible for spreading contour work throughout this island, and that history is accredited to me, very few estate owners now would believe me.

But then this very same man was trying to make a name for himself. First of all, he put me on the short work, to prove how much money he could save. Then he decided to go further and cut down the rate because I was ploughing by the acre then. I wouldn't bite it. To give up a job at that time took some guts. My wife was expecting my first child. I start looking for a job. We suffered for about two months when I get a job with the bus company because I had got my bus licence in the gap between coming back and getting the job on the plantation. It was 1949 to be exact that I got the job on the buses, and I work on that till March 1956 and then I come to Britain. They were short of labour on the London Transport, and London Transport send their representatives down here to recruit men. People were very keen to get selected. You sat a test for London Transport. It wasn't anything big, more common sense than anything. You knew (if you passed) the same day and you were advised to prepare yourself and then await the Labour Office to write to you and tell you the day you were going to travel. That wasn't long. I think we knew inside three weeks.

So there I was. I had already travelled – because I went back to America in 1953 for a short spell. There I was working for the government in a job which was considered very reasonable, a bus driver, the pay wasn't bad, the working conditions were very fair and it was what I like. I was happy. I was married. I was sure by then that the woman I married to was right for me. My mother was here, a mother I loved very much so it would have to be something to make me feel I would want to go abroad again. I knew that the money was slightly better to start with in Britain, but the main thing that attracted me was to see Britain. So much was taught down our throats about the Mother Country and so forth and we really believed that we're going home to a Mother Country, a place that's going to be loving and nice. And I, despite the fact that I had travelled before, was very, very keen to come to England more than any place else. That was my first motivation, my first attraction. Then also, when I was in the States and I saw these trains I thought I wouldn't mind driving one of them so then when I was asked to choose between whether I would go for a bus driver or work on the trains, I choose to go on the trains.

I had just the idea which were instilled into us (about England). We were told that the place and everybody in it was nice, virtually angels.

I mean, that's the story that was told to us down here from the time we were training school from Britannia, raise the flag on Jubilee day and drink your lemonade, you know, we think of England. The Union Jack and the National Anthem. And we thought this is a good chance to go to England, everybody up there is going to be nice and lovely, we were virtually told that everybody up there was a Christian. That's true and we believed it.

The mass emigration started in 1956. The first lot was in '55 and I was in the second lot, '56. But prior to then, you was getting nothing, whether people was up there and didn't want to say what they were going through, or there wasn't sufficient people to spread enough about it, or people, even if they hear things, they probably won't believe it, they probably don't tell it to anybody else. I can assure you that up to when I left (for) England in 1956 I had nothing but a hundred per cent good picture of England and everybody else that is in England. I felt I was going to a place which would be second to Heaven, and that is true. I found, in short, that the English could teach hypocrisy better than anybody else on earth. First of all, it was difficult to detect whether an Englishman is pleased with you or not. I find too, in England, that people didn't like to see you earn too much money. You had one job, you went and took another job, they treat that as if you commit another crime. And if you bought something better than them, or even as good as them, they didn't like that much either. I find that they suffer with, the indigenous population as a whole, an inferiority complex in the sense that they've got to have somebody one step above them, and if they think that you're a step beneath them, you got no right coming up to their level. Not so in America – and I'm talking about the Midwest now, I don't talk of the South as America – they won't matter if you own the same mansion, four cars if you like.

We docked at Southampton and it was gloomy. But that didn't surprise me because I was told about the weather conditions. Gloomy, very gloomy. Every house had a chimney stick up and the smoke going up and the smog. But I would be dishonest if I say I was surprised because I realise I was down on the docks, I wasn't in the city, cor I was telling myself I was going to see something better later on. The Liaison Officer met us and took us to Paddington, to the various addresses he had allocated for us. I had a bed for myself, but there was three or four of us to one room. No proper facilities laid on for our food and the bath situation wasn't the best. But from experience I realise he did the best he could. He didn't have a big choice as all of us experienced later, because to get somewhere for us as immigrants, black immigrants, coming up there was something like America. I was out in two weeks flat. I went to Balham, to stay with a relative (Vernon) who was living with a

Barbadian. I stood there until I was considering bringing my wife up then I had to get somewhere more suitable. This next was a room in Mitcham, in a house that a Jamaican owned but there was a clash of ways and I had to decide if my wife ent going to be happy then I'll have to find somewhere else. I went to Earls Court then, and it was closer to my work. We had this room which I don't think was twelve feet, ten feet and the same length. It had two divan beds and just one single ring, no stove and we shared the bathroom and toilet. No where to wash our clothes, do the laundry. We paid four guineas for that. My wife come up in 1956 and the children in 1957. I thought when I went there I am going to stick this out for about ten years. That's what I told myself.

First I was sent into training school as a stationman. We had three weeks there. My first station was King's Cross, then I went to Gloucester Road, was promoted there after three months from stationman to foreman–ticket collector and got a station foreman in another three months. I was the first black man to be promoted to station foreman on London Underground. When I got my promotion I was on very good terms with everybody on the station and I think that help to get me accepted. I think it was accepted, even if, underneath, they had feelings of envy, because I beat Englishmen to the post. But I knew a thing or two by then about being tactful. You had to be tactful.

I resign from that in 1961. Although the job was a prestigious one, moneywise, it wasn't enough. By then I was doing four jobs. I was selling washing machines and vacuum cleaners. I was doing electrical wiring for my landlord, the famous Peter Rachman. And then I realised that there was a big demand for light removals and I managed to get a deposit and put on a van and went doing light removals. I made do with four hours sleep but at that time the first concern was about how to keep your family in house, in food and clothes. My wife didn't work, she had a small baby.

I came by Peter Rachman out of necessity. People weren't letting you accommodation one, because you were black and two, if you had children. That was a double portion of prejudice and Peter Rachman saw this opportunity to do business. People say he exploit it. I take care how I use the word because if it wasn't for him lots of people would have to sleep on the street. I only wanted somewhere to live and that was what cause me to go with him. Necessity. I just couldn't get any place other than his place at the time. Once I decided to send for the children then that's what led me to Peter Rachman. Once I prepared to pay the price, he didn't ask no more questions. I paid eleven guineas for a flat with three rooms. That is a lot of money at the time, my flat pay as a foreman was eight pounds. My big week taking home thirteen pounds, and if it's a flat week, you see I can't pay my rent at all. And sending back to my mother, and for Beulah.

I was living in Westbourne Park Road and was actually indoors the night the rioting started. Underneath me was a club run by black men and they throw petrol bombs inside that club. That start going up in fire and we were on the first floor. You got the choice of either having to stand and get roast, or go out and get a bottle or chain in your head, or a knife. I was in that limbo. We could look outside and see the battle going on. People like us wanted to stay out of trouble, we just huddle ourself together and pray. I didn't go out. And I was worried about staying in. The smoke was coming up, and I was living on the first floor. On the ground floor was a tailor shop, Trinidadian fellow. There was two more families above me. The fire brigade came along and put out the fire and that was my prayer heard. But believe you me, we didn't get a check from the fire brigade nor the police. They never ask us anything. We know we prayed. My children was very excited and worried about this. The fire brigade did turn up and put it out and the police turn up for the commotion and then once they got them away from that area and there was no longer fire, they went away. No one ever came and knock on the front door and ask us, 'Are you alright? How you feel? Are you in shock? How are the children?' Nothing. It never happen.

We was in that area from 1957 to 1961, renting, furnished flats. We left that area in 1961. By then I had been invited by one of Rachman's agents to take over some flats, let them off. I was given what I thought was a genuine lease agreement. I trusted them. I let, sub-let, and I was getting for myself a very small commission. That help me, that was my way of subsidising my own income. Then they wanted a bit more money for these places, so if they charged me more, I would have to charge the sub-tenants more, and they were people who were already struggling. I just didn't feel I could do it. It wasn't a very pleasant experience at all. But to tell you the truth, to this day, I don't have any sour thoughts about Peter Rachman. Along with the bad he do by exploitation, as I far as I am concern, he provided a service where no one else wanted to. If it wasn't for Peter Rachman when people, including myself, might have had to sleep on the pavements with their children. Lots of things was written about him, but I haven't seen that bit written, that bit wasn't perceived, wasn't seen about the man. I wasn't prepared to pay the higher rents because I wasn't prepared to charge the higher rents. I thought if this is going to get me a stigma of exploitation and corruption, I'm going to get out of it. So I had to make my exit. We moved from there to New Cross.

We had rented a house, and had a bit more unpleasant experience. We had to leave. I was in tears. I was in tears every day for a long time.

My wife was devasted and I said to her, 'Right, there's only one answer for us. The next flat we go to, by the grace of God, will have to be our last place.' I was trying everywhere. The council help me with what was almost a hundred per cent mortgage, and I managed to get this shelter of my house. 1965, July. I was elated. That was one of the glorious experiences, to get my own place.

At this stage, I am only doing one job. Took a job working at the chocolate factory, delivering, so I am beginning to feel the pinch again. The vacuum business gone. The electrical wiring had gone, so I decided that I want to do some driving instructions. I went to nearly all the driving schools that around, and none of them would take me on. None. One man, took me out for assessment. He said, 'You did better than most who apply, but I'm not going to take you on, for the same reason that the others didn't take you on. I am not prejudiced, but we got people in this country who are. If I take you on, I'm going to lose my business. You happen to be the wrong colour.' But I am determined I want to do it. I said, 'I will open my own driving school.' We put our money together and buy a little car. I pin up a little sign. I got a few cards and write them up. I got my first customer. A Jamaican. Then I got his friend, then I got his friend's friend, then they start coming in. In no time I had clients enough, and I never look back.

I gave up the delivery and now I only got the driving school. And then with that, I decided to do grocery and greengrocery. Always try to get one step ahead, feeling that with a family it's not wise to ship all your sugar in one basket, so we started this little business, but I folded it up shortly after and went back to London Transport, as a bus driver. After two attempts, I got promotion as a driving instructor for London Transport. I was the first black man who ever done it. I want to go higher now. I want to be a senior official. I got drop on the first time, but the second time I got it. You're one below the chief of staff. I'm the only one, up to this day, who made it. I retired as such. That is my story.

> Peter is Beulah's eldest son. He was born in Reading in 1967 and has a brother ten years younger than himself. He is not married, but has two children by his girlfriend from whom he has now separated. Although he trained to be a professional footballer, he did not pursue football as a career. He is now a car trader, and manages a local football side in his spare time.

I played a lot of sport, so my childhood was always spent out on a cricket field, playing field, doing some kind of recreation. In the home there were certain rules and regulations like tidy up the house, after dinner, washing up. Cutting the lawn. Basic things, which had to be complied with, which were never really broken.

Most weekends I stayed with my gran and she would take us to church. Sunday School. But when I was eight and nine, I was always playing football, so that stopped, luckily, because it's quite boring for a child to go to church and listen to all that. So my church days were very numbered really. I didn't really see a lot of my grandfather because of the distance. When the family were going up London to see him, I was always the member of the family that wasn't able to go there, because of football commitments. It wasn't really often that we saw him. But we were still very close, we still had a very good relationship. My mum told me about the situation, between my gran and grandfather, when I was young so it never seemed odd to me at all. One thing with my mother, she's always told me about our family. I knew all about our family, from her great-grandmother, to my gran, and my grandad. I suppose I saw more of my father's family, growing up. My grandmother, as I said, was always in the church, whereas my dad's parents weren't really into the church. And their house, from my dad's side of the family, was like the meeting-place. My dad comes from a very large family and with all the grandchildren and wives and aunties and uncles it was like a big congregation. This gran would usually just cook a big pot, and who turned up turned up. There was always food there. But after my gran and grandad went back to Barbados, I think we lost that kind of meeting-place, and people moved, and it become a lot more spread out.

My parents moved house when I was seven or eight. My mum and dad worked hard, saved a little bit of money, and obviously wanted to move to a better area. I think they were worried about my schooling, because the area we were in was like a hard kind of area. I think they were worried about the influences I would be picking up with. When we moved out here, I was the only black kid in the school. I think it would have affected a lesser child than myself. I've always been brought up in a good home, and a strong home, mentally and physically, and the name-calling, and all the problems racially, never bother me. I think me being so good at sport, I mixed with people and they accepted me. When they saw how good I was at football and cricket they wanted me in their team. So through sport, that brought down a lot of barriers for me. Race was never an issue, really, because it wasn't important. I knew who I was, I knew what I was, and whatever people thought about me, at the end of the day, is not really important. That's how I've always been brought up by my parents.

I suffered more racial prejudice from teachers than from the children, not by calling me 'black bastard', but through my school work, through things happening at school, detentions for things I'd never even done. I felt I was getting all the pushing and all the helping in sport, but the academic side of it, I didn't get any help. At school, I was a very, very intelligent person, but never got the push and help to make that blossom. And they weren't bothered about it. All they were bothered about was that I was winning trophies for the school. It's only when you look back at it, that you can see it. Mum was very aware of it, always telling me about it. But I wasn't really bothered, because I just wanted to play football and cricket. But my mum was very on the heels of all the teachers. My mum, being the kind of person she was, had been very well-educated, was up the school, knew her rights, knew what I was entitled to as a child, knew what she was entitled to as a parent, and stood for that. I think I was seen as a child that, 'We can't mess him about, otherwise his mum'll be up the school, and she won't just be rearing up and shouting, she'll be ringing up the governors, and ringing up the Race Relations Board.'

I left school at fourteen, because I was playing football. The school was becoming bad in every way. I wasn't going anywhere, I wasn't learning anything. I was playing football and had the chance to go and play for Chelsea. I left in the fourth year, under the supervision of one of the Chelsea team managers. I trained, I played football everyday but I went to college, like, twice a week. But my academic work really stopped then. My mum must have said, 'If he's got the chance to be a footballer, then he's going to put a hundred per cent effort into that.'

I spent four years with Chelsea, playing the youth team, and the reserve team. I didn't actually get into the first team. The wage was only small, but in my last year, I signed a professional contract, and I was then on something like a hundred pounds a week. It was good money. I don't know if I could have made it to the first team, being the kind of person I am. Committed, in the sense that I was good at football, but my personality is one that I find it hard to concentrate and toe the line and there were certain things and responsibilities as an apprentice which I didn't like doing. When you're an apprentice, you're at the bottom of the ladder and you have to take the rubbish and accept it until you get on the top of the ladder. If you're not prepared to go through that, then you're not going to get anywhere. I think there's a similarity in life. It's like our parents. My parents had to go through a lot. If they never went through it and endured it, they wouldn't have what they have today. They wouldn't be retired now at fifty, going to Barbados. I wasn't prepared to do that. I think I was silly not doing it, but I'm not sorry that I'm not a footballer.

I was unemployed for a little while, when I left Chelsea. I was temping various jobs, rubbish jobs. My parents weren't prepared for me to lounge around the house all day and not do anything. So for them, I had to be out of the house, finding jobs, just for them. One job, I was washing dishes and I remember a cousin of ours, he really liked me, he thought I was still at Chelsea. I was washing the dishes. All of a sudden, he come to the counter and he saw me, in the back. I can imagine how he felt. It was a downer on him and it was a downer on me. From then, I said, regardless of how my parents feel, I'm not doing anything like that. What they had to do when they came here, is up to them. They had to do it. I don't have to do it, and I'm not doing it. I'm not washing no more dishes, I'm not sweeping out any toilets to make them happy, to say I've got a job.

I found a job after that, working in printing. Stayed there for about three or four years, but that was my choice. Left there through boredom. Went into an estate agency, as a sales negotiator. But I'm a kind of person that I can't do anything for too long, because I just get bored. So I ended up leaving there as well. That was the last proper job I had, working for somebody else. I don't like working for other people, doing their hard work, and them making the rewards off of me. I might as well do it myself. I've tried various things. Now, I'm a car trader. I don't really know anything about cars. I met up with a friend of the family, a mechanic, a white guy. I'm streetwise into what is a good car, what is a good price. If I get bored of that, then I'll sell up and do something else. If we want to work, we work. If we don't want to work, we don't. But the rules are mine and my friend's.

But there's racism in the car trade. A white person don't want to sell a black man a car cheap, knowing that he's going to make money off him. Or if there's a car going to sell, they will keep it between the traders, they won't let the black boys get a piece of the money. With me and my white friend, with the buying side of it, off white people, I send him. And like, with the blacks, I will deal with the blacks. So between the two of us, we're doing all right. What can you do? At the end of the day, you've got to look after yourself.

My mum and dad talked all the time about Barbados. It's surprising really, being here so long. You wouldn't really feel that they would have brought a lot from Barbados with them. But the knowledge that my mum had of the island, and the love of the island. It's amazing, to still have that inside of them. I don't know if it's the black culture, but speaking from my experience as being half Barbadian, is the ability to comprehend things. My great-gran, she was very, very good at recalling things. The same with my mum, the same with my dad.

I must have been about thirteen the first time I went. My mum and dad gave me such a good insight into what the place would be. It was like, for me, going home. I knew what to expect. It's meant to be a Third World country, but that didn't bother me any. I went there with an open mind, knowing what to expect. Mum and Dad had told me about how hard life was, but how happy they were. They made the best out of what they had. But things were hard, things that we take for granted here, are very difficult to come by. Like water, my dad would tell me stories of getting up at six o'clock in the morning, to go and walk six or seven miles to milk the cows, and then walk back home and then go to school. My gran used to run a market stall in town and she would walk to town with all the food that she was going to sell. A lot of people think of Barbados as this wonderful place, paradise, exotic. It is like that, it's very beautiful. But another side of it is the poverty. I went out there knowing both sides.

There's not a close-knit community here now and we've strayed from back home. That's what I saw when I went back home to Barbados. That's not our nature. We are a close people, and that's the only way we could have got through back home, by being close, by sharing the food, the sisters raising the brothers so that their mum could go out to work, by going out and milking the cows, by going out and bringing home the water. That was the only way my parents survived, through being a close family. And, all of a sudden, and I don't know what it is, when we've come here, and my generation of people, not my mother and dad's so much, because they're still tight, and they're still strong, but my generation of people, because now they can see this money that is out there, and that it can be made, certain values go out the window, certain family values, and friend values. They're not interested. They just want money, flash car, jewellery, clothes. They're not bothered about family values any more. Those family values that made us a strong people, we've come here and those values have gone out the window, and that's why we can't get forward as people any more.

I think that's to do with the westernising that we've had. Coming here, we've been westernised. Without people like my mum and dad, and my gran, telling the younger generation, and the younger generation wanting to listen how it was in the olden times, then they've got nothing to clutch on to. It means nothing to them. I'm another generation of parent, and if I don't tell my kids about Granny Violet and Grandad Roy, and about my mum and about how bad things were when they were alive, and cook them rice and peas and chicken and West Indian dishes, then they're not going to know anything else. They'll just do what they want to do, because they don't care about our parents going through a lot of problems, or slavery. It means nothing to them. Unless I give my kids those values, they're not going to have them.

White people get on with blacks alright, but we're not a threat to them, because we haven't got anything. We'll never be a threat until we come together and have our own businesses and own things and make money and handle money. You see, it's the direction that western society, white people want us to go. And when you don't go in that certain direction is where you now become a problem to them. When I was nine, the first time I heard this phrase was 'chip on your shoulder.' I come home and asked my mum, 'What does this chip on my ... I ain't got no chip on my ... what does this mean?' It wasn't that I was being wrong, or mischievous, all it was is that I was disagreeing with another person's views. That was the thing that always haunted me through my school life. If I didn't comply to somebody's views, a teacher's views, they'd say, 'Oh, he's got a chip on his shoulder' or 'he's a problem child.' But why do I have to agree with something that I don't feel is right? That is the path that a dominant person, or a dominant race, wants the next race to do down. It doesn't want them answering back. He wants him to 'put that there,' 'do that,' clocking it round the clock. When you want to set up a business for yourself and make money, then you're a problem. As long as we're always the workers, the workers are not a problem to the manager. A man that wants to be successful at being manager is a problem to the manager. Until we realise that, until we've got lawyers, doctors, policemen, and every influential people in jobs, then we'll always be the workers, and we'll never be no threat.

I love my kids now. A lot of people say that I'm hard on my kids. I reprimand them for things that you wouldn't do with other children. But I can only give them what my parents gave me. Respect. I've still got installed all those good habits that they brought me up and taught me, and I've got to install them in those children. People say money is not important. Their mother can love them more than me, but what's she got to offer them? Love. But love, at the end of the day, don't pay bills and pay nursery fees and pay for private school. At the end of the day, you need money. I love to give those children what I want to give them. So that's why I've got to be out for myself, making my money, so that I can give them things that I want to give them. Opportunity. I think that's the most important word, that if they said, 'Daddy, I want to be a lawyer,' then I should be in a position to do the best, and make him a lawyer. Or, if my kids say to me, 'Dad, I can't get on with school.' I want to say, 'Alright, this is my business, car trading, you come and learn this with me.' But that's the opportunity I've got to be able to give those kids. The white kids have got the head start like that.

Notes

1 'Meat' is dialect for cattle fodder, typically the tops of the sugar cane.
2 Fumigate. One of the first domestic insecticides available in the West Indies was retailed as 'Flit' and the word entered into the vocabulary as the verb 'to flit'.

Bibliography

Aron, R. (1962) *Peace and War: A Theory of International Relations*, London, Weidenfeld & Nicolson.

Banton, M. (1967) *Race Relations*, London, Tavistock.

Barraclough, G. (1964) *Contemporary History*, London, C.A. Watts.

Barthes, R. (1957) *Mythologies*, Paris, Editions du Seuil.

Beckles, H. (1990) *A History of Barbados*, Cambridge, Cambridge University Press.

Beckles, H. and Shepherd, V. (eds), (1993) *Caribbean Freedom: Economy and Society from Emancipation to the Present*, Kingston, Ian, Randle/London, James Currey.

Besson, J. and Momsen, J. (eds), (1987) *Land and Development in the Caribbean*, London, Macmillan.

Bonnett, A. and Llewellyn. W.G. (eds), (1989) *Emerging Perspectives on the Black Diaspora*, Lanham, University Press of America.

Bottomley, G. (1992) *From Another Place: Migration and the Politics of Culture*, Cambridge, Cambridge University Press.

Brock, C. (ed.) (1986) *The Caribbean in Europe*, London, Frank Cass.

Bryan, B. Dadzie, S. and Scafe, S. (1985) *The Heart of the Race: Black Women's Lives in Britain*, London, Virago.

Burton, J.W. (1967) *International Relations: A General Theory*, Cambridge, Cambridge University Press.

Butterfield, H. and Wight, M. (eds), (1966) *Diplomatic Investigations*, London, George Allen & Unwin.

Chamberlain, M. (1989) *Growing Up in Lambeth*, London, Virago.

Cohen, R. (1987) *The New Helots: Migrants in the International Division of Labour*, Aldershot, Avebury Press.

Cottle, T. (1978) *Black Testimony: The Voices of Britain's West Indians*, London, Wildwood.

Cross, M. and Entzinger, H. (eds), (1988) *Lost Illusions: Caribbean Minorities in Britain and the Neth~rlands*, London, Routledge.

Cross, M. and Keith, M. (eds), (1993) *Racism, the City and the State*, London, Routledge.

Davison, R.B. (1962) *West Indian Migrants*, London, Oxford University Press.

Davison, R.B. (1966) *Black British*, London, Institute of Race Relations, Oxford University Press.

Dahrendorf, Ralf (1982) *On Britain*, London, BBC Books.

Dodgson, E. (1984) *Motherland: West Indian Women in Britain in the 1950s*, London, Heinemann Educational.

Egginton, J. (1957) *They Seek A Living*, London, Hutchinson.

Elton, Lord. (1945) *Imperial Commonwealth*, London, Collins.

Field, F. and Haikin, P. (1971) *Black Britons*, London, Oxford University Press.

Foner, N. (1979) *Jamaica Farewell: Jamaican Migrants in London*, London, Routledge and Kegan Paul.

Foot, P. (1965) *Immigration and Race in British Politics*, London, Penguin.

Fryer, P. (1984) *Staying Power: The History of Black People in Britain*, London, Pluto Press.

Giddens, A. (1990) *The Consequences of Modernity*, Cambridge, Polity Press.

Gilroy, P. (1987) *There Ain't No Black in the Union Jack*, London, Unwin Hyman.

Gilroy, P. (1993) *The Black Atlantic: Modernity and Double Consciousness*, London, Verso.

Glass, R. (1961) *London's Newcomers*, Cambridge, Mass., Harvard University Press.

Gmelch, G. (1992) *Double Passage: The Lives of Caribbean Migrants Abroad and Back Home*, Ann Arbor, University of Michigan Press.

Glazer, N. and Moynihan, D.P. (1975) *Ethnicity: Theory and Experience*, Cambridge, Mass., Harvard University Press.

Goulbourne, H. (1991) *Ethnicity and Nationalism in Post-Imperial Britain*, Cambridge, Cambridge University Press.

Green, J. (1990) *Them: Voices from the Immigrant Community in Contemporary Britain*, London, Secker & Warburg.

Griffin, F.J. (1995) *"Who Set You Flowin'?"*, New York/Oxford, Oxford University Press.

Gus, J. and Humphry. D. (1972) *Because They're Black*, Harmondsworth, Penguin.

Halbwachs, M. (1980) *The Collective Memory*, New York, Harper and Row.

Hebdige, D. (1987) *Cut'n'Mix*, London, Methuen.

Hercules, T. (1989) *Labelled a Black Villain*, London, Fourth Estate.

Hinds, D. (1966) *Journey to an Illusion: The West Indian in Britain*, London, Heinemann.

Hiro, D. (1973) *Black British White British: A History of Race Relations in Britain*, London, Penguin.

Hobbes, T. (1962) *Leviathan*, (1651) Oxford, Clarendon Press.

Hobsbawn, E. and Ranger, T. (eds), (1983) *The Invention of Tradition*, Cambridge, Cambridge University Press.

Huxley, E. (1964) *Back Streets, New Worlds*, London, Chatto & Windus.

Tajfel, H. and Dawson, J. (1965) *Disappointed Guests: Essays by African, Asian and West Indian Students*, London, Oxford University Press/Institute of Race Relations.

Hood, C. (1970) *Children of West Indian Immigrants: A Study of One-Year Olds in Paddington*, London, Institute of Race Relations.

Husband, C. (ed.), (1975) *White Media and Black Britain*, London, Hutchinson.

Johnson, H. (1988) *After the Crossing: Immigrants and Minorities in Caribbean Creole Society*, London, Frank Cass.

Kasinitz, P. (1992) *Caribbean New York: Black Immigrants and the Politics of Race*, Ithaca, Cornell University Press.

Kerridge, R. (1983) *Real Wicked Guy: A View of Black Britain*, Oxford, Blackwell.

King, A.D. (ed.), (1991) *Culture, Globalization and the World System: Contemporary Conditions for the Representations of Identity*, Basingstoke, Macmillan.

Kritz, M., Keely, Charles and Tomasi, Silvano (eds), (1981) *Global Trends in Migration*, New York, Center for Migration Studies of New York.

Lamming, G. (1953) *In the Castle of my Skin*, London, Longman.

Laurence, K.O. (1994) *A Question of Labour. Indentured Immigration into Trinidad and British Guiana 1875–1917*, Kingston, Ian Randle/London, James Currey.

LePage, R.B. and Tabouret-Keller, A. (1985) *Acts of Identity: Creole Based Approaches to Language and Ethnicity*, Cambridge, Cambridge University Press.

Levine, B. (ed.), (1987) *The Caribbean Exodus*, New York, Praeger.

Lewis, O. (1976) *Five Families: Mexican Case Studies in the Culture of Poverty*, (first published USA 1959). London, Souvenir Press.

Lewis, O. (1964) *Children of Sanchez. Autobiography of a Mexican Family*, (first published USA 1961), London, Penguin.

Little K. (1947) *Negroes in Britain: A Study of Race Relations in English Society*, London, Kegan Paul.

Littlewood, R. and Lipsedge, M. (1989) *Aliens and Alienists: Ethnic Minorities and Psychiatry*, London, Unwin Hyman.

Look Lai, W. (1993) *Indentured Labour, Caribbean Sugar: Chinese and Indian Migrants to the British West Indies 1838–1918*, Baltimore, Johns Hopkins University Press.

Marshall, T., McGeary, P. and Thompson, G. (eds), (1981) *Folksongs of Barbados*, Bridgetown.

Marshall, W. (ed.), (1987) *Emancipation*, Vol II, National Cultural Foundation/ Department of History, UWI, Cave Hill, Bridgetown.

Miles, R. and Phizacklea, A. (1984) *White Man's Country: Racism in British Politics*, London, Pluto Press.

Millett, R. and Marvin Will, W. (eds), (1979) *The Restless Caribbean: Changing Patterns of International Relations*, New York, Praeger.

Momsen, J. (ed.), (1993) *Women and Change in the Caribbean* Kingston, Ian Randle.

Mullard, C. (1973) *Black Britain*, London, Allen & Unwin.

Palmer, R. (ed.), (1990) *In Search of a Better Life. Perspectives on Migration from the Caribbean*, New York, Praeger.

Parnwell, M. (1993) *Population Movements and the Third World*, London, Routledge.

Pastor, R. (ed.), (1985) *Migration and Development in the Caribbean: The Unexplored Connection*, London, Westview Press.

Patterson, S. (1964) *Dark Strangers: A Study of West Indians in London*, London, Penguin.

Peach, C. (1968) *West Indian Migration to Britain: A Social Geography*, London, Oxford University Press.

Peach, C. (1991) *The Caribbean in Europe: Contrasting Patterns of Migration and Settlement in Britain, France and the Netherlands*, Warwick, University of Warwick, Centre for Research in Ethnic Relations, Research Paper in Ethnic Relations no. 15, October.

Petras, E.M. (1988) *Jamaican Labor Migration: White Capital and Black Labor 1850–1930*, Boulder and London, Westview Press.

Philpott, S.B. (1973) *West Indian Migration: The Monserrat Case*, London, Athlone Press, 1973.

Prescod-Roberts, M. and Steele, N. (1980) *Black Woman: Bringing It All Back Home*, Bristol, Falling Wall Press for Housewives in Dialogue.

Puckrein, G. (1984) *Little England: Plantation Society and Anglo-Barbadian Politics, 1627–1700*, New York, University Press.

Rex, J. (1988) *The Ghetto and the Underclass: Essays on Race and Social Policy*, Aldershot, Avebury.

Rex, J. and Tomlinson, S. (1979) *Colonial Immigrants in a British City*, London, Routledge and Kegan Paul.

Richardson, B. (1983) *Caribbean Migrants, Environment and Human Survival on St. Kitts and Nevis*, Knoxville, University of Tennessee Press.

Richardson, B. (1985) *Panama Money in Barbados, 1900–1920*, Knoxville, University of Tennessee Press.

Rosenau, J. (ed.), (1961) *International Politics and Foreign Policy*, New York, The Free Press.

Ross, E. (1994) *Love and Toil: Motherhood in Outcast London, 1870–1918*, Oxford, Oxford University Press.

Rutherford, J. (ed.), (1990) *Identity, Community, Culture and Difference*, London, Lawrence and Wishart.

Said, E. (1993) *Culture and Imperialism*, London, Chatto & Windus.

Samuel, R. (1994) *Theatres of Memory*, London, Verso.

Samuel R. and Thompson, R. (1990) *The Myths We Live By*, London, Routledge.

Schelling, T. (1960) *The Strategy of Conflict*, Cambridge, Mass., Harvard University Press.

Schiller, N.G., Basch, L. and Blanc-Szanton, C. (eds), (1992) *Towards a Transnational Perspective on Migration: Race, Class, Ethnicity and Nationalism Reconsidered*, New York, Annals of the New York Academy of Sciences.

Selvon, S. (1956) *The Lonely Londoners*, London, Longman.

Shepherd, V. (1993) *From Transients to Settlers: The Experience of Indians in Jamaica, 1845–1950*, University of Warwick/Leeds, Peepal Tree Books.

Shepherd, V., Brereton, B. and Bailey, B. (eds), (1994) *Engendering History: Caribbean Women in Historical Perspective*, Kingston, Ian Randle/London, James Currey.

Shore, L. (1982) Pure Runni*ng: A Life Story*, London, Hackney Reading Centre at Centreprise.

Stark, O. (1991) *The Migration of Labour*, Oxford, Blackwell.

Sutcliffe, D. and Wong, A. (1986) *The Language of Black Experience: Cultural Expression Through Word and Sound in the Caribbean and Black Britain*, Oxford, Blackwell.

Sutton, C. and Chaney, E. (eds), (1994) *Caribbean Life in New York City: Sociocultural Dimensions*, New York, Center for Migration Studies of New York.

Thomas, B. (1973) *Migration and Economic Growth*, Cambridge, Cambridge University Press.

Thomas-Hope, E. (1992) *Explanation in Caribbean Migration*, London, Macmillan.

Todaro, M.P. (1976) *International Migration in Developing Countries*, Geneva, International Labour Organisation.

Tonkin, E. (1992) *Narrating Our Past*, Cambridge, Cambridge University Press.

Tonkin, E. McDonald, M. and Chapman, M. (eds), (1989) *History and Ethnicity*, ASA Monograph, London, Routledge.

Walcott, D. (1977) *The Star-Apple*, New York, Farrar, Strauss and Giroux.

Wallerstein, I. (1979) *The Capitalist World Economy*, Cambridge, Cambridge University Press.

Walvin, J. (1973) *Black and White: The Negro in English Society, 1555–1945*, London, Allen Lane.

Watson, J. (1973) *Between Two Cultures: Migrants and Minorities in Britain*, Oxford, Basil Blackwell.

Western, J. (1992) *Passage to England: Barbadian Londoners Speak of Home*, London, UCL Press.

White, J. (1986) *The Worst Street in North London: Campbell Bunk*, London Routledge.

Williams, R. (1975) *The Long Revolution*, London, Pelican.

Wood, W. and Downing, J. (1968) *Vicious Circle*, London, SPCK.

Articles

Bach, R. (1982) 'Caribbean Migration, Causes and Consequences', *Migration Today*, 10(5) pp. 6–13.

Barrow, C. (1986) 'Finding the Support: Strategies for Survival', *Social and Economic Studies*, 35(2).

Barrow, C. (1977) 'Migration from a Barbados village: Effects on Family Life', *New Community*, 5:381–91.

Baud, M. (1991) 'Families and Migration: Towards an Historical Analysis of Family Networks', *Economic and Social History in the Netherlands* 5, pp. 83–107.

Bertaux, D. and Thompson, P. (1993) Introduction, *International Yearbook of Oral History and Life Stories* Vol. II, Between Generations: Family Models, Myths and Memories, Oxford, Oxford University Press, pp. 1–12.

Bertaux-Wiame, I. (1979) 'The Life History Approach to the Study of Internal Migration', *Oral History*, Vol 7, no. 1.

Bhabha, H. (1993) 'Between Identities', *International Yearbook of Oral History and Life Stories*, Vol. III, Migration and Identity, Oxford, Oxford University Press.

Brockman, C.T. 'The Western Family and Individualisation: Convergences with Caribbean Patterns', *Journal of Comparative Family Studies*, 18(3) pp. 471–80.

Chamberlain, M. (1990) 'Renters and Farmers: The Barbadian Plantation Tenantry System, 1917–1937', *Journal of Caribbean History*, 24(2) pp. 195–225.

Chamberlain, M. (1994) 'Family and Identity: Barbadian Migrants to Britain', *International Yearbook of Oral History and Life Stories*, Vol. III, Migration and Identity, Oxford, Oxford University Press.

Cohen, R. 'Rethinking "Babylon": iconoclastic conceptions of the diasporic experience', *New Community* 21(1) pp. 5–18.

Conway, D. (1990) 'Emigration to North America: the continuing option for the Caribbean', *Caribbean Affairs* (Trinidad) 3(2) pp. 109–119.

Cooper, D. (1985) 'Migration from Jamaica in the 1970s: Political Protest or Economic Pull?', *International Migration Review*, 19(4) pp. 728–745.

Davin, A. (1978) 'Imperialism and Motherhood', *History Workshop*, 5.

Dean, D.W. (1987) 'Coping with Colonial Policy: The Labour Government and Black Communities in Great Britain, 1945–51', *Immigrants and Minorities*, Vol. 6, November.

Ebanks, G. George, P.M. and Nobbe, C.E. (1979) 'Emigration from Barbados', *Social and Economic Studies*, 28(2).

Greenfield, S. (1983) 'Barbadians in the Brazilian Amazon', *Luso-Brazilian Review*, 20(1) pp. 4–64.

Hall, C. (1993) 'White Visions, Black Lives: the Free Villages of Jamaica', *History Workshop Journal*, 36, Autumn.

Harris, C. (1993) 'Britishism, Racism and Migration', paper presented at 25th Annual Conference of the Association of Caribbean Historians, Mona, Jamaica.

Hinds, D. (1980) 'The "Island" of Brixton', *Oral History: The Journal of the Oral History Society*, Vol. 8, No. 1, Spring.

James, W. (1984) 'A Long Way From Home: On Black Identity in Britain', *Immigrants and Minorities*, 5(3) pp. 258–84.

Lindsey, L. 'Halting the Tide: Responses to West Indian Immigration to Britain, 1946–1952', *Journal of Caribbean History*, Vol. 26 (1).

Lunn, K. (1989) 'The British State and Immigration, 1945–51: New Light on the

Empire Windrush', *Immigrants and Minorities*, Vol. 8, March.

Maunder, W.F. (1955) 'New Jamaican Emigration', *Social and Economic Studies*, (4).

McElroy, J. and de Albuquerque, K. (1990) 'Migration, Natality and Fertility: Some Caribbean Evidence' *International Migration Review*, 24(4) pp. 783–802.

Miles, R. (1991) 'Migration to Britain: The Significance of a Historical Approach', *International Migration*, (Switzerland) 29(4) pp. 527–543.

Newton, V. (1987) The Panama Question: Barbadian Emigration to Panama, 1880–1914', in Woodville Marshall (ed.) *Emancipation* Vol. II, Bridgetown, National Cultural Foundation/Department of History, University of the West Indies, Cave Hill.

Paul, K. (1992) 'The Politics of Citizenship in Postwar Britain', *Contemporary Record: The Journal of Contemporary British History*, Vol. 6:3, Winter.

Petras, E. M. (1980) 'The Role of National Boundaries in a cross-national labour market', *International Journal of Urban and Regional Research*, 4(2) pp. 157–194.

Portelli, A. (1981) 'The Peculiarities of Oral History', *History Workshop Journal*, 12, Autumn.

Richardson, B. (1980) 'Freedom and Migration in the Leeward Caribbean, 1838–48', *Journal of Historical Geography*, Vol. 6:4 pp. 391–408.

Roberts, G.W. (1955) 'Emigration from the Island of Barbados', *Social and Economic Studies*, 4(3).

Rubenstein, H. (1983) 'Remittances and Rural Underdevelopment', *Human Organisation*, 42(4).

Samuel, R. (1995) Editorial, *History Workshop Journal*, 40, Autumn.

Segal, A. (1985) 'Caribbean Realities', *Current History*, 84 (500) pp. 127–130, 134–5.

Segal, A. (1991) 'The Caribbean: Small is Scary', *Current History*, 90 (554) pp. 105–8, 138.

Sherwood, M. (1981) 'Black Contract Workers in Britain 1940–1945', paper presented at the Commonwealth Conference of the Society for the Study of Labour History, Coventry, September.

Skotnes, A. (1994) 'Some Reflections on Migration and Identity', in *International Yearbook of Oral History and Life Stories*, Vol. III, Migration and Identity Oxford, Oxford University Press.

Smith, M. (1991) 'Windrushers and Orbiters: Towards an Understanding of the "Official Mind" and Colonial Immigration to Britain', *Immigrants and Minorities*, Vol. 10, November.

Tidrick, G. (1966) 'Some Aspects of Jamaican Emigration to the United Kingdom, 1953–1962', *Social and Economic Studies*, (15).

Thompson, A. (1966) 'Historical Writing on Migration into the Commonwealth Caribbean: A Bibliographic Review of the Period, c.1838–c.1938', *Immigrants and Minorities*, Vol. 5, no. 2, July.

Watson, H. (1982) 'Theoretical and Methodological Problems in Commonwealth Caribbean Migration Research: Conditions and Causality', *Social and Economic Studies*, 31(1).

Economic Commission of Latin America, (1981) *Barbados Experimental Migration Survey – a Preliminary Analysis of the Results of the first Three Rounds*, UN Cepal/Carib.

Archive Sources

BARBADOS, DEPARTMENT OF ARCHIVES (BDA)

Pam A 45. Barbados (Governors), *Rules and Regulations framed and passed by the Governor in Council, under the Authority of the Emigration Act (1873) on the 23rd September 1873.*

Pam A 61, Pam A 104, A 220 *Information Booklet for Intending Emigrants to Britain*, Broad Street, Bridgetown: Advocate Co. Ltd (undated). Barbados, Government Printing Office (undated).

Pam B141. Payne, E. (1968) *Lecture Series and Panel Discussion*, UWI/University of Sussex Centre for Multi-Racial Studies, Barbados, Cave Hill, 1968. Barbados, Department of Archives.

Pam B 394. (1946) *West Indian Census, 1946*; Census of Agriculture (in Barbados); preliminary tables. Bridgetown, Census Office, (Census Office Bulletin No. 7).

Pam C 9. Governor R.W. Rawson, *Report on the Population of Barbados, 1851– 1871*, Barbados, Barclay and Fraser, 1872.

Pam C 28. (1954) *Report of the Joint Committee appointed by the two Houses of the Legislature to Examine the Question of Over Population in Barbados and to Make Recommendations for Dealing with this Problem, 1953.* Barbados, Advocate Co. Ltd.

Pam C 58. *The Report of the Committee Appointed to draw up a Detailed Scheme for the Settlement of Barbadians at Vieux Fort, St. Lucia, 15 November 1937.* (Head of Committee, S.J. Saint, Chairman).

Pam C 93. (1960) *Report of Delegation Appointed to visit Dominica to examine the possibilities of a land settlement scheme there for Barbadians, 1960*, Barbados: Government Printing Office.

Pam C 676. *Barbados Emigration Commission Report 1895*, Chairman, Henry A. Bovell.

SRL 9. *Annual Report of the Labour Department*, (1955–1966), Bay Street, Barbados: Government Printing Office.

SRL 49. *Annual Reports of the Post Office Department* (1963–1968), Bay Street: Government Printing Office (undated).

LABOUR DEPARTMENT FILES – CHIEF LABOUR OFFICER

E5010/1 – E5010/1. Vols I, II, III, IV, V *Hospitals and Nurses*, 1954–1968.

E5010/1. *Emigration to the UK (non-sponsored). Returns from Shipping*, 1956.

E5010/1. *Regional Economic Committee of the British West Indies, British Guiana and British Honduras*, 1956.

E5010/B1/1. *Welfare Liaison Scheme, Monthly Reports*, 1955–1963.

E5010/B/1. *Welfare Liaison Scheme, Monthly Reports*, 1955–1963.

E5010/B1/Vol. II. *Welfare Liaison Scheme, Monthly Reports*, 1955–1963.

E5010/7. Vols I–IV *London Transport Board*, 1956–1973.

E5010/7. Vols I–IV *London Transport Executive*, 1957–1958.

E5010/7 (TJ), E5010/8/1. Vol. IV *British Transport Commission*, 1957–1965.

E5010/14/Vols. II–IV *Problems with Emigrant Workers*, 1959–1964.

E5010/15, E5010/17, E5010/18, E5010/20, E5010/22, E5010/24. *Specific industries, Travel Agency Arrangements.*

E5010/29/3. *Commonwealth Immigrations Advisory Council Reports*, 1963–1965.

E5010/29. *Commonwealth Immigration into Britain*, 1961–1968.

E5010/29/1. *Emigration to the UK: Racial Discrimination*, 1962.

E5010/29/3a. *Requests from Emigrants to Return Home*, 1971.
R5010/30. *Lyons & Co*, 1970–1974.
E5010/31. *Social Welfare: Responsibility for Minors Emigrating*, 1962.
R5010/32. *Employment of Coopers and Orderlies*, 1963–1964.
E5010/33. *Brereton Catering Co. Ltd*, 1964.
E5010/34. *Midland Motor Omnibus Company: Expansion of sponsored scheme.*
E5010/35. *Repatriation of Barbadians from UK*, 1964.
E5010/36. *Grand Metropolitan Hotels*, 1965.
E5010/37. *British Hotels and Restaurants Association.*
E5010/39. *Recruitment for Training as Moulders*, 1967.
E5010/41. *Admission to Medical Institutions.*
E5010/43. *Hotel Workers.*
E5010/46. *Hilton Hotel.*
E5010/48. *Postmen.*
E5010/49. *Police College*, 1965–1970.
E5010/50. *Disbursement of Advances to Barbados High Commission*, 1969–1970.

Government Sources

MINISTRY OF TRADE, INDUSTRY AND LABOUR: EMIGRATION AND EMPLOYMENT OF BARBADIANS IN BRITAIN (MTIL)
L10/2. Vols II, V, VI, *Employment of Barbadians Abroad (women): student nurses in the UK.*
L10/10. Vols I, IV, V, *Emigration of West Indians to the UK*, 1955–1959.
L10/11. Vols I, II, IV, *Employment of Barbadians in the United Kingdom: Hotel Workers*, 1955.
L10/19. Vols Ia, II, *Employment of Barbadians in the UK – recruitment for LTE.*
L10/21. Vol III, *Emigration to UK Housing of Emigrants in UK*, 1960–1966.
L10/23. Vols I, II, *Reports of the Barbados Immigrants Liaison Service.*
L10/25. *Confectionery Workers, Training and Emigration*, 1956–1966.
L10/35. Vols I–IV, *Barbadian Immigrants in the UK, children of*, 1959–1962.
L10/41. *Employment of Barbadians Abroad – Lyons Teashops*, 1962–1971.
L10/42. Vol II, *Repayment of Loans from Emigrants in UK Collection.*

NATIONAL SOUND ARCHIVE, BRITISH LIBRARY
Barbados Migration Project (M. Chamberlain). Tapes and transcripts.
National Life Story Collection, London.

UNIVERSITY OF THE WEST INDIES
Barbados Plantation Tenantry System (M. Chamberlain). Tapes. Department of History, Cave Hill, Barbados, University of the West Indies.

Index

232